Religion and State

Religion and State

The Muslim Approach to Politics

L. Carl Brown

 Columbia University Press   New York

Columbia University Press

Publishers Since 1893

New York   Chichester, West Sussex

Library of Congress Cataloging-in-Publication Data

Brown, L. Carl (Leon Carl) 1928–

Religion and state : the Muslim approach to politics /
L. Carl Brown.

p. cm.

Includes bibliographical references and index.

ISBN 0–231–12038–9 (cloth: alk. paper) —

ISBN 0–231–12039–7 (pbk: alk. paper)

1. Islam and state—Islamic countries.

2. Islam and politics—Islamic countries.

3. Islamic countries—Politics and government.

I. Title

BP173.6 .B76 2000

297.2'72—dc21   00–022700

Casebound editions of Columbia University Press books
are printed on permanent and durable acid-free paper.

Printed in the United States of America

Designed by Audrey Smith

c 10 9 8 7 6 5 4 3 2 1

p 10 9 8 7 6 5 4 3 2 1

Contents

Religion and State

Introduction

A few years ago pundits and politicians discovered Islam—yet again. This sister religion of Judaism and Christianity was suddenly seen to determine the politics of the more than one billion Muslims in this world. Indeed, Islam, it was believed, prescribed a particular form of politics: secularism, or the separation of *din* (religion) from *dawla* (state), was inconceivable. Nor could there be any opting out of worldly concerns. Muslims must work to achieve the divinely ordained political community in this world, the *dunya*. Thus, the three *d*s, *din*, *dawla*, and *dunya*, cohered to provide a distinctly Islamic approach to political life.

Pundits and politicians of earlier times had regarded Islam differently. One of the few Arabic words with Islamic resonance that our grandparents would have recognized is kismet, meaning fate or destiny.[1] Muslims, it was believed, were fatalists, disinclined to believe that human exertions could shape events significantly. What was *maktub* (written, that is preordained by God) would surely occur.[2]

The most recent Western perception of Islam and politics is surely linked to the last months of 1978 and early 1979 when a seventy-eight-year-old Muslim cleric who had lived the previous fourteen years in exile forced an autocrat from his throne and began a revolution. Ayatollah Khomeini had rallied a mass movement in Iran that overthrew the Pahlavi dynasty—which President Jimmy Carter had earlier labeled an "island of stability" in a volatile region—putting in its place an Islamic government.

Two years later, in October 1981, Egyptian President Anwar al-Sadat was gunned down by assassins following, as they claimed, the dictates of Islam to eradicate this "pharaoh" and work to achieve a legitimate Islamic government.

Thereafter it seemed as if every Muslim country has confronted the challenge of adapting politics and governance to the requirements of Islam. Some governments claimed to be Islamic. These would include, in addition to Iran, Pakistan and Sudan. Adding confusion to these new developments, the Saudi Arabia regime, which since its creation in the 1920s had viewed itself as the very epitome of Islamic orthodoxy (and been dismissed by many modernist Muslims as hopelessly old hat), was now accused by radical religious forces of lacking Islamic legitimacy.

Many other governments in Muslim countries have sought to adopt a religious coloration, for example by insisting that all legislation must conform to the corpus of Muslim religious law known as the *Shari'ah*. Radical religious groups have met such efforts, however, with derisive dismissal. And there are many such groups. Their names, once alien to Western ears, have entered into the Western lexicon—Hizbullah, Hamas, Takfir wa al-Hijra, FIS, and many others. Ironically, the older Muslim Brethren, once the bad boy of Middle Eastern politics in the eyes of establishment politicians and Western diplomats, was now earning in some circles the rubric of moderate.

These new religious forces have often been intent on overthrowing established government in any way necessary, including assassination and terrorism. Bringing about Islamic rule would also require shaking off foreign influence. This has meant eradicating both Western economic, political, and military hegemony as well as Muslim fascination with Western ways (Westoxification).[3] Thus, recent years have witnessed acts of violence and terrorism against Western interests not only throughout the regions of predominantly Muslim populations but even in New York, Paris, and elsewhere.

The existence today of Islamic governments, radical Islamist political groups, and terrorist incidents is incontrovertible. These are hard facts, not perceptions. Are we, then, to conclude that politicians and pundits are finally getting it right? Are we now coming to understand the true nature of Islam in its relation to politics? Such a judgment would be in line with the thinking of the radical Muslim ideologues themselves. They insist that there is, has been, and always will be only one true Islam valid "for all time and place" (*li kull makan wa zaman*, in Arabic).[4]

The notion that radical Islamist politics as preached and practiced today more correctly reflects the Islamic norm is also held by many non-Muslim observers ranging from serious specialists convinced that Islam offers a clarity of doctrine and a historical continuity distinguishing it from Judaism,

Christianity, or other world religions to commentators who have found a new threat to "our way of life" after the end of the cold war. Indeed, it might be maintained that the present-day West has returned to its centuries-old image of Islam as the traditional enemy vaunting a religion of the sword. Jihad (holy war) ranks alongside kismet as one of the few Arabo-Islamic terms long recognized in the West. Firmly rooted in the Western subconscious is the image of Islam as a peculiarly aggressive and impenetrably xenophobic religion.

It is the argument of this book that both the radical Islamist spokesmen and those disparate non-Muslim observers have it wrong. Yes, they are strange bedfellows, but they converge in positing an Islam existing outside of history, an unchanging Islam. They are conflating theology and history. They are confusing the ought and the is.

No serious person maintains that the this-worldly manifestation of, say, Christianity is the same today as it was in the time of Luther or Aquinas or Augustine or Paul. One accepts Christianity's diversity throughout time and space. Isn't it plausible to expect roughly the same of Islam in history?

Roughly the same is, indeed, to be expected in terms of diversity, complexity, and change characterizing the history of Muslims. Still, restoring Islam and Muslims to history also imposes the task of seeking out the distinctive strands of Muslim experience throughout the centuries that have produced an identifiable civilization. A useful way to illuminate the distinguishing characteristics of Islam in relation to politics may well be to compare this religion with its two Semitic sisters, Judaism and Christianity.

Such is the aim of this book. It presents the case that we can better understand present-day politics among Muslims by keeping two requirements in balance: 1. accepting the reality of historical diversity and change among Muslims (just as among other people) while 2. identifying what may be said to be distinctive in Muslim thought and action concerning politics. This is no more than the historian's usual task of balancing continuity and change, but it has not always been brought to bear in studying Muslims.

The first seven chapters will sketch the historically conditioned broad outlines of Muslim political thought. Thereafter the guiding theme becomes that of the great transformations and upheavals Muslims have been experiencing beginning some two centuries ago.

It will be argued here that mainstream Muslim political thought in premodern times tended toward political quietism. Moreover, Muslim political history, in contrast with much of Christian history, has been characterizd by a largely successful attempt to bar government from proclaiming (and then enforcing) religious orthodoxy.

From this it follows that although radical Islamist groups today claim that they are only restoring Islam to an earlier worldly model established during the time of the Prophet Muhammad and his followers they are, in fact, introducing striking innovations. These innovations, being reactions to existing circumstances, are decked out as reconstructions of an earlier "golden age." This should not shock. All serious political thought (and even more religio-political thought) is a response to immediate problems. Once we integrate Islam and Muslims into ongoing history we should expect the Islamists to adapt past ages, past formulations, and past doctrines to present purposes, but we must be prepared to find signficant innovations as well.

A broad comparison between today's Muslim world and Europe of the Reformation can be suggested, however distasteful that comparison may be to both the Islamists and the many champions of Western "exceptionalism." Just as the leaders of the Reformation in Europe set in motion revolutionary religious and political changes while contrasting a presumably purer past with present corruption, so may today's Islamists be revolutionary in impact even as they preach a return to the past.

Q

A healthy rule in present-day writing asks that authors avoid the role of "omniscient observer" and state their assumptions and prejudices, to the extent these can ever be understood. Here are mine: I have studied and at times lived among Muslims of the Middle East and North Africa, mainly the Arab countries, since 1953. My knowledge of other Muslims (the majority) is less personal and less thorough. I am an old-fashioned historian of the modern period emphasizing political and, to some extent, intellectual history. I am not a student of theology, and my selective dipping into Muslim and Christian theological studies while preparing this book has made me acutely aware of what an awesome discipline theology is. My approach to this subject is more mundane, more historical, more sociological (if I can presume to use that latter designation).

I feel very much at home in that part of the Muslim world where I have lived, and I hope that I have been able to avoid the detached subject-object or self-other approach that is often thought (excessively in my view) to characterize Western scholarship of the Muslim world. I am intellectually fascinated by establishment-challenging religious movements, of whatever religion, but they disturb me. To say that they are distasteful would be entirely too weak. I simply do not like those individuals, in past history or present times, who believe that God has given them a clear message of what is required and has also mandated that they employ any means necessary to impose that message on others. I would go so far as to insist that such arrogance (as I see it) offers a poor parody of Islam or, for that matter, of Judaism and Christianity. Given this prejudice, I have made a conscious effort to be fair to those religious radicals whose ideology and actions I deplore. Whether I have succeeded in depicting them fairly (perhaps even too kindly?) is for the reader to judge, but my heart is with those who, possessing a fearful respect for human limitations, work to make things better without risking the possible chaos and suffering revolutions usually bring.

If I have a hidden agenda in writing this book it has now been unveiled. I would very much like to see present-day Muslim political thought and action draw more on its mainstream doctrines and theology in order to restore, appropriately updated where necessary, the best of its rich heritage of tolerance and a keen sense of solidarity that also shields basic individual rights against potentially abusive state power. I would wish to see an Islam that calls for the creation of, in the oft-cited Qur'anic passage, "a community of the middle way."[5] Such Muslim spokesmen exist today. May they increase in number and influence. For the present, however, those of a much harsher, more Manichaean message appear to be dictating the terms of the debate.

Part One

The Heritage

1.

Setting the Stage: Islam and Muslims

Who are the Muslims? Where are they to be found? How many are they? Many people assume that most Muslims are Arabs. In fact, Arabs make up only about one-fifth of the total world Muslim population.

Others, even if aware that the Middle East contains many inhabitants other than Arabs, are inclined to think that the Muslim world and the Middle East are roughly coterminous. It is true that the Middle Eastern population is about 90 percent Muslim, but all the Muslims of the Middle East still add up to a minority of the world's Muslim population. Even when defining the Middle East broadly to embrace the entire Arab world from Morocco to the Arabian Peninsula plus Iran, Israel, and Turkey the Muslims thus included are only slightly more than one-third of the world's Muslim population.

The largest Muslim state, Indonesia, is not in the Middle East. Indeed, the first four Muslim states in terms of population are all outside the Middle East—Indonesia, Pakistan, Bangladesh, and (surprising to many) India with over 100 million Muslims.

There are approximately half again more Muslims in the states of the former Soviet Union than in all of the Fertile Crescent states (Iraq, Israel, Jordan, Lebanon, and Syria), and the Muslims of Nigeria outnumber the Muslims of the entire Arabian Peninsula by roughly two to one.

The total world Muslim population is estimated to be slightly more than one billion. This gives a ratio of roughly six Muslims in the world for every ten Christians. There are slightly more Muslims than Catholics. Muslims outnumber all Protestants combined by almost three to one.[1]

Muslims are a close second to Christians (315 million as against 356 million) in the continent of Africa. They outnumber Hindus in all Asia (812 million versus 776 million) and are far ahead of the third largest group, the Buddhists (349 million). There are more than twice as many Muslims as all Christians throughout Asia.

Islam is, thus, by far the largest religious community in the Afro-Asian world with almost 400 million more than the Hindus, and outnumbering Christians by almost five million and Buddhists by a ratio of three to one.

In worldwide terms Muslims account for somewhat more than one-fourth of the total membership of the principal religions in terms of numbers of adherents (Christianity, Islam, Hinduism, Buddhism).

Islam began in the Middle East, as did Judaism and Christianity. Unlike its two sister religions, however, Islam has never suffered a statistically significant loss of its followers in the land of its origin. At different times and in response to different challenges the center of gravity of Christianity and Judaism (in demographic and cultural terms, at least) moved from the Middle East to Europe and the lands of largely European settlement, i.e., roughly what is now loosely labeled the West. Islam, always a proselytizing religion like Christianity, also expanded, but never at the expense of its Middle Eastern core area.

This may partially explain why so many outsider observers associate Islam with the Middle East even though the region accounts for a minority of the world's Muslims and has been in that minority status for centuries. Among Muslims, as well, there is a decided tendency to consider the Middle East both the homeland and the heartland of *Dar al-Islam* (the abode of Islam).

Many important aspects of Islam serve to remind Muslims of this special attachment to the Middle East. God chose to give what Muslims deem the final revelation in the Arabic language, and from the rise of Islam to this day Arabic has been the vehicle of Muslim ritual and theological communication. It is perhaps no exaggeration to say that Arabic is to Islam what Hebrew, Greek, and Latin all together are to Christianity.

Muslims everywhere face toward the Holy *Ka'ba* in Mecca in prayer. Pilgrimage to Mecca—the Hajj—is a ritual obligation that all Muslims whose health and wealth permit are enjoined to fulfill at least once in a lifetime. The number of Muslims who have made that pilgrimage throughout the centuries is impressive. In recent years over two million Muslim pilgrims have come to Mecca each year during the pilgrimage season.[2] Only slightly less holy in Muslim eyes is Madina, roughly 270 miles north of Mecca where Muhammad gathered his earliest converts and founded a religio-political community. It was also at Madina that the Prophet died in 632

C.E., and this city—the second holiest in Islam—served as the seat of the caliphate (the leadership of the Muslim community) in the crucial first few years of Islamic history after the death of Muhammad.

The third holiest city of Islam—Jerusalem—is also very much in the center of the Arab Middle East. It was from Jerusalem that the Prophet Muhammad, as related in the Qur'an, made his miraculous ascent to heaven. Jerusalem was also the first *qibla* (direction toward which Muslims are to face in prayer). Only a later Qur'anic revelation changed the *qibla* to Mecca.

Two other holy cities, especially venerated by the Shi'i Muslims, are also located in the Middle East heartland. They are Najaf, where Ali, the fourth caliph and son-in-law of the Prophet Muhammad, is believed to be buried, and Karbala, which witnessed the martyrdom of Ali's son, Husayn (on the tenth day of the month of Muharram in 61 A.H. or 680 C.E., commemorated thereafter by Shi'i Muslims as the principal day of mourning in the liturgical year). Both Najaf and Karbala are located in modern Iraq.

The formative years of what might be called political Islam are also solidly embedded in a Middle Eastern geographical context. As a result, many other Middle Eastern place names resonate with religio-cultural connotations to Muslims wherever they may be: Damascus, the capital of the first Muslim dynasty, the Umayyads (661–750), and Baghdad, the capital of the succeeding long-lived Abbasid dynasty (750–1258) evoke religio-political memories for Muslims much the way the names of Rome and Constantinople call forth the Christian religio-political heritage.

Also located in the Middle Eastern heartland are many of the later imperial and cultural capitals of Islam, including Cairo, founded as a new Islamic capital city in 969, Istanbul, wrested from the Byzantines in 1453 by the Ottomans and serving as their imperial capital until the end of the Ottoman Empire following the First World War, and Isfahan, the old Persian city that later became the resplendent capital of the Safavid Empire (1500–1736).

For all these reasons there is an understandable tendency among both Muslims and non-Muslims to emphasize the Middle Eastern dimension of Islam, past and present, and accordingly to give less attention to the majority of the world's Muslims who live outside the Middle East.

Observers are also likely to attribute to Islam behavioral patterns that are more properly to be traced to the Middle Eastern cultural legacy. There is no easy answer to this problem of perception. The Middle Eastern matrix of Islam is a historical fact. Moreover, the area of the Middle East that provided the arena for the activities of the Prophet Muhammad and the first few generations of his followers continues to stand out in Muslim consciousness as a distinctive, if not, indeed, a holy land. At the same time, Muslims everywhere are aware that many mundane and unholy activities take place in the Middle East and have done so for centuries.

The prudent observer should seek a middle path in weighing the Middle Eastern role in Islam as a religion and as a culture. The Middle East and Middle Easterners are perhaps more important to an understanding of Islam than any comparable territory or similar number of people, but, for all that, the Middle East is home for only a minority of the world's Muslims. Any effort to isolate the special Islamic element in shaping the political life of Muslims must give those peoples and regions beyond the Middle East due consideration.

The different peoples making up *Dar al-Islam* can be classified according to a number of criteria. There are, for example, states with Muslim majorities as opposed to those states in which they are a minority (See tables 1.1–1.3).

Muslims may also be divided according to cultural areas or regions with common mores and traditions in which such basic matters as language, gender roles, child rearing, cuisine, housing, play, and patterns of politesse bind people together and make them different from other peoples with other mores and traditions. A rough-and-ready breakdown of such separate Muslim cultural areas might be as follows:

> The Arabian Peninsula
> The Fertile Crescent
> Anatolia and the neighboring areas of Turkic language and culture
> The Iranian plateau, Afghanistan, and Persian speaking portions of
>   former Soviet Central Asia
> The Nile Valley (Egypt and Sudan)
> Northwest Africa (the Maghrib)
> West Africa
> East Africa
> Northwestern Indian subcontinent (largely now Pakistan)
> Northeastern Indian subcontinent (largely now Bangladesh)
> Central and Southern Indian subcontinent
> The East Indies (Indonesia, Malaysia, and Brunei)
> The old Muslim populations in Europe (Albania and Bosnian
>   Muslims)
> The new Muslims minorities in Europe (Arabs and Turks in Western
>   and Central Europe)
> Smaller minorities (e.g., the United States, Philippines, Latin
>   America)

Table 1.1 States in Which 75 Percent or More of the Population
Are Muslims

	Total Population (000,000 rounded)	Percent Muslim
Afghanistan	24.8	99%
Algeria	30.0	99.9%
Azerbaijan	7.7	93.4%
Bahrain	.6	81.8%
Bangladesh	127.6	88.3%
Comoros	.5	99.3%
Djibouti	.7	97.2%
Egypt	63.3	90%
Gambia	1.3	95%
Guinea	7.5	86.9%
Indonesia	203.0	87.2%
Iran	61.5	99.0%
Iraq	21.7	97%
Jordan	4.7	96.5%
Kuwait	1.9	85%
Libya	5.7	97%
Maldives	.3	100%
Mali	10.1	90%
Mauritania	2.5	99.5%
Morocco	28.1	99.8%
Niger	9.7	88.7%
Oman	2.4	87.7%
Pakistan	141.9	95%
Qatar	.6	95%
Saudi Arabia	20.8	96.6%
Senegal	9.7	92%
Somalia	6.8	99.9%
Sudan	33.6	72%
Syria	15.3	86%
Tajikistan	6.1	85%
Tunisia	9.4	99.5%
Turkey	64.6	99.8%
Turkmenistan	4.7	87%
United Arab Emirates	2.7	96%
Uzbekistan	24.1	88%
Yemen	16.4	99.9%

Table 1.2 States with Muslim Majorities Ranging from 50 Percent to 75 Percent

	Total Population (000,000 rounded)	Percent Muslim
Albania	3.3	70%
Brunei	.3	67.2%
Burkino Faso	11.3	50%
Chad	7.4	53.9%
Eritrea	3.8	69.3%
Kyrgzstan	4.7	70%
Lebanon	3.5	55.3%
Malaysia	22.1	52.9%
Sierra Leone	4.6	60%

Table 1.3 Selected States with Significant Muslim Minorities Either in Total Numbers or as a Percentage of the State's Population

	Total Population (000,000 rounded)	Percent Muslim
Bosnia and Herzegovina	3.4	40%
Cameroon	15.0	21.8%
China	1,243.0	1.4%
Cote d'Ivoire	15.4	38.7%
Ethiopia	58.4	30.0%
Guinea-Bissau	1.2	30%
India	984.0	12.0%
Israel	5.7	14.6%
Kazakstan	5.8	47%
Macedonia	2.0	30.0%
Nigeria	110.5	43%
Philippines	73.1	4.6%
Tanzania	30.6	35%

Even the tiny 2.4 percent in China amounts to 18 million Muslims. There are an estimated 105 million Muslims in India. A few midsized states, not listed, have Muslim minorities constituting a larger percentage of the total population than found in the Philippines, e.g., Ghana, 16.2 percent, Malawi, 16.2 percent, Mozambique, 13 percent, Yugoslavia, 19 percent, or even Singapore, with 15 percent. Information on the Philippines (4.6 percent or 3.3 million) was listed, because leaders of that tiny minority have adopted an adamant "Muslim nationalist" position.

Source: Britannica Book of the Year, 1999.

Yet another way of distinguishing the world's Muslims is according to the different denominations of Islam. Just as Christianity can be divided into Catholic, Orthodox, and Protestant plus several smaller sects Islam also has its divisions. They are, however, fewer than in Christianity and with sharply different proportions. The overwhelming majority are Sunni Muslims. *Sunni* is an Arabic word meaning custom or tradition. It is often translated into English as "orthodox," which is an accurate enough description of the Sunni Muslim self-image. Muslims who are not Sunnis, however, do not accept that they are thus heterodox. Sunnis account for roughly 84 percent of the world's Muslim population.

Virtually all of the remaining Muslim population is composed of the various Shi'a groups constituting 16 percent of the total Muslim population.[3] Shi'a, another Arabic word, means partisan or follower, and it is used to designate those Muslims who believe that the religious leadership (*imama*, anglicized to imamate) rightly belonged to Ali, the son-in-law of the Prophet Muhammad, and thereafter to his descendants. The Shi'a can in turn be divided into three numerically disproportionate groups—Twelver, Sevener, and Zaydi Shi'a, the great majority being Twelver Shi'a. The number twelve indicates the count of imams, beginning with Ali and followed by his two sons, Hasan and Husayn, who were physically present in this world to lead the community before the last in the line (the twelfth) left the visible world and went into occultation (*ghayba*).

These Shi'i imams are deemed to have been without sin and have a special relationship to God. Moreover, it is believed that the return of the occulted, or hidden, imam will signal the end of time and the consummation of the divine plan. This amounts to a striking similarity of Shi'i Islam and Christianity as contrasted with Sunni Islam and Judaism. Shi'ism and Christianity both posit a more imminent God in the form of an individual presence in this world, human but partaking of divinity (the imam or Christ). Judaism and Sunni Islam, by contrast, both stress a more transcendant God.

The Twelvers account for by far the majority of the world's Shi'a Muslims. They constitute the overwhelming majority in Iran, are also a majority (over 60 percent) in neighboring Iraq, in Bahrain and Azerbaijan, and are clearly the largest community in multiconfessional Lebanon. In other countries they have minority status. (See table 1.4).

Another, much smaller, number of Shi'is are customarily classified under the rubric of Seveners, for they believe that a different son of the sixth imam succeeded to the imamate. This son, Ismail, predeceased his father, but those who became the Sevener Shi'is either believed that Ismail remained alive or

Table 1.4 States with Significant Shi'i Muslim Populations[a]

	Total Population (000,000 rounded)	Percent Shi'a	Percent Sunni	Total Muslim
Afghanistan	24.8	15%	84%	99%
Azerbaijan	7.6	"mostly"		93.4%
Bahrain	.6	61.3%	20.5%	81.8%
Iran	61.5	93.4%	5.6%	99.%
Iraq	21.7	62.5%	34.5%	97%
Kuwait	1.9	30%	45%	85%[b]
Lebanon	3.5	34%	21.3%	55.3%
Pakistan	141.9	20%	75%	95%
Saudi Arabia	20.8	3.3%	93.3%	96.6%
Syria	15.3	12%	74%	86%
Tajikistan	6.1	5%	80%	85%
United Arab Amirates	2.7	16%	80%	96%
Yemen	16.4	46.9%	53%	99.9%

Source: Britannica Book of the Year, 1999.
a Not a complete listing. Shi'i minorities may well be underestimated in certain cases. The Lebanese figures are at best "guestimates."
b Includes 10 percent "other Muslim."

that Ismail's son should have succeeded to the imamate. Thus, the name Ismaili is still used to identity those Shi'is of this persuasion. Much more could be said about the role of Sevener Shi'is in Muslim history, just as minority or "extremist" groups often provoke the majority or "mainstream" bodies to more clearly define their positions. For present purposes it will suffice to record the following: the most important political challenge posed by the Sevener Shi'i was that of the Fatimids in the tenth century c.e. They seized political control in the Maghrib, Egypt and geographical Syria, seriously threatening the Sunni Abbasid caliphate ruling in Baghdad.[4]

As Fatimid power waned, Sevener Shi'ism took a radical turn, spawning the "Assassins," from the Arabic word for hashish users, made famous in Western history by their confrontation with the Crusaders. The Bohra and Khoja Isma'ilis, the latter followers of the Agha Khan, are descendants of these radical Sevener Shi'i groups. Most of these Ismailis are now Indian Muslims of quietist bourgeois orientation. They can perhaps be compared, in terms of this evolution, to today's Quakers, Amish, and other Christian groups who evolved from sixteenth- and seventeenth-century Anabaptists, Shakers, and others who were once quite revolutionary.

Many Ismailis now live as important diaspora communities in East Africa and Britain.

Also evolving from Sevener Shi'ism are the Druze, who typify the type of religious community that is nonproselytizing, has an esoteric doctrine, and has been able to keep its tight-knit communal nature by having chosen a geographical refuge area sufficiently remote (and infertile) to dissuade political power situated in the cities and plains from interfering. The Druze have lived for centuries in the mountainous regions divided today between Lebanon, Syria, and Israel.

Another such group are the Alawites, or Nusayris, whose early history is also extremist. The Alawites, however, represent a radical offshoot from Twelver, not Sevener, Shi'ism. Also a mountainous people, they constitute about 12 percent of the Syrian population. Traditionally at the bottom of the Syrian socioeconomic ladder, the Alawites in recent years have exercised political control under the leadership, since 1970, of Hafiz al-Asad. They are an intriguing example of upward mobility via the military and mobilization politics (the Syrian Ba'th party).

The third Shi'a group are the Zaydis, who are found in Yemen. They are named for the brother of the fifth Shi'i imam, Zayd, who challenged the more quietist political posture of his nephew, Ja'far al-Sadiq, the sixth imam. Zaydi Shi'ism, in its political or worldly terms, permits any descendant of Ali to be imam provided he exerts his right, including by force of arms. Zaydi Shi'ism also bridges the sharp theological divide separating Sunnis and other Shi'is, for they accept as a less than ideal imamate the rule of the first three caliphs before Ali.

Another small Muslim sect that, like the Ismailis, evolved from revolutionary beginnings are the Ibadites found in remote areas of Tunisia and Algeria and constituting the majority religion in Oman. They trace their origin to the Kharijites (seceders), who, as rigorists, turned against Ali after he had agreed to arbitration in his struggle with the Umayyad Mu'awiya. The descendants of the Kharijites, classic examples of the uncompromising, he-who-is-not-with-us-is-against-us religious stance, have long since moved to an essentially accommodationist attitude in worldy affairs.[5]

Many other smaller offshoots of mainstream Islam could be listed if one moved on further east to the Indian subcontinent or, for that matter, elsewhere.[6] Even the above cursory listing of smaller Muslim sects to be found in the Middle East risks giving a distorted image of Islam in today's world. It is much more pertinent to think of Sunni and Twelver Shi'a Islam as constituting mainstream or "orthodox" Islam (using *mainstream* and *orthodox* simply as quantitative measures without positive or negative connotation), for these two account for over 95 percent of the total Muslim population. Moreover, sticking to a quantitative scale, the overwhelming predominance of Sunni Islam throughout the centuries and to this day is indisputable.

Accordingly, in this broad-ranging effort to take the measure of Islam in its relation to politics and, in the process, to highlight the historical roots of Muslim attitudes toward politics, the Sunni Muslim story gets the most attention. Twelver Shi'ism, important in its own right, also offers a useful comparison and contrast with Sunni Islam. Twelver Shi'ism will thus also figure prominently. The minority sects of Islam, however, will be treated only to the extent that they clarify the story of mainstream Islam.

2.

Islam, Judaism, and Christianity in Comparative Perspective: An Overview

Paul Bowles's novel, *The Spider's House*, offers the following musings of a long-time resident in Morocco:

> Stenham smiled: unaccountable behavior on the part of Moslems amused him, and he always forgave it, because, as he said, no non-Moslem knows enough about the Moslem mind to dare find fault with it. "They're far, far away from us," he would say. "We haven't an inkling of the things that motivate them." There was a certain amount of hypocrisy in this attitude of his; the truth was that he hoped principally to convince *others* of the existence of this almost unbridgeable gulf. . . . This pretending to know something that others could not know, it was a little indulgence he allowed himself, a bonus for seniority. Secretly he was convinced that the Moroccans were much like any other people, that the differences were largely those of ritual and gesture, that even the fine curtain of magic through which they obscured life was not a complex thing, and did not give their perceptions any profundity.[1]

Bowles is right on target. There is a deep-rooted Western tendency to obscure Islam and Muslims through veils of esoterica and—in extremis—even to suggest that entirely different rules of logic and evidence are required to take the measure of Islam and Muslims. This is nonsense. Muslims *can* be understood, just like other people. They can also be misunderstood, just like other people. Avoiding the assumption that Muslims are "not like us," let's proceed comparatively.

Islam, Judaism, and Christianity:
Some Comparative Generalizations

Islam should not be all that strange to those who have grown up in a Jewish or Christian environment. It is a sister religion, the last of the three great monotheistic religions, all three of which share a common worldly home-land—the Middle East.

Jews, Christians, and Muslims worship the same God, believe in revelation, holy scriptures, heaven and hell, and have similar attitudes toward history and the role of humankind in fulfilling the divine purpose. If one is to think in global terms, which would seem to be the only acceptable norm in this age, then the most significant dividing line is not among any of the three Semitic monotheistic religions but between all of them and the other major world religions such as Hinduism or Buddhism.

In earthbound historical terms Islam grew for the most part out of a Jewish and Christian heritage. If, from one perspective, Christianity started as a Jewish heresy, then from a similar way of viewing the matter Islam began as a Judeo-Christian amalgam.

This much is even accepted theologicaly by Muslims, although of course the fact of Islam's largely Judeo-Christian matrix is expressed differently. In theological terms Muslims view Muhammad as the last in a line of prophets beginning with Abraham and continuing through Jesus. Muslims believe that Muhammad brought God's final revelation, the "seal of prophecy."

Muslim theologians take the position that God began with a partial revelation contained in the Old Testament (the Hebrew term, *Torah*, being used in the Qur'an) deeming in His wisdom that such was all His human believers were then able to absorb. More of His revelation was later given through Jesus in the New Testament (the Arabized form of gospel—*injil*—appearing in the Qur'an). Later, having determined that the world was ready, God gave the final and perfected revelation through His chosen messenger, Muhammad. This was the Qur'an.

Anyone with even a passing knowledge of the way the early Christian Church distinguished itself from Judaism should be able to follow such Muslim theological reasoning with a sense of both familiarity and empathy.

Accordingly, many of the most venerated names in the Bible figure with equal holiness in the Qur'an in their Arabized form. These include Abraham (Ibrahim), Moses (Musa), Jacob (Ya'qub), David (Dawud), Solomon (Sulayman), John the Baptist (Yahya), and Jesus, ('Isa) who is revered as a prophet but not as the son of God.

Islam, thus, offers an abundance of familiar signs along the way to any Jew or Christian. It can be argued that the more Jews or Christians know of their own religious heritage the better able they are to understand Islam. Not surprisingly, many of the most perceptive studies of Islam by non-Muslims have been made by those well conversant with their own Jewish or Christian tradition. Such would include, from an earlier generation, the Jew, Ignaz Goldziher, the Protestant, Duncan M. MacDonald, and the Catholic, Louis Massignon. Another famous triad of contempories would be the Jew, S. D. Goitein, the Protestant, Wilfred Cantwell Smith, and the Catholic, Louis Gardet. The late Marshall G. S. Hodgson deserves special mention.[2] Hodgson's devout Quakerism, with the Quaker emphasis on the "inner light," certainly would appear to have helped him appreciate the distinctive Islamic mix of legalism and mystical devotionalism, of practicality and piety. Moreover, experiencing Christianity from within the tradition of Quakerism, which largely rejects the notion of a clergy, Hodgson was well placed to interpret an Islam that has neither clergy nor any equivalent of the Christian sacraments.

Why, then, is Islam so poorly understood in the West? Or, even worse, why is it so often distorted? The sad history of Christian-Jewish relations suggests the answer, reminding us that common religious origins and even many shared religious values do not guarantee fellow feeling.

When groups of people (whether religious communities, political parties, or nation-states) share a common origin but split away from each other to form organizationally separate entities, the more normal human result is acute antipathy if not downright enmity. The Stalinist rage against Trotskyites, the brutal Pakistani repression of what later emerged as the new nation of Bangladesh, and the harsh Christian polemics and Christian conduct against Jews over the centuries all illustrate this theme (and many other examples, religious and secular, could be cited). When the issue revolves around ideological and organizational integrity (in a word, group identity), the bitterest enemies are the former fellows who refused to go along. The most brutal fights are often between kinsmen, not strangers.

Islam, throughout most of the long history of Christian-Muslim encounters, has been the enemy. In Christian eyes Islam has been a heresy that, to make matters worse, was until modern times also often a military threat.

The Jewish view of Islam (as of Christianity) was necessarily different. It was the perspective of a vulnerable small minority living among and accommodating as best it could to a dominant majority. Jewish history thereby provides a significant minority view-from-within perspective on both Christendom and *Dar al-Islam* (as does the history of minority Christian communities living in Islamic countries), but in terms of global politics the great confrontation was always between Islam and Christendom.

Nor was the animosity any less from the Muslim side as regards the Christian West. Or if animosity was less from the Muslim side in earlier centuries it was largely because the Christian West did not threaten the Muslim world militarily nearly so much as Muslim political power threatened Europe. The Crusades were something of a sideshow seen from the Islamic heartland. The infinitely more important military concern of Muslim peoples during those years centered on the martial nomadic tribes in Central Asia who reached a peak of power under the Mongols.

Equally, the Reconquista, which cleared the Iberian peninsula of Muslim control, was more than matched during those centuries by the steady Muslim destruction of the Byzantine Empire with the accompanying Islamization of Anatolia (the fall of Constantinople in 1453 was the dramatic climax to a process that had been going on for centuries) and the penetration of Islam deep into southeastern Europe. Armies of the Ottoman Empire even laid seige to Vienna in 1529 and again as late as 1683.

The Muslim reaction to the West in modern times, which may be seen as ranging from ambivalent admiration to suspicious antipathy, is in many ways a great reversal of roles between the two sister civilizations. Just as medieval Christendom deemed Islam a heresy and feared Muslim military power, so the Muslim world in modern times sees the Christian West as stubbornly clinging to an incomplete revelation but frightfully powerful militarily and technologically.

The one constant element in Muslim-Western relations throughout the centuries is that of religious suspicion and politico-military confrontation. The kinship binding together Judaism, Christianity, and Islam is a demonstrable fact, but the antipathy dividing them politically is an equally powerful fact. For this reason the handful of theologically trained Jewish and Christian scholars who have made, and still make, important contributions to our understanding of Islam have been vastly outnumbered throughout the centuries by both theologians and the laity who approach the subject with a marked animus. The same holds for Muslim perceptions of Judaism and Christianity and, by extension, of Western civilization.

The burden of this sad legacy must not be minimized. Confining our attention to Western perceptions of Islam (and not the reverse, equally fascinating but best left to another occasion), a sensitive individual who begins to watch for subtle signs of Western bias regarding Islam can only be dismayed. From the greats of our literature (e.g., Dante) to the stereotypes of present-day political cartoons, the legacy lives on to distort our image of Islam, a sister religion and culture.

We must be fully aware of these pervasive cultural biases concerning

Islam and Muslims, but we can—with conscious effort—manage to see things clearly. One of the most encouraging developments in modern scholarship has been the rise of the scientific study of religion, including the comparative sociology of religions. Although resisted and misunderstood by traditionalists in all religions, this scholarly approach is not antireligious or even irreligious (although, admittedly, many of its practitioners do adopt intellectual postures ranging from skeptical to disdainful). The comparative study of religions provides a scientific methodology and a shared vocabulary for analyzing and interpreting the impact of religion in this world. Equally important, it gives us a common base—that transcends any single religion or culture—from which to study any particular religion or religions in general.

This seemingly simple step marks a decisive turn in religious history. Instead of studying one's own religion solely in order to strengthen one's faith, and instead of studying other religions in order to proselytize or to resist the proselytizing efforts of others, the purpose of the scientific comparative study of religions is to advance knowledge and understanding. Such knowledge and understanding will not undermine religious faith, nor will it necessarily strengthen religious faith. It does, however, provide a clear path for the inquiring mind to transcend the limits of an individual's own culture and thus to see that culture in the context of other cultures, *sub specie aeternitatis*.

In this spirit let us begin with a very broad-ranging comparison of the three great monotheistic religions—Judaism, Christianity, and Islam, keeping in mind the cultural burden of the past, but consciously transcending this obstacle to understanding by adopting a scientific value-free outlook.[3] These general points of comparison between the three religions can serve to set the stage for our discussion of Islam and politics.

Q

To begin with an important general finding, a comparison of the three Semitic religions readily reveals that Judaism and Islam have much more in common than either does with Christianity. Judaism and Islam posit a much more transcendent deity and a more rigorous monotheism. They have nothing equivalent to the Christian notion of the incarnation. This is why the old usage *Muhammadan* to label Islam or Muslims is incorrect and even abusive. It assumes that Muhammad is to Islam as Christ is to Christianity. Not at all, for to Muslims Muhammad was fully human with no divine attributes. Indeed, the Islamic religious outlook makes it extremely difficult for Muslims to understand the Christian doctrine of the Trinity, even less to view it sympathetically. To Muslims the idea of God-in-man comes across as *shirk* (literally, association, thus meaning the linking of any person or thing with the ineffable God), and *shirk* is the gravest of sins in Islam. Some years ago I sat in on a discussion between an eminent Egyptian *'alim* and an equally eminent Catholic priest famed for his rich, nuanced scholarly study of Islam. An exhilarating atmosphere of mutual respect and mutual understanding reigned, but then the *'alim* raised the issue of the Trinity, bringing in its wake a discussion characterized by misunderstanding and even animosity poorly papered over by scholarly politesse on both sides.

This antipathy to any idea of an immanent God well characterizes Sunni Islam, but the exalted role of the imams in Shi'i Islam, by contrast, does bear some comparison to that of Christ in Christianity.

Islam and Judaism both place great emphasis on the law. Both religious systems conceive of a comprehensive religio-legal system covering all aspects of the individual's relations to others and of the individual's relation to God. Everything is taken into account and set out in detail—times of prayer, foods that may be eaten and manner of ritual slaughter of animals, almsgiving, inheritance, and even such minor details as the use of a toothpick.

This emphasis on the religious law in both Islam and Judaism is to be contrasted with the Christian concept of liberation from the curse of the law (Galatians 3:13) and of justification through faith alone, all this being especially the theological contribution of Saint Paul.

What are the practical social and political implications of these distinctions? Islam and Judaism may be seen as giving more emphasis to obeying the rules, Christianity to the intent that lies behind action, to faith. It has even been suggested that the hallmark of Islam is well summed up not so much in its emphasis on orthodoxy (right thinking) as on orthopraxy (right conduct). The same can be suggested for Judaism.

In another sense, Islam and Judaism emphasize rather more the running tally of a believer's deeds and misdeeds, with the implication that the more favorable the balance the stronger the individual's position before God.

Christianity places more emphasis on the disjuncture between God's grace and man's deeds. One cannot earn a place in heaven. Salvation is an act of divine grace, a theological position reaching its logical extreme in Calvinism. This aspect of Christianity may be seen in the importance Christians give to the parable of the prodigal son (Luke 35:11–32) or of the shepherd leaving his ninety-nine sheep to find the one lost sheep (Luke 15:4–7).

Islam and Judaism stress instead the virtue of consistent, constant fulfillment of God's law. The Orthodox Jew embracing the "yoke of the law" as being in itself a liberating and fulfilling experience is matched by the Muslim regard for the *Shari'ah* (the entire corpus of Muslim religious law). The Christian image of the law has an almost opposite sense (e.g., Romans 3:28, 7:6, and 10:4).

The very word, *Shari'ah*, has the original sense of the path to the watering place, a striking image for a religion born in arid Arabia, where one's very life depended upon planning itineraries to reach the rare oasis in good time. The this-worldly and social implications of Islam, as of Judaism, may be compared to an extended journey across a difficult but passable terrain. To arrive safely at the destination one must plan ahead and reach the various intermediate stages in good time. The Shari'ah may be seen as the map setting out the route for this worldly journey. Another powerful Muslim expression that conveys the same sense is *sirat al-mustaqim* (the right path). It figures in the opening prayer (*al-Fatihah*) of the Qur'an.

This similarity between Judaism and Islam and the contrast of each to Christianity deserves emphasis. Let a few modern scholars help to nail down the point. With her flair for the striking phrase, Patricia Crone has written: "If Christianity is Judaism gone soft, Islam by contrast is Judaism restated as an Arab faith: like Judaism, it is strictly monotheist where Christianity is trinitarian, it is shaped as an all-embracing holy law where Christianity is antinomian, and it finds its social embodiment in a learned laity where Christianity has its priests."[4]

"It is now fairly well known," Seyyed Hossein Nasr has observed, "that the very concept of law in Islam differs from what is prevalent in the West and that sacred law in Christianity refers to the spiritual and moral principles enunciated by Christ, whereas the sacred law, *Shari'ah* in Islam, involves not only principles but also their application to daily life in the form of legal codifications."[5]

To Marshall Hodgson Islam is "the religion of sober moderation, and most Muslims would distrust Paul's grand defiance of reason and of nature or an exaltedly private *credo quia absurbum.*" The Muslim, he notes, "seeks not so much consolation as *guidance* from his faith." In comparing the opening sura (chapter) of the Qur'an, the *Fatiha*, with the Lord's Prayer in the Bible, Hodgson points out that the former asks for guidance, the latter for forgiveness.[6]

Such general comparisons of the three monotheistic religions necessarily involve some distortion. These three rich, complex, and long-lived religious traditions cannot be so neatly categorized. Many exceptions are to be found. Nor do the distinctions adequately envelop the total action and lifestyle of even the quintessential Jew or Christian or Muslim. The Christian does care about compiling a record of piety and good deeds. The Jew and the Muslim affirm God's omnipotence and thus His ability to save whom He wills. In crasser terms, Christianity is more than seeking salvation at the last moment after a long span of hell-raising.[7] Judaism and Islam are more than religions of calculated prudence. Still, as broad brush portraits they may have some utility.

In one important respect Judaism is the exception while Christianity and Islam are similar. Both are proselytizing religions. This statement, in turn, evokes the hoary Western image of militant Muslims offering the infidel the harsh choice of conversion or the sword. And what about the Islamic doctrine of jihad, which can be translated as holy war, that is, religiously mandated war, against the infidel?

This much can be said for present purposes: the Muslim concept of jihad is an important principle of the faith. Indeed, the scholarly consensus is that jihad just missed becoming the sixth "pillar of Islam," joining the five canonically sanctioned "pillars" (profession of faith, prayer, fasting, almsgiving, and pilgrimage). Moreover, Islam provides for a clear "we-they" bifurcation between the Muslim community, the Dar al-Islam and everybody else, or the *Dar al-Harb* (literally, the abode of war). Nor can it be denied that from its earliest years the Islamic community by means of an amazing series of conquests became a religio-political community, indeed an empire. This status was attained by Christianity only some three centuries after Christ with the conversion of Constantine in 312 C.E.

On the other hand, the historical reality is that political authority in the early Muslim empire made little effort to convert. Indeed, at times political authority sought to slow down those voluntary conversions for the most practical (or, if you prefer, basest) of reasons—to maintain the aristocratic status of the Arabo-Muslims and to avoid losing tax revenues (the *jizya*, or special tax, paid by non-Muslims in return for protection [*dhimma*] and freedom from military duty). Moreover, the principle of "no compulsion in religion" (Qur'an 2:256) has stood throughout the centuries as a bar against forced conversions.

Jihad can in fact be compared to the Christian doctrine of just war.

> Jihad, like just war, was conceived by its early theorists basically as a means to circumscribe the legitimate reasons for war to so few that peace in inevitably enhanced. Jihad, like just war, is grounded in the belief that intersocial relations should be peaceful, not marred by constant and destructive warfare. The surest way for human beings to realize this peace is for them to obey the divine law that is imprinted

on the human conscience and therefore accessible to everyone, believers and unbelievers. According to the medieval view Muslims are obliged to propagate this divine law, through peaceful means if possible, through violent means if necessary. No war was jihad unless it was undertaken with right intent and as a last resort, and declared by right authority. Most Muslims today disavow the duty to propagate Islam by force and limit jihad to self-defense. And, finally, jihad, just like just war, places strict limitations on legitimate targets during war and demands that belligerents use the least amount of force necessary to achieve the swift cessation of hostilities.[8]

A good first step in comparing the three monotheistic religions is to accept that all three contain a militant, even violent, tradition. One need only read Deuteronomy 20:16–17: "In the cities of those nations whose lands the Lord your God is giving you as a patrimony, you shall not leave any creature alive. You shall annihilate them." Or, skipping millennia, one comes to the period of the Crusades and then in modern times such symbolic markers as the rousing "Battle Hymn of the Republic" or "Onward, Christian Soldiers."

All three religions have, however, evolved rules (honored, alas, often in the breach) to restrict under what circumstances one can legitimately engage in warfare as well as what restraints apply in the conduct of war.

As for the two proselytizing religions, Christianity and Islam, it can be suggested that both claim the right to seek converts but neither now goes so far as to champion the right to use military forces against those who would resist such peaceful proselytizing. Interestingly, the more violent and activist modern-day Islamists, in any case, see themselves as engaged in a desperate defensive battle against the religious (or secular) West. They are not so much bent on seeking new converts. The major thrust of their message can be summarized as defense against the outside infidel and jihad against the internal infidel (that is, those Muslim rulers deemed to have strayed from the true Islam).

In terms of class analysis traditional Islam is marked by an urban bourgeois outlook. It is a religion of carefully elaborated rules, of contractual relations, of keeping accounts and weighing in the balance. Christianity, especially during its formative period, was the religion of a proletariat. Later, with the alliance of church and empire, the situation became more complex, but certainly something of Christianity's nonbourgeois (antibourgeois?) origins remained. The Muslim scriptures, like the Jewish Bible, contain what might be labeled bourgeois images.[9] By way of illustration, Judaism: "You have been weighed in the balance and found wanting"

(Daniel 5:27); Islam: "Give full measure and full weight, in justice" (Qur'an 6:153); Christianity: "And Jesus looking upon him loved him, and said to him, 'You lack one thing; go, sell what you have, and give to the poor, and you will have treasure in heaven; and come, follow me.' At that saying his countenance fell, and he went away sorrowful, for he had great possessions" (Mark 10:21–22).

This point, in turn, may serve to clear up one tenacious Western misconception about Islam. This is the notion of Islam as the religion of the desert, Islam as the religion of nomadic simplicity. In actual fact Islam grew up in the cosmopolitan trading city of Mecca, and its principal early leaders were sophisticated Meccans. Islam evolved in this world not essentially as a religion of the desert and of nomads but as a religion of oasis urbanites living in symbiosis with the desert and the nomads.

The nomadic tribes of Arabia did provide the manpower for the early Muslim conquests, but leadership came from the cities. Moreover, the nomadic contribution to the growth of Islam rapidly decreased while that of the urban and sedentary areas continued to grow. Early on, the political center of Islam left Arabia for the much more urbanized and sedentary Fertile Crescent with Damascus as capital of the Umayyads (661–750) and Baghdad created by the Abbasids (750–1258) as their capital.

Thereafter, Islamic political fortunes were always linked to great cities commanding well-populated hinterlands—Cairo, Cordova, Isfahan, Delhi, Fez, Istanbul. Thinly populated Arabia was the cradle of Islam, its two holy cities—Mecca and Madina—remain the religious hub of Islam, and Arabia has from time to time sent out or nurtured other Muslim messengers (the last major example being Muhammad ibn Abd al-Wahhab in the eighteenth century), but within less than a generation after the death of Muhammad Arabia had lost its political centrality and was never to regain it.[10]

Finally, on this point of the urban and bourgeois nature of Islam it is well to note that Islam is the only major world religion to have been founded by a successful businessman. The prophet Muhammad before his "call" (the Christian usage is appropriate to the Muslim context as well) had been an active participant in Mecca's caravan trade. This was a complex business offering seventh-century equivalents of joint-stock enterprises, long-term and high-risk investments with the possibility of significant gains given good organization and effective market analysis. A caravan with as many as one thousand camels would be en route from, say, Mecca to Damascus for some forty days, and careful long-range planning for provisions and protection on the journey was required. Not surprisingly, many of the religious messages in Islamic scriptures have been expressed in the language of merchants.

Another matter linking Islam and Judaism while distinguishing both from Christianity is the role of the religious specialists, or—using the Christian term—the *clergy*. In the sense that Christianity uses this word there is no clergy in Islam or Judaism. There is no equivalent body of specially trained individuals, institutionally separated from the rest of society, organized in a chain-of-command hierarchy from parish priest to pope and given monopoly control over significant religious acts (the sacraments) as well as over the interpretation of dogma.

Every religion, however, and certainly every scriptural religion does possess a clergy in the sense of identifiable religious specialists with some authority (even if ill-defined and less than total) over the faith and the faithful. Such a group in Islam, comparable to the Jewish rabbinate, are the *ulama* (singular *'alim*). The terms translates literally as "the learned," i.e., learned in Islamic religious studies.

Throughout the centuries and to the present day those who would become ulama must spend many years of study, usually as seminarians, slowly absorbing a large and—in theory —unchanging corpus of religious knowledge. Their status as learned men is earned through book learning of a very traditional sort.

They are the guardians and transmitters of the bookish religious tradition. They are the teachers, the theologians, and the pastoral priests of Islam. From their ranks come also those called *fuqaha*,[11] those learned in the science of *fiqh*, or Islamic law, who provide the qadis (judges) and muftis (jurisconsults) of Islam.

In this sense there is certainly a Muslim clergy, but these religious specialists of Islam are more comparable to Jewish rabbis than to Christian clergy.

Another major category of Muslim religious specialists are the sufi leaders. What is the difference between an 'alim and a Sufi shaykh? In simplest terms the ulama are the guardians and expositors of the Islamic theological and legal tradition, the sufis the champions of the Islamic mystical tradition. The latter may be seen as the Muslim equivalents of holy men or gurus or shamans or saints. Their followers are usually grouped into special religious fraternities or *tariqas* (interestingly, yet another word with the meaning of "path"). The Sufi leader—who may be called shaykh or *pir* or *baba* depending on the prevailing linguistic/cultural tradition in the different parts of the Muslim world—is also a religious specialist, a learned man but in his case well versed not so much in the scriptural *'ilm* of the ulama as in *ma'rifa* (which can be well conveyed by the Christian term *gnosis*, or esoteric, direct, illuminist knowledge of the divine plan).

Here, again, Islam is more like Judaism than Christianity. Sufis are not organizationally linked to the ulama. There is nothing equivalent to the way in which the Catholic Church was able to channel and control mystical tendencies by permitting different religious orders to develop, nothing equivalent to the Catholic distinction between secular and regular clergy (the former being pastoral priests, the latter members of special religious bodies such as the Dominicans, Franciscans, or Jesuits).

Nor does Islam, any more than Judaism, offer an equivalent to the pronounced tendency within Protestantism wherein those of more antinomian or gnostic or immanentist persuasion reject the existing established churches and form separate sects.

In Islam, just as in Judaism, there is the potential for tension between the religion of the ulama and the sufis, the religion of the head and the heart, the religion of law and of illumination. This potential tension is sometimes realized (the anti-Sufi stance of the Wahhabis in modern times being an example), but usually the two religious tendencies, personified by the ulama and the Sufi shaykhs, have managed to reach a working accommodation, at times even a symbiotic relationship.

Looking at the matter sociologically, a clear distinction emerges between the organizational path chosen by both Islam and Judaism as opposed to Christianity. Islam and Judaism make no attempt to bring all such tendencies together into an explicit organizational hierarchy. Islam and Judaism, instead, settle for a more unstructured approach to the basic issues of organization and hierarchy to be found in all religions.

What then is the specifically Muslim form of "church government," and what influence does this pattern of religious organization have on politics and society in Muslim lands? We next turn to those questions.

3.

Muslim "Church Government"

In Islam, unlike Christianity, there is no tradition of a separation of church and state, of religious organization as contrasted with political organization. At least, this is the oft-repeated statement contrasting the two religions. There will be occasion to suggest important modifications to this assertion, but let it serve as a point of departure.

One simple reason for this difference between Islam and Christianity is that Islam knows no "church" in the sense of a corporate body whose leadership is clearly defined, hierarchical, and distinct from the state. The organizational arrangement of Muslim religious specialists, or ulama,[1] makes an *institutional* confrontation between Muslim church and Muslim state virtually impossible. An 'alim may speak out against a ruler, but there is no canonical way he can summon a Muslim "church council." Nor has he any opportunity to pass his charges up the Muslim religious hierarchy until a Muslim equivalent of pope or council or synod renders a judgment binding on all members of the "church." This, at least, holds as a broad generalization (with reservations and exceptions to be noted) for Sunni Islam. As for Twelver Shi'ism, the actions of Ayatullah Khomeini and the mullahs in Iran suggest that the clergy there are more nearly a recognizable "church" hierarchy. This Sunni-Shi'i distinction calls for separate treatment.

Sunni Islam

Taking the majority Sunni case first, to argue that no distinctive corporate body equivalent to the church in Christianity exists in Sunni Islam is not to suggest that the ulama have no group identity or that the ulama, individually or collectively, have had little impact on politics. On the contrary, throughout the ages Muslim religious spokesmen have confronted Muslim rulers—ever so circumspectly at times, but occasionally in thundering condemnation. The ulama have often led or been intimately involved in movements toppling rulers from power.

The contrasting roles in the modern era of Muhammad ibn Abd al-Wahhab (1703–1787) and Shaykh Muhammad Abduh (1849–1905) exemplify the range of ulama involvement in this-worldly politics. The former represented the typical Muslim challenge from the periphery to the political center. He preached a rigorous puritanical religion from the central Arabian Peninsula, and his followers took up arms against other Muslims seen as lax to the point of apostasy.

Egypt's Muhammad Abduh, by contrast, was trained at al-Azhar and spent his life not in the hinterland but at one of the representative urban centers from which political power and cultural norms have radiated throughout Islamic history. After a brief flirtation with radical politics in his early years, Abduh chose the path of meliorist reform while working with the powers that be, including foreign overlords, the British having established their military occupation of Egypt in 1882.[2]

Both Ibn Abd al-Wahhab and Abduh garnered a following among the ulama as well as the people at large. Each in a different way left an imprint on religion and politics that survives to this day. The special type of Sunni Islam that outsiders call Wahhabism continues as the official religion of Saudi Arabia.[3] Indeed, the very existence of Saudi Arabia as a sovereign state is inextricably linked to the work of Muhammad ibn Abd al-Wahhab.

Abduh was the pioneer and principal champion of the Salafiyya school of Islamic modernism, which insists that Islam, properly understood, is perfectly attuned to the liberal, democratic, and scientific values of the modern world. The Salafiyya ideology has strongly influenced two quite different movements:

1. The Muslim Brethren (founded in 1928), which, still in existence and now representing what might be labeled moderate fundamentalism, served also in the decades following its creation as the chrysalis from which later emerged many of today's radical Islamist movements.
2. The diffuse cluster of ideological options embracing the various gradations of religious liberalism, secularism, and what might be called Muslim Erastianism.

Many examples of moderate or radical ulama impact upon constituted political authority, such as personified by Abduh and ibn Abd al-Wahhab, can be cited going back to the earliest days of Islam. Time after time the ulama refused to be "lions under the throne" and instead defined religious limits to royal authority.[4] Time after time religious leaders took to the periphery and organized religio-political challenges to the political center, often overthrowing and replacing the existing dynasty in a recurring geopolitical dialectic brilliantly interpreted centuries ago by the celebrated Ibn Khaldun.[5]

At this point we need to address what might appear to be a contradiction between two general assertions thus far advanced:

1. A confrontation between Muslim "church" and Muslim state is virtually impossible, since there is no such organizationally structured Muslim body of "clergy," but

2. Muslim religious leaders from earliest times to the present day have resisted and at times challenged and even overthrown Muslim rulers. Anyone who can win over the ulama or in other ways achieve a standing as a valid religious spokesman is in a position to pose a serious organized challenge to government.

The two points can be reconciled. Perhaps one way to understand the general Sunni Muslim arrangement of religious and political power is to realize that the very amorphousness of Muslim religious structures has provided religious spokesmen protection against state control.

The state can give office and other perquisites to the Muslim clergy it favors, but throughout Muslim history the state has been circumspect in its dealings with religious spokesmen, even state-appointed officials, for two complementary reasons: 1. Assertive state action against religious spokesmen risks setting off a reaction that the state cannot easily control and 2. there is usually no need to contemplate such action since the Muslim clergy lack the institutionalized framework to stand as an organized body against the state. Indeed, in the modern era the Sunni ulama have tended to become organized not so much as a discrete corporate body but as part of the state apparatus.

A Muhammad ibn Abd al-Wahhab in eighteenth-century Arabia or his numerous predecessors may take the Muslim equivalent of nailing their doctrinal theses to the church door at Wittenberg, but there is no Muslim pope to bring the issue to trial. The Sunni ulama have almost never acted in an organized fashion as if they constituted an institutionally distinct, hierarchically arranged body. This refusal to organize, to confront, to let things proceed to a showdown provides the Muslim clergy a certain protection against state control.[6]

Or perhaps a more subtle statement of the relationship is that neither state officialdom nor religious spokesmen have sufficient motivation to push matters to confrontation. The state has the organizational means but usually no great need to impose conformity on the ulama. The ulama lack the organizational framework—by contrast with the Catholic Church in its confrontation with the state in medieval Europe—but are usually not pressed by the state to abandon either doctrine or actions that they deem fundaments of the faith.

In religio-political confrontations that do occur many of the ulama continue to serve the state, and even sometimes take the offenders (in the eyes of the government) to task for violating legitimate Islamic practice. Just as often, however, the establishment ulama would take a more circumspect position, neither confronting the government nor anathematizing (if that Christian term may be used) the opposition. Other ulama might go over to the challenger either actively or quietly and behind the scenes. Many other ulama would adopt a wait-and-see attitude.

Examples in modern times of "establishment" ulama cooperating with political authority include the following:

1. In c. 1800 Hammuda Bey of Tunis ordered his ulama to write a rebuttal to a proselytizing letter sent by Wahhabi adherents. A leading Tunisian 'alim wrote a scathing response in Arabic rhyming prose (saj').

2. Then, in the 1933, still in Tunisia but now a French protectorate, a qadi in Bizerte ruled that Tunisians who had adopted French citizenship thereby lost their status as Muslims and could not be buried in Muslim cemeteries. Pressed by the protectorate authorities to solve the problem (being exploited by the young Habib Bourguiba and those destined to create the nationalist Neo-Destour Party) the chief Maliki and Hanafi ulama issued a fatwa announcing that Muslims adopting French citizenship could regain their Muslim status provided they "repented." This satisfied neither the protectorate authorities nor—even less—the nationalists. Demonstrations against these ulama continued, and the protectorate authorites got out of their plight by creating separate Muslim cemeteries for Tunisians granted French citizenship.

3. Following the 1979 Egyptian-Israeli peace treaty, the Egyptian government prevailed upon the leading ulama of al-Azhar to issue a statement supporting the accord. The ulama cited the *Al-Hudabiyya*

agreement reached between Muhammad and the Meccan leadership in the early period of the Prophet's leadership to justify the peace treaty with Israel. Earlier, however, 150 ulama meeting at al-Azhar on August 7, 1960, had issued a proclamation calling on Muslims throughout the world to "adopt an attitude of jihad against the Shah of Iran's recognition of Israel."[7]

For this reason religio-political challenges throughout Islamic history have often been set in motion, quite literally, by voices crying in the wilderness (e.g., Muhammad ibn Abd al-Wahhab from the heart of the Arabian Peninsula, the founder of the Sanusiyya order from a remote oasis in southeast Libya, or the Sudanese mahdi from Aba Island, far removed from Khartoum). Such action would then lead to a variety of possible outcomes: the most extreme would be either the downfall of a dynasty (the Mahdist forces overrunning Khartoum and establishing their government in Sudan) or the disgrace, and perhaps death, of the religious leader (the many defeated and thus "false prophets" noted in Western literature during the colonial period). Another alternative could be the failure of the religio-political challenger to win over the political center but the building of a new, viable sectarian movement in the hinterland (Sanusiyya in Libya or Wahhabiyya in Arabia).

Politics aplenty in all this, but nothing quite like the institutionalized church-state confrontations of European history. It is, instead, rather more like European church-state cooperation in confronting heresy raising its head in the hinterland.

Of course, the state has always had—and still has—great power to influence the ulama. Throughout much of Sunni Muslim history, and especially in modern times, the state has assumed the right to appoint and dismiss qadis, muftis, and teachers in Muslim seminaries, has exercised control over financial aspects of Muslim religious properties such as mosques, madrasas (religious schools), and the institution of waqf (endowment funds earmarked for religious purposes), and has used state police power to punish, imprison, and exile recalcitrant Muslim religious leaders.

In certain cases state control over the Muslim religious establishment became so pervasive that the ulama virtually became an arm of government. The best example was the Ottoman Empire, in which the ulama were largely integrated into the state apparatus. Such a development is perhaps best explained by the Ottoman's having possessed the most elaborate bureaucracy of any Muslim empire. For that matter, the roots of Ottoman government can be traced, at least in part, to the earlier Byzantine political tradition that the Ottomans built upon even while destroying the Byzantine Empire.

Not even the Ottoman Empire, however, attempted to impose religious doctrine. Nor did the members of the Muslim religious establishment holding government office make such an effort. This is all the more significant in that the Ottoman Empire developed institutionalized structures that might have made such moves possible.

For example, from the nineteenth century on the Ottomans did make an effort to breathe new life into the old idea of the ruler as caliph or, in effect, the religious leader of all Muslims as well as the sovereign over Ottoman subjects, regardless of their religion. This tendency, which peaked during the reign of Sultan Abdulhamid II (1876–1909), was an interesting example of cross-cultural feedback. The classic idea of the caliph as religious and political leader of the Muslim *umma* had remained throughout the centuries the centerpiece of Muslim political theory, but statements on the subject by Muslim scholars had long been quite divorced from operative reality. The caliph in such writing was as removed from the real world as was the Platonic philosopher-king, and the only historical approximation of such an ideal was deemed to have lapsed after the reign of the "rightly guided caliphs," Muhammad's first four successors—Abu Bakr, Umar, Uthman, and Ali. (This, of course, is the Sunni formulation. Shi'i Muslims believe that Muhammad's son-in-law, Ali, should have directly succeeded, then followed by Ali's progeny.)

Thereafter, the title of caliph when bestowed upon Muslim rulers had been essentially an honorific, an inflation of throne titles common to most monarchical systems. The title was not seen by rulers or the ruled as a serious claim to either the historical caliphate or, even less, what might be called the idealized caliphate.

The West, however, had long misperceived the Ottoman ruler as a "Muslim pope," and as the West increasingly interfered in Ottoman affairs in support of Christian Ottoman subjects it seemed natural to Sultan Abdulhamid II that he should, indeed, be the Muslim "pope" and stand up for Muslims everywhere. Just such an arrangement had been prefigured as long ago as 1774 in the Treaty of Kuchuk Kaynarja between the Ottoman Empire and Russia.[8] Moreover, the idea of the Ottoman sultan as both religious and political leader made more sense in Abdulhamid II's day, by which time the empire was becoming overwhelmingly Muslim, having lost almost all of its Balkan provinces where Christians predominated. The result was Pan-Islam.

Sultan Abdulhamid II did not, however, opt for any Muslim caesaropapism. He supported religious figures, sponsored the building of the Hijaz Railroad to connect Damascus with the holy cities of Mecca and Madina (funds were raised from all over the Muslim world by individual subscriptions) and was ever alert to gestures or acts that could enhance his position as leader of the entire Muslim umma. This is as far as he went. He did not try to decide religious doctrine, nor did he seek to exercise tighter control over the religious leadership.

In the Ottoman Empire there also developed the imposing office of *shaykh al-Islam*. This official, with his office in Istanbul, the imperial capital, came to be regarded as the principal mufti or, as it were, the mufti of last resort. This office could have stimulated the development of an organized and distinctive judiciary that might have more readily confronted the Ottoman executive. Something like a separation of powers as in the political thought of Montesquieu or in American governmental practice might have emerged. Nothing of the sort developed. The office had great prestige, but sultans appointed and dismissed whomever they wished, making a change on the average of every three or four years.[9]

Nor did the Muslim ulama attempt to nominate their own candidate or to support the continued tenure of an existing shaykh al-Islam. Individual holders of the office did from time to time get involved in high politics (such as issuing a fatwa to depose a reigning sultan), but no institutionalized power emerged from these activities. If the sultan was not really a Muslim pope, the shaykh al-Islam did not become one either. He was not even the Muslim equivalent of the archbishop of Canterbury.

In sum, the Sunni approach to church government is more akin to the Jewish. It rejects clerical hierarchy or centralizing procedures for establishing doctrine and law as well as for rewarding or punishing individual believers (Islam developed only limited and seldom used equivalents to penance, indulgence, anathema, or excommunication, all of which were for centuries fully institutionalized in Christian practice). Sunni Muslim political experience is, however, more like that of the Christian West—a religious establishment with close ties to government with both claiming to represent the majority population. A word now is in order concerning the quite different "church government" of Shi'ism.

Shi'i Islam

Shi'ism is legitimist, to adapt Western political terminology. The imamate, Shi'is assert, should have gone directly to Ali, the son-in-law of the Prophet Muhammad, and it should have remained thereafter from generation to generation in the Alid family line. As noted earlier, the majority Shi'i community believe that there were, counting Ali, twelve such imams in legitimate succession, the twelfth imam, having disappeared from worldly view, has since been in a state of occultation (*ghayba*).[10] Shi'a eschatology anticipates the return of the twelfth imam as the mahdi (the divinely guided) who will usher in the golden age and the consummation of God's plan.

This bedrock principle of the imamate in Shi'ism would not, however, necessarily produce a hierarchical, corporate Shi'i clergy. The role of the imam/mahdi in Shi'ism bears comparison to the role of the messiah in Judaism and of Christ's Second Coming in Christianity. Judaism has no clergy but instead a rabbinate (very much like the Sunni ulama). Christianity developed a corporate body—the church—and a clerical hierarchy. This divergent historical experience indicates that a religious system positing an occulted leader possessing divine or near-divine attributes (a Jewish messiah, a Christian Christ, or a Shi'i imam) could accommodate either a body of religious specialists who might be a nonhierarchical clustering of individuals and groups (as the rabbinate) or a corporate body arranged hierarchically (as the Catholic Church). Or the result might well be something in between the two. This latter possibility may best define the Twelver Shi'a clergy.

Shi'ism emerged as a fully elaborated theological system during a period of Sunni political power first under the Umayyads and then their rivals and successors, the Abbasids. To compress a complex story into a few words, the patristic age of Shi'ism involved moving toward a "spiritualization" of the imamate in order to avoid confronting existing political authority. In the same way and for the same reason there grew up the important Shi'i tenet of *taqiyya* (dissimulation), permitting believers to deny or dissimulate their beliefs if exposed to danger.

This prudent, politically quietist stance vis-à-vis worldly power continued in large measure among the Twelver Shi'i community until the sixteenth century[11] when a radical millenarian Shi'i movement, that of the Safavids, burst upon the scene in Iran. Iran, now rightly seen as the heartland of Twelver Shi'ism, was actually converted to that faith only in the sixteenth century under the aegis of this radical religio-political dynasty. The nineteenth-century Orientalist interpretation of Shi'ism as representing pre-Islamic Iranian culture and Sunnism reflecting pre-Islamic Arab culture has been proven to be an anachronism.

Twelver Shi'ism in today's world can summarily be presented in terms of the following evolution since the sixteenth century: the virtually messianic and charismatic authority of early Safavid Shi'ism was later routinized (to apply Max Weber's formulation) with the body of ulama (or mullahs, the term more in use in Iran) regaining control over religious doctrine and practice. The turbulence following the overthrow of the Safavid dynasty in 1722 could only strengthen the claims of the ulama to religious leadership, for the ensuing political leadership lacked any special religious aura. Moreover, the last major example of political leadership seeking to impose religious doctrine ended in complete failure. This was the effort by Nadir Shah (ruled 1736–1747) to effect a Sunni-Shi'i merger. The Shi'i ulama emerged victorious as defenders of the Shi'i faith.

Something approaching political stability was again reached with the advent of the Qajar dynasty (1794–1925), but the autonomy of the Shi'i clergy was not threatened since the Qajars claimed no special religious mandate to leadership as had the Safavids.

The eighteenth century in Iran also witnessed a confrontation between two schools of thought dividing the Shi'i ulama—the *Akhbari* versus the *Usuli*. The former held a position more like that of Sunni Islam in arguing that there was no need for independent scholarly judgment and interpretation (*ijtihad*). The Qur'an plus the statements of the Prophet Muhammad and the imams (*akhbar*)[12] were considered sufficient guidance to the faithful, thereby ruling out the use of human reason or of *ijtihad*. The *Usuli* school, on the contrary, affirmed the need for human reasoning and ijtihad in each generation.

Ultimately the Usuli school won out. This meant that the faithful required the guidance of a reasoning religious specialist, in a word, an 'alim who was a *mujtahid* (one who engages in ijtihad). There was to be no Protestant-like "priesthood of all believers." Instead, every believer needed to follow a mujtahid who would be for that believer a *marja'-e taqlid* (a source of imitation). The more influential of the clerical sources of imitation came to be called ayatullahs (literally, sign of God). Then in the early nineteenth century the Shi'i clergy developed the additional idea that the optimal arrangement was that of a single *marja'* to whom all others deferred. The Shi'i ulama were becoming more nearly a distinctive and even, in a sense, a corporate body. That all this makes Shi'i "church government" more like that of the Catholic Church has been noted by several observers. For example, "The triumph of the usuli school and the emergence of the institution of the supreme source for emulation are as important in the history of modern Shi'ism as the victory for papal power at Vatican I was for modern Roman Catholicism."[13] Or,

> In the first half of the nineteenth century, Shi'ism markedly diverged from the general Islamic pattern, becoming more similar to Western Christianity. As was the case with the papacy in medieval Western

Christianity, in sharp contrast to Byzantine caesaropapism and its Russian heir, it was the successful institutional translation of the separation of the religious and the political spheres that subsequently gave the Shi'ite hierocracy tremendous *political* power as the independent custodians of religion and of the sacred law.[14]

Even so, the Shi'i ulama did not develop the kind of strict hierarchy as seem in Roman Catholicism from parish priest to pope. Nor is there any body of eminent Shi'i clergy designated to select that single marja' equivalent to the College of Cardinals empowered to elect each new pope. The question of who becomes recognized as an ayatullah or a marja' has no such hard-and-fast rules. Rather, one becomes an ayatullah not by election but rather by informal accretions of religious scholarly opinion that so and so is deemed worthy of the august title. There is almost a post facto aspect to the process: after enough religious scholars have come to so designate an 'alim whom they choose to follow, the title of ayatullah accrues to the man by a sort of emerging consensus. Something of the same approach characterizes the designation of an ayatullah as the single marja' of his time. Interestingly, efforts by political authority to designate the marja' have been resisted.

Another important aspect of the Shi'i ulama vis-à-vis the state and worldy affairs is that they, unlike their Sunni counterparts, have managed to rely financially more on contributions given directly to them by their followers. Of course, political authority from the time of the Safavids to the end of the Pahlavi dynasty offered the ulama official positions and financial inducements, but the Shi'i ulama never became nearly so "bureaucratized" as did their Sunni peers in, for example, the Ottoman Empire and the post-Ottoman successor states. That a revolution in Iran was led by the ulama whereas Islamic radicals in most countries with Sunni majorities are largely from outside the ranks of the ulama dramatically illustrates how such structural differences impact on political dynamics. Indeed, the Sunni Islamic radicals often accuse the leading Sunni ulama of being catspaws of the government.

It remains to say a word about relations between religion and politics, betweeen "church" and "state" in today's Iran. Put simply, was the revolution that sent Muhammad Reza Shah into exile and produced the Islamic Republic consistent with earlier Iranian history? Did it accord with what we might call Shi'i political ideology?

Precedents for ulama activism are be found. There was the important role of the ulama in the Tobacco Concession boycott or during the 1906 Constitutional Revolution,[15] not to mention the earlier religio-political movement that ushered in the Safavid dynasty and converted Iran to Twelver Shi'ism. Even so, the political ideology advanced by Ayatullah Khomeini and the political reality of a government actually led by mullahs represents a sharp break with tradition. Khomeini scornfully dismissed any argument for not only political quietism but also political prudence. Instead, the ulama in the absence of the Hidden Imam had, in his view, the responsibility of actively "commanding the good and forbidding the evil." The ulama could neither retire to their prayers and their private lives nor counsel others to do so. They could not tolerate non-Islamic practices by those in authority with the excuse that all government was necessarily illegitimate in the absence of the Imam.

Although Khomeini was careful to insist that the religious leaders were fallible, unlike the Imam, who was *ma'sum* (divinely inspired and sinless), they were, in his judgment, obliged to assume the Imam's worldly burdens of guiding the community. Moreover, to Khomeini, such guidance went far beyond the more traditional role of advising rulers. It even exceeded the activist tradition of thundering against the misdeeds of rulers and working to replace them. The ulama were to participate actively in governance, and this is just what happened in the Islamic Republic of Iran, with the office of *velayat-e faqih* (guardianship of the jurisconsult) as set out in Khomeini's earlier writings being assumed by him until his death.[16]

In sum, the ulama in both Sunni and Shi'i Islam are an identifiable body of religious specialists. They attain this status following an extended period of formal training, just as is the case with Christian clergy. They then usually move into professional careers as teachers, preachers, judges (qadis), jurisconsults (muftis), or mosque officials in some other capacity. Just as the Christian clergy have ranged in eminence and theological sophistication from an Augustine or Thomas or Tillich to those with only a smattering of the basics so, too, there have been leading ulama throughout the centuries from a Ghazali, an Ibn Taimiyya, a Muhammad Abduh, or an Ayatullah Khomeini alongside those only slightly above the Muslim "laity" in religious learning. To this extent the idea that there is no "clergy" in Islam may be compared to the Protestant cry of the priesthood of all believers. Neither maxim is completely false but neither embraces the whole truth.

Always distinguishable from those pursuing civil or military positions in government, the ulama have nevertheless at times been so absorbed into governmental activities as to be deemed virtually part of the bureaucracy. Such a development characterized the Ottoman Empire as well as most of the Ottoman successor states. The Shi'i ulama of Iran have managed to keep a greater group identity and separation from government—until with the Islamic Revolution beginning in 1979 they became government itself. Will this revolutionary change survive and become the norm? Only time will tell.

The ulama, Sunni or Shi'i, provide one important key to understanding the relationship of Islam to politics, and clearly assertions such as "no separation of church and state in Islam" or "no priesthood in Islam" fail to capture the more complex reality of Islamic history.

4.

The Historical Bases of Traditional Muslim and Christian Political Theory

Most Muslims and most Christians have for centuries lived as majority communities ruled by governments that are at least nominally of the same faith. Even the religio-political struggles within Christendom and Islamdom have usually been intrafaith, such as Protestant versus Catholic or Sunni versus Shi'i.

Not so for the Jews. Throughout most of their history Jews have lived as tiny vulnerable minorities. Under such circumstances there was little practical need for a specifically Jewish political theory. Questions concerning the extent to which government, or the political community, should be guided by Jewish religious teachings simply had little relevance to the worldly situation of Jews. Indeed, only with Zionism and the creation of Israel did the need arise for defining the interaction of religious and political life in a state with a Jewish majority.

What, however, should the believer render unto Caesar when the particular caesar in question is of the same religious faith? Even more, what if this caesar presumes to be the defender of the faith, to seek religious legitimation for his rule? Such has been the lot of most Christians and most Muslims throughout the centuries, and it follows that Christian and Muslim thinkers have been obliged to address the questions of religion and the state in a way that Jewish thinkers have not.

From the historical perspective Jesus's instruction to "render therefore unto Caesar the things that are Caesar's and to God the things that are God's" (Matthew 22:21) represented the political wisdom of a tiny minority seeking protection against government and the larger society by prudently refusing to get involved in politics. Jesus's reply to the question of whether it was lawful to pay taxes to Caesar was not an answer but a prudent evasion.

Any clear answer would have harmed Jesus's mission. If he had replied yes, he would lose favor with the many antigovernment and antiestablishment forces. If he had advised against paying taxes, he would likely have faced harsh governmental action. The evasive answer Jesus gave was relevant to the political situation he and his small band of followers confronted, just as this kind of political withdrawal remained relevant for most of subsequent Jewish history.[1]

The maxim "render to Caesar" does not, in short, really answer the question that later majority Christian communities faced, and it represents only an early phase of the Christian community's development in this world. It is also clear why no equivalent of "render to Caesar" figures in the Qur'an or in the hadith literature. Islam grew up in political success. The question of accommodating to non-Muslim worldly authority did not arise.

Christianity and Islam began in almost diametrically opposite political circumstances, but within a few centuries both religions faced similar political questions growing out of similar political reality. Both had become universal religions whose followers were of different languages and cultures. Both religions had spread over vast territories, and throughout most of the areas conquered for Christianity or Islam the faithful eventually became a majority of the population. Moreover, within the vast territorial expanses that made up Christendom and *Dar al-Islam*, political power was in the hands of those professing the faith.

The situation was never static. Exceptions always existed. Islam gave way to Christianity in Iberia, Christianity to Islam in Anatolia. Christianity continued to push out with great success in various parts of the world, Islam with similar success in other parts. The earliest Christian churches of the Holy Land and the Eastern Mediterranean lost their dominant positions and survived as ever decreasing minorities within the world of Islam. Nebulous and shifting zones of Christian-Muslim confrontation and coexistence such as now pertain in much of Africa have always existed. There have always been significant Christian minorities living among non-Christian majorities and ruled by non-Christian rulers. The same holds for Muslims.

Yet after all the changes over time and the many exceptions are duly noted it remains true that most of the world's Christians and most of the world's Muslim have lived for most of the time as majority communities in polities controlled by their coreligionists. This highlights the radical and traumatic situation Muslims have faced in modern times when they found themselves directly or indirectly dominated by non-Muslims.

It is, accordingly, appropriate to use the more familiar history of Christian political theory as a yardstick for clarifying and interpreting Islamic political thought. Only a tantalizing sampling of broad generalizations can be mentioned, but perhaps the unavoidable distortion that comes with such simplifications can be offset by a perspective that emphasizes the shared circumstances of Islamic and Christian political traditions.

Politically both religions went through a process of compromises with and adjustments to the world. In Max Weber's terms there was a "routinization of charisma." Not all the believers accepted this in good grace. Within the two religious communities small groups have always come forward to resist such "routinization" with its inevitable adjustments and compromises that institutionalization necessarily bring. For these resisters nothing but a totally consistent application of the perceived religious truths, come what may, would suffice. Of such stuff are martyrs made, and not a few bigots as well.

These all-outers in the two religions have played an important role in posing the political questions to be resolved, but if the all-outers had won, neither Christianity nor Islam would have become, or have remained, universal religions. They would, instead, have continually split and resplit into smaller sects. Consensus politics is the cement of universal religions, even if this process is at times obscured by being carried out within the framework of authoritarian systems.

The Western Christian compromise with the world of politics went somewhat as follows: Christianity evolved from a proletarian outcast community to become the state religion in the Roman Empire.[2] The church government and the pattern of church leadership that had become effectively institutionalized before Rome embraced Christianity did not, however, go out of existence. Instead, church and state existed side by side.

Both church and state claimed otherworldly sanction. Both claimed this-worldly authority. Neither ever totally dominated the other. In the extended confrontation that ensued polemicists on both sides (usually clergymen or of clerical training whether supporting pope or emperor) created the corpus of medieval political thought that, together with the earlier Greco-Roman legacy of political philosophy, makes up the bedrock on which later Western political thought rests.

In the process, the existence of an organized church with its own hierarchy of leadership closely linked to but institutionally distinct from the state was accepted. The necessity and legitimacy of government was accepted. The need for government to conform to a religious standard of conduct was accepted. Only the questions of who was to determine that standard and who to judge whether it was being met were left unresolved.

The Reformation and Counter-Reformation brought additional problems obliging new adjustments. These new adjustments were long in coming and took a heavy toll in human suffering along the way, but eventually there emerged the notion of the secular state, a political entity that was to be judged by religiously based principles of morality but in no way controlled by or even accountable to any religious body.

The medieval church-state arrangement and the modern idea of a secular state that is religiously neutral were both the results of working compromises. The more reasonable among the partisans of pope or emperor, just as later the more reasonable Catholics and Protestants, seeing that doctrinal purity and logical consistency spelled continued strife, settled for a nebulous but manageable middle ground between the extremes. The ideological results of such compromises are always complex if not at times confused, making them vulnerable to the persistently logical attacks of the *pur et dur* intellectually inflexible. Such, it might be argued, is the customary fate of consensus politics, whether in the religious or the political field, but most of all in the area where religion and politics come together.

Muslim compromise with and adjustment to the world of politics took an interestingly different route. The Muslim community started, of course, from a different point. Muhammad and his immediate successors presided over both a new religious community and an imposing, rapidly expanding new polity. The early Christian church was, by contrast, a politically insignificant body that shunned worldly political ambition (believing the end of time was nigh). Facing the early Muslim community was the question of how to organize a state appropriate to the new religion.

Even this way of expressing the worldly development of Islam is not quite right, implying as it does a body of religious founders more or less consciously providing for a political apparatus. There was no Muslim church putting together a Muslim state. Rather, the new Muslim community—the *umma*—developed from a worldview that perceived religion and politics as a seamless web, that thought of this world and the world to come as a continuum. This perception is well expressed in the hadith of the Prophet, "Work for this world as if you would live forever. Work for the world to come as if you would die tomorrow."

In theological terms the early Muslim community did not accept that the end of time was nigh, nor that the believer should renounce this world in preparation for the world soon to come. In political terms the early Muslim community gave religious valuation to this-worldy matters. It accepted the religious imperative of implementing God's plan in this world.

Accordingly, the historical period extending from the time Muhammad was first called by God through the rule of the four rightly guided caliphs—roughly two generations—has always been viewed by Muslims as the golden age. It was the time when God's divine plan was believed to have come closest to being achieved.

Of course, the time of Jesus and the early apostles is equally Christianity's golden age. The enduring political import of these two golden ages, however, differs sharply. Those Christians of later centuries looking back on the primitive church as model for their times were inclined toward separatism and sectarianism. Any effort to reconstruct the early Christian Church involved logically (and psychologically) renunciation of the imperfect world and the creation of a small body of the totally committed who would form their own community, open only to those accepting their demanding standards.

The Muslim reformer seeking to get back to the piety and the purity of the Islamic golden age could not opt out of the existing imperfect umma. The Muslim reformer's model was not, and is not, that of a small, tight-knit, vulnerable, and totally committed tiny community in but not of this world. It is, instead, that of a dynamic, politically successful great society accepting God's charge to maintain a divinely guided umma both in this world and the world to come.[3]

The Christian harking back to the Christian golden age would be motivated to repudiate the snares of this world, the Muslim to call for a reordering of this world according to God's plan.

The Christian neotraditionalist could be reconciled to political insignificance and minority status even within Christendom, but not the Muslim, who would feel compelled to bring back into being the powerful, politically significant early umma.

Contrast, for example, the sociopolitical implications of Paul's effort to raise the spirits of the insignificant (in worldly terms) church at Corinth with the Qur'anic passage (revealed three years after Muhammad had become leader in Madina) calling for unity and community:

> For consider your call, brethren; not many of you were wise according to worldly standards, not many were powerful, not many were of noble birth; but God chose what is foolish in the world to shame the wise. God chose what is weak in the world to shame the strong. God chose what is low and despised in the world. (lst Corinthians 1:26–28)

And hold fast, all of you together, to the cable of Allah, and do not separate. And remember Allah's favor unto you; how ye were enemies and
He made friendship between your hearts so that ye became as brothers by His grace. . . . And there may spring from you a nation who
invite to goodness, and enjoin right conduct and forbid indecency. Such
are they who are successful. (Qur'an 3:103–104)

For this reason the Muslim "patristic age" is infinitely more important to
Islam and to Muslims as a source of political ideas than the Christian equivalent is to Christianity and Christians. The Christian thinker looking for
models of the Christian approach to politics would be pushed to go beyond
the Christian golden age, which has, after all, very little to say about politics.
For this very reason Christian political theory (or, more largely, political
theory emerging from a Christian context) has paid great attention to such
matters as church-state relations in medieval Christendom, to the theological struggles of the Reformation and Counter-Reformation, and to the religio-political implications of the rise of the secular state.

Political theory in the Christian context has, in other words, always
ranged over a broad field of historical experience. There has been a corresponding deemphasis of the early church period as a political model.

Not so for Islam. The Muslim period of the Prophet and the four rightly
guided caliphs stands splendidly alone as the significant model to which
Muslims concerned with political philosophy should repair. Even the Shi'i
political tradition gives overwhelming importance to essentially the same
period, although different interpretations are placed on the same historical
facts. The Shi'a contend that only Ali and his lineal descendants should have
succeeded to the calphate. Moreover, the "patristic age" for Shi'ism extended
somewhat beyond the age of the Sunni four rightly guided caliphs to include
the martyrdom of Husayn (61 A.H./680 C.E.). In a sense the principal branch
of Shi'ism that recognizes twelve imams from the family of the Prophet
beginning with Ali might be said to have a "patristic age" extending until the
ghayba of that twelfth imam in 869 C.E. Even so, the historical period from
which the political (and other) doctrines of Shi'ism are largely derived is that
encompassed by the mission of Muhammad, the imamate of his son-in-law,
Ali, and of the next two imams, Ali's sons Hasan and Husayn.

This is not to dismiss the many important points distinguishing Sunni
and Shi'a approaches to politics or to overlook the complex religio-political
history of the early Muslim community, but it does seem valid to insist that,
by contrast with Christianity, Islam in all its varieties looks back to its earliest years for its political model.

The decisive importance of early Muslim historical experience provides common ground on which virtually all later Muslims concerned with Islam and politics have chosen to take their stand. The neotraditionalist Hasan al-Banna, who founded the Muslim Brethren in 1928, emphasized the early Muslim community as the political model to be emulated. So, too, did the radical Shi'a political activist Ayatullah Khomeini.

At the same time, the modernist Ali Abd al-Raziq, arguing for a Muslim equivalent of separation between church and state, attempted to make his case by reinterpreting the religio-political history of the origins and early development of the caliphate. Equally, the radical 'alim from Egypt's al-Azhar, Khalid Muhammad Khalid, set out to justify a socialist approach to politics by appealing to examples from the time of the early Muslim community.[4]

Indeed, observers of Muslim political thought in modern times have often noted, sometimes with patronizing sympathy, sometimes with superciliousness, that those Muslims who seek democracy argue that Muhammad was the first democrat and the early Muslim community the first democracy, those advocating socialism depict Muhammad as the first socialist and the early community as the first socialist state, and so on as political styles change. Even certain Muslim communists went so far as to urge that Muhammad and the early community prefigured the idealized communist society.

What this persistent attitude of mind does reveal is the continued importance of the early Muslim community as political model. The idealized early community as a reservoir of Muslim political ideas must not be ignored by anyone who would understand the political rhetoric of Muslims past, present, and—so we are persuaded—future.

Other political traditions unrelated or at best loosely tied to the early Muslim umma model did emerge in Islamic societies. There was the rich heritage of Greek political thought developed by Muslim philosophers. There was also the literature of the "mirrors for princes" or practical guides to rulers. Nor should the borrowings from political traditions absorbed into the expanding Islamic civilization (such as the Sassanian, Byzantine, and Mongol) be ignored. Without careful attention to these other traditions the student of Islamic history throughout the ages would be quite at a loss to explain what daily governance was actually like and why.

Nevertheless, these other political traditions were not effectively integrated with the paradigmatic model of the early umma. Instead of a symbiotic relationship between the different political traditions there developed more nearly a compartmentalization.

Muslim philosophers studied and developed Greek philosophical thought but all the while accepted the clear distinction between *fiqh* (Islamic law) and *falsafa* (speculative philosophy).

Those writing tracts for rulers on how to rule were careful to honor the God-given Islamic religio-political model but were more concerned with practical advice than the religious model.

Imposing state structures were created starting with those early years when the Muslim center of political gravity shifted from Mecca and Madina to Damascus and later Baghdad. The ensuing fourteen centuries have witnessed many distinctively Islamic dynasties marked for longevity, territorial expanse, and cultural achievement. A roll call of selected dynasties suffices to make the point—Umayyad, Abbasid, Fatimid, Almohad, Mamluk, Seljuk, Moghul, Safavid, and Ottoman. A venerable tradition of government developed throughout the centuries, one that acknowledged the primacy of the political model set out in the early community but made little effort to work out the implications of that ideal umma model for one's own times.

In other words, mainstream Muslim political thought throughout the ages has protected inviolate the idealized early community by resisting the temptation to relate too precisely the pristine model to stubborn reality. The model of the early community remains thus an unsullied norm, but in the terminology of modern political science the maxims derived from the idealized model are not readily operationalized. To those understanding political theory in terms of the post-Machiavellian Western tradition,[5] it almost seems as if the strictly Muslim political theory (as distinguished from the philosophical writings of Muslims or the "mirrors for princes" penned by Muslims) is satisfied to affirm that the good ruler should rule well, not really defining either "good" or "well" more explicitly but insisting that the answer is readily to be found in the Qur'an, the Sunna, and the practice of the early community.

Is this to say that Muslim thinkers were ignorant of—or deliberately ignored—the great differences in scale between Muhammad's ruling a small community in Madina and a caliph or sultan ruling a far-flung empire from Damascus or Baghdad or Delhi or Istanbul? No.

Did Muslim thinkers turn their backs on such precise questions as taxation, administration, rules of war, or the treatment of minorities? Again, certainly not. Muslim philosophers, theologians, and jurists have written tomes on just such subjects. Moreover, until modern times—and the shattering impact of the West on Islamic peoples—the broad lines of such writings were all part of the educated man's intellectual baggage.

One is tempted to put it this way: no Muslim Thomas Aquinas attempted systematically to integrate religious and other-than-religious sciences in a way that could provide guidance in political philosophy. Yet such a statement will not do, either, for it overlooks the really impressive efforts at philosophical/theological synthesis by such Muslims as al-Ghazali and Al-Ash'ari, not to mention the more strictly philosophical tradition of political thought culminating in the masterful work of Ibn Khaldun.

The most that can be said is that the writings of Muslims on what we Westerners would label political theory did seem rather more inclined to stay within one of the separate traditions—either philosophy or theology or practical guides for princes—and to steer clear of attempts to relate the one tradition chosen to the other two, even though all three were known to educated Muslims.

Another way to illuminate this distinction between Christian and Muslim approaches to political theory is to let Martin Luther exemplify a strand in the Christian approach that has no Muslim equivalent. Luther wrote,

> A man who would venture to govern an entire community, or the world, with the Gospel would be like a shepherd who would place in one fold wolves, lions, eagles and sheep together and say, "Help yourselves, and be good and peaceful among yourselves; the fold is open, there is plenty of food; have no fear of dogs or clubs!" The sheep, forsooth, would keep the peace and would allow themselves to be fed and governed in peace, but they would not live long.[6]

Many Muslim thinkers would not disagree with the import of Luther's remarks, but one would look in vain for a Muslim thinker who would assert so categorically that the Muslim scriptures did not constitute a completely adequate guide to mundane political practice.

Nor is this to say that the gamut of Muslim political thinking reveals either a blind or willfully stubborn idealism. On the contrary, the mirrors for princes literature is of a very practical nature, arguing, in effect: This is the way the world is. This is how people must be managed by rulers.

Even so, no Muslim writer went so far as to assert, or even suggest, that the necessary answers to daily political problems were not to be found in the Muslim scriptures.

Why this difference between classical Muslim and Christian political theory? That elusive issue is addressed in the next chapter.

5.

Unity and Community

A weakness of much cross-cultural scholarship is a tendency to move, often quite unconsciously, from the legitimate inquiry of how "they" are different from "us" to the more dubious question: "Why can't they be like us?"

The best antidote to such superciliousness is to study first what the alien culture sought to achieve and did achieve by the choices made. Thereby, the political problems arising from the confrontation between the cultural values adopted and the ongoing historical development can be more clearly seen from within.

From this internal perspective it is not so much that Muslim societies failed to link Islamic thought with political practice but that the Muslim self-image gave preeminent importance to the ideals of unity and community. To clarify this interpretation of Islamic political thought let us recall two fundamental points already adumbrated in a somewhat different context.

First, the clear relevance of early Muslim political theory for all later thinking about the role of the state and the political community coupled with the natural tendency of any scriptural religion to emphasize the historical period during which those scriptures were revealed combined to give the political model of the idealized early *umma* an unchallenged role in later Muslim thinking about politics.

Second, since a hierarchically structured clergy charged with establishing doctrine never developed in the Islamic community there was—viewing the matter politically—no effective institutional way to reconcile differences between religious dogma and political practice.

Rulers learned that they could usually get the acquiescence of their subjects provided they did not try to impose orthodoxy. Subjects learned that they could deviate in their religious belief and practice provided they did not openly challenge government. Certain ulama could resist the blandishments of government office, others could accept, and all could accommodate in a system wherein no one—not even the caliph—presumed to speak ex cathedra (to use the Catholic term) on religious dogma.

Expressing this point somewhat differently, it might be said that societies—just like individuals—do not go out of their way looking for problems to solve. They tend to tackle problems that cannot be avoided. The early Muslim community developed in a way that facilitated the compartmentalization, isolation, and, thus, nonresolution of potentially explosive issues involving religion and politics.

In the Christian development, especially in the Latin Church, members of the religious hierarchy, right up to the pope, had to decide on issues presented or forfeit the claims on which the institutional church was based. The same obligation to take a stand faced the emperor unless he was willing to grant by default this authority to the pope.

Since the caliph was not an emperor warily watching lest a religious establishment encroach on his power and the ulama were not an organized body possessing a clear chain of command and eager to prevent the ruler from asserting authority in the religious field, Muslims usually found it easier to rock along with a certain indeterminancy.

At the same time, all could and did appeal to the Islamic golden age—the time of the early umma—because it was 1. religiously satisfying, 2. religiously and politically appropriate, and 3. politically safe, there being no easy way in which the differing interpretations of what was required of the umma would be challenged or tested.

This is not to deny that Muslim history was from the earliest days filled with religious confrontation and, indeed, civil war. Since, as has been seen, Islam—unlike Christianity—early achieved astonishing political success in the form of a vast new sovereignty, extending within the lifetime of those who had known the Prophet Muhammad from Morocco to India, the normal tensions of politics ineluctably involved the religious community.

Yet, if the Muslim umma was caught up in the cut and thrust of politics, Muslim political thought evolved in a way that safely shielded the Islamic religio-political idea from worldly compromise. The first step in this evolution had been taken with the denial of the right to fix orthodoxy to any individual or group (whether caliph or ulama).[1]

The next step, after reducing worldly political authority's interest in imposing orthodoxy, was to remove from worldly political authority the temptation to reopen the issue. This was achieved by the Muslim community's moving in the direction of political quietism. Government was to be obeyed provided it did not actively prevent pious Muslims from carrying out their religious obligations. An implicit quid pro quo had been struck between the umma and its rulers. If the rulers refrained from interfering in matters of faith, the ruled would obey and not insist on any specific religious principles of political conduct.

"O ye who believe! Obey Allah, and obey the messenger and those of you who are in authority."[2] This Qur'anic admonition became the scriptural foundation for a submissive attitude toward political authority that reached its fullest flowering in the oft-cited maxim "Better sixty years of tyranny than one hour of anarchy."

In this way the Muslim community found an answer to the question of what must be rendered to Caesar even when the particular caesar was a professing Muslim engaged in very un-Islamic practices. Such a ruler was to be obeyed but not granted any sanctity. To speak in terms of medieval Western political thought, Islam rejected the divine right of kings.

The idea of the caliphate or imamate did, of course, offer the possibility of a Muslim equivalent of the divine right of kings, but the historical development did not take such a turn in the Islamic world. Admittedly, the notion of the ruler being "the shadow of God on earth" would certainly seem to introduce the Muslim equivalent of the divine right of kings. And this lofty designation for the ruler, probably traceable to earlier Sassanian notions of monarchy, was used even by such rigorous Muslim purists as Ibn Taimiyya (1263–1328), the hero of many present-day Muslim fundamentalists. On balance, however, this exaggerated title may be seen as fitting into the bleak acceptance that even harsh government was better than anarchy.

The caliphate or imamate became, instead, an abstracted ideal not expected to be applied in the real corrupt world. Rather than a divine right of rule, Islam came to recognize a divinely sanctioned need for rule.

The distinction is important. The Islamic tradition asserted, in effect, that mankind's need for government was so overwhelming as to make the quality of that government decidedly secondary. "Prayer is permitted behind any imam, pious or impious. . . . Revolt is prohibited even if the ruler is unjust."[3] So wrote a highly regarded twelfth-century Sufi scholar. That such a ruling should come from an eminent Sufi is especially significant, for Sufism often sheltered the Muslim equivalent of Christian antinomian and gnostic tendencies.

If even within Sufism—the most likely refuge for radical, antiestablishment sentiments—there was a strong tendency to accept without protest whatever government came forward through the workings of the worldly wheel of fortune, then one could hardly expect to find well-developed political protest elsewhere.

A later Muslim scholar, writing in the age of political chaos following the Mongol invasions, took matters a step farther, even justifying the rule of a usurper "as a means of assuring the public order and unity of all Muslims." Moreover, if that ruler is in turn overthrown, then the victor becomes imam "for the reasons we have already presented, that is, the well-being and unity of the Muslims."[4]

All this seems to argue that Muslim political thought categorically rejected the right of rebellion against an unjust government. This would be going too far, and it should be emphasized yet again that Islamic culture, like its sister Semitic cultures—Judaism and Christianity—is too rich and complex to be so neatly labeled.

An account often cited by Muslims eager to demonstrate the right of rebellion—indeed, the duty to oppose an unjust government—concerns the second caliph, Umar, who called upon the people to correct him should he inadvertently make a mistake. One of the congregation brusquely told Umar to have no fear on that score, for any such deviation would be corrected "with our swords." Umar, it is related, then praised God for such an umma.[5] Several statements of this sort attributed either to the Prophet Muhammad or to one of his companions are to be found in Muslim literature. For example, "And we have heard the Prophet of God, may God bless and save him, say, 'If men see evil and do not change it, God will swiftly blind them with His punishment.' "[6]

Yet, on balance, the weight of Muslim tradition was on the side of political submission. The same Caliph Umar, often singled out in the hadith literature as the epitome of early Arab boldness, is related to have admonished, "If he (the ruler) oppresses you, be patient; if he dispossesses you, be patient."[7] There are also numerous hadiths of this sort attributed to Muhammad.

This picture of a traditional Muslim attitude toward politics characterized by resignation and patience must appear totally at variance with the Western image of Islam as a religion of the sword always eager to engage in jihad. It is certainly true that Islam, like Christianity, has always been a proselytizing religion. The religious merit of not only defending the faith but extending the borders of *Dar al-Islam* has always been stressed, but the old Western stereotype of countless forcible conversions to Islam ("Islam or the sword") is grossly inaccurate. As a general rule, it can be suggested that there were no more forcible conversions in Islamic history than in Christian history.

What the West has largely ignored, and many present-day Muslims have forgotten, is that throughout most of Muslim history until modern times the problem of a non-Muslim political threat seldom arose, and when it did arise it seldom continued for long. This is yet another way of emphasizing that Islam, unlike Christianity, early achieved political success, and thereafter the situation facing most Muslims most of the time was that of accommodating to political reality within a largely self-contained, self-confident, and self-sufficient Muslim world.

The West, like most people everywhere and at all times, sees the outsider too much from its own perspective. Thus, in Western lore the Christian Reconquista in Spain and the earlier Crusades in the Eastern Mediterranean loom large, but they are reduced in importance when viewed from within the vast Dar al-Islam. Spain was at the western limit of Islamic expansion, and its loss posed no threat to the Islamic heartland. Moreover, while Islam was losing Iberia it was gaining Anatolia at the other end of the Mediterranean. The Crusades, as already noted, were something of a sideshow from the Muslim viewpoint. Not only were they of limited territorial penetration but even these Crusader gains did not long survive.

Indeed, the peak of Muslim political success came in the sixteenth century, following the Reconquista, with the flowering of the Ottoman, Safavid, and Moghul Empires.

In this vast territory, from Northwestern Africa to the Eastern reaches of South Asia, most of the Muslims for most of the time confronted problems of adjusting to at least nominally Muslim regimes. The political fortunes of most Muslims were, in this regard, comparable to those of Christians in medieval Europe. Caesar and subjects professed the same religion.

Accordingly, the tradition of political resignation and submission grew up within Dar al-Islam, with limited regard for the world beyond. It was a vast political world subject to considerable turbulence (just as medieval Christendom), but with rare exception (the Mongol invasions being the most important) the threats to political order and responses to political challenges were securely within the confines of an Islamic culture. The tradition of political resignation and submission thus evolved as an Islamic response within a well-established Islamic culture.

To some extent the predominant Muslim political tradition evolved toward a position bearing some similarity to the political teachings of Jesus and Paul. That is, both the early Christian and the developed Muslim political attitudes involved 1. an acceptance of existing political authority however unjust as preferable to anarchy 2. with a concomitant decided preference for avoiding contact with government to the extent possible 3. as the best way to preserve the purity and cohesion of the religious community.

Christianity after the time of Jesus and Paul embarked on a political path leading to institutionalized church-state confrontations and a meshing of religion and politics that spawned a complex and often contradictory corpus of political theory.

Islam took another path following its golden age of the Muslim "early church," with the result

> that there was no Islamic political doctrine. There was a fervent but vague aspiration, more external to the actual states. . . . To the extent that jurists had formulated a few concrete rules, these did not reveal this general aspiration except in form, and, far from having had some sort of influence on the evolution of the actual institutions, they adapted to them somehow or other—and these institutions resulted from the combination of all the historical, social, national and other circumstances of the Muslim world, which owed nothing to the intervention of Islam as a doctrine.[8]

As with all great choices made by a civilization, the option ultimately embraced by most Muslims concerning politics and political theory had many and divergent results. On the negative side the result was a corpus of religious-inspired political theory that offered little practical guidance for either ruler or subject while the much more pragmatically oriented "mirrors for princes" literature steered clear of the really fundamental questions of politics (who should rule, the limits of loyalty, etc.), it being in the very nature of this genre of political writing to avoid questioning established political authority or established religious doctrine.

The Muslim philosophical tradition also paid obeisance to the established religious orthodoxy while carrying out its philosophical speculation in an arcane language designed to protect the philosophers from scrutiny by the rigorously orthodox ulama. This they achieved, but at the price of letting their lucubrations remain peripheral to everyday life, both political and religious.

Thus the three strands making up the political philosophy of Muslims (the religio-legal, the mirrors for princes, and the philosophical) did not sufficiently mingle to create through the continuing dialectic of ideas and experience an integrated political tradition. Political speculation, instead, remained utopian in theory and pessimistic as regards the real world with the two spheres—theory and practice—remaining compartmentalized. The result was what would appear to most Western observers, viewing the matter from their quite different heritage, as an underdeveloped political tradition.

The positive aspect of these political choices that became a part of Islamic culture is equally imposing, if not even more so. By rejecting anything equivalent to the Christian church/state confrontation and by shielding the ideal of the Muslim umma from any tampering on the part of the body politic, whether rulers or rebels, Muslims were largely able to avoid the sectarian splintering that has characterized Christianity.

By contrast with Christianity, the uniformity of Islam—in ritual, law, custom, in aesthetic expression embracing art, architecture, music, and calligraphy—is striking.[9] Islamic culture, it might well be argued, abandoned the effort to prescribe in any detail what the ruler or the ruled should do in the matter of worldly politics in order better to concentrate on the overriding aspiration of maintaining the unity of God's umma.

"And hold fast, all of you together, to the rope of Allah, and do not separate. And remember Allah's favor unto you: how you were enemies and He made friendship between your hearts so that you became as brothers by His grace . . . and there may spring from you a nation."

"Ye are the best community that has been raised up for mankind. . . . And if the people of the Book (i.e., Jews and Christians) had believed it had been better for them."

"Thus We have appointed you a nation of the middle that you may be witnesses over mankind."[10]

This sense of community as set out in the Qur'an is emphasized with even greater intensity in many hadiths attributed to Muhammad. The following are typical examples:

> "He who separates himself even a single span from the community, removes the noose of Islam from his neck."
>
> "The hand of Allah is with the community. He who stands alone stands alone in hell."
>
> "Muslims are like a single body, if any part hurts all are pained or have fever."
>
> "The believer is to the believer like (the several stones of) a building. Each supports the other."
>
> "He who seeks to divide your community, slay him."[11]

On this important point Islam is shown to be, again, closer to Judaism than to Christianity. Although clearly more like Christianity in being a religion with millions of adherents spread over a large segment of the globe, as well as a religion most of whose followers live in states in which their core-ligionists constitute the majority, Islam has—for all its cultural and territo-rial diversity—maintained among its adherents a communal solidarity much more like that of Judaism.

This amazing communal solidarity binding together millions of believers across time, space, and cultures did, however, necessarily come at the cost of other matters not so carefully nurtured. All of which brings the subject squarely back to politics, to what might be labeled the tradition of political pessimism that will be discussed next.

6.

The Roots of Political Pessimism

Islamic political thought or, more precisely, Muslim attitudes toward politics and the state produced a paradox that can be expressed as follows:

1. Islam emphasizes the religious importance of man's deeds in this world. Islam decidedly does not turn its back on mundane matters. Islam, moreover, grew up in early political success. Thereafter, the overwhelming majority of the world's Muslims usually lived free of political threat from non-Muslims—until modern times. Muslims cling to the ideal of the early *umma*, which, unlike the early Christian Church, was a this-worldly religio-political community par excellence.

2. Yet, this very Islam with such characteristics created a political culture that nurtured a pessimistic attitude toward politics and, out of this political pessimism, a submissive attitude toward government. While never developing anything like the Christian separation of church and state, Islamic culture did foster a de facto separation of state and society.

This separation of state and society was never explicitly recognized as legitimate. The idealized early umma as led by the Prophet and thereafter the four rightly guided caliphs (and the equivalent imamate of Shi'ism) was the only legitimate model of Islamic government.

If the early umma can hardly be overemphasized as the exemplar to be singled out in all later Muslim political thinking, it would be equally difficult to exaggerate the extent to which actual Muslim history involved a depoliticized society of Muslims who accepted government as a necessary evil but chose to have little to do with it.

This important development in the historical experience of Muslim peoples can be highlighted by contrasting the resulting traditional Muslim attitude toward politics with that of modern America. A venerable American response upon hearing about something deemed unjust or absurd or simply not to one's liking is, "There ought'a be a law." This simple statement contains an implicit political theory. It bespeaks an optimistic attitude toward politics, an affirmation that things can be corrected by group political activity.

The response of the typical Muslim from the time the tight-knit early Muslim community became an intercontinental empire right down to the present day would not likely be "There ought'a be a law." Much more in keeping with the political culture would be, "God forbid that the ruler learn of this." The typical Muslim reaction to worldly shortcomings has been to suffer in silence rather than bring the matter to the attention of political authority, for fear that an activist government would only increase the sum total of human misery, largely in the form of exorbitant taxation.

The traditionalist Islamic attitude toward *actual* government (as opposed to the traditional Islamic concept of the ideal government) is neatly summed up in the Jeffersonian dictum that the government that governs least governs best.

Again, let it be quickly conceded that this stark contrast between the modern American and traditional Muslim attitude toward politics necessarily distorts a much more complicated reality. There is, of course, a healthy dose of pessimism and cynicism in the American political tradition, too—well summed up in another saying: "You can't beat City Hall." Or the story told some years back by Representative Brooks Hays of Arkansas of the school teacher who, when asked on election day if she voted, testily retorted, "I never vote. It only encourages them."

Nor should it be overlooked that a tradition of petitioning authority for redress of grievances, and the concomitant tradition that the ruler should be accessible for just such petitions, was one of the most important customs that the early Muslim community adopted from Arab society.

Moreover, many, perhaps most premodern societies have tended to adopt a pessimistic attitude toward politics. The theological assumption of medieval Christendom viewing this world as a vale of tears can be set alongside that of traditional Islam.

Yet, after all reservations and nuances are duly noted it still seems fair to characterize traditional Muslim attitudes toward politics as decidedly pessimistic. Why? One possible reason has already been suggested. It was the price paid in order to achieve and then protect two considerable assets: 1. keeping the God-ordained community beyond the grasp of fallible or corrupt human hands, and 2. maintaining the unity of the umma against sectarian splits by making theological disputes well-nigh impossible to adjudicate by worldly authorities, whether "church" or state.

Another possible reason is suggested in the comparison with medieval Christendom that also tended toward political pessimism. Both Christendom and the traditional premodern *Dal al-Islam* involved the ideal, and to an appreciably lesser extent the reality, of political ecumenicalism. There was in theory only a single legitimate state coextensive with the totality of Christendom and the Dar al-Islam, respectively. Imperial government transcending barriers of culture, language, and geography was the norm.

In imperial systems the ideal of individual subjects personally presenting their petitions to the ruler may not be repudiated in theory, but it becomes virtually meaningless in fact. One need only reflect on the clear qualitative differences between, on the one hand, the early caliphs in Arabia who personally led the prayers in the mosque and resolved problems face to face with petitioners and claimants and, on the other hand, a Harun al-Rashid (reigned 786–805), caliph of an Abbasid empire extending from Morocco to India, who is said to have kept himself posted on what was really going on by strolling the streets of Baghdad at night incognito.

Traditional empires, in short, whether East or West, Roman or Abbasid, Hapsburg or Ottoman, tend to be based on a clear separation between rulers and the ruled. Moreover, the rulers are a small elite often distinguished from the ruled by different language, culture, and lifestyle. Nor is this separateness necessarily resisted by those ruled. There is usually little or no agitation on the part of the great mass of subjects to break into the ruling class or in any other way to "get a piece of the political action," as the breezy American idiom would put it. In traditional empires—East and West—those ruled not only accept this separation but act so as to keep the walls dividing rulers and ruled in good repair.

To this common structural aspect of traditional empires should be added the political inheritance that Islam was fated to receive. Islamic civilization, in moving its political center out of the Arabian Peninsula and into the Fertile Crescent and the Nile valley, inherited the centuries-old Western Asian imperial tradition. The Umayyads ruling from Damascus and the Abbasids ruling from Baghdad found all about them not just the brick and stone of earlier empires but also ideas and customs concerning politics. Just as the evolving architecture of Islam reflected the earlier legacy so too did their politics build on the traditions of the Romans, Byzantines, Achaeminids, and Sassanids, not to mention pharaonic Egypt.

It was this tradition (and the several imperial legacies cited above can be seen as variations of a single Western Asian approach to politics) that caused such notions as the ruler being "the shadow of God on earth" to gain some partial acceptance in the political thought of Muslims. It was this tradition that provided the matrix out of which evolved the Muslim mirrors for princes writings.

Islam, thus, quickly inherited all the appurtenances of traditional empires—viziers, bureaucracy, a royal mail and intelligence service, an army and taxation controlled from the imperial center.

All of this, which was fairly well in place as early as the reign of the Umayyad caliph Abd al-Malik (ruled 685–705), stood in stark contrast to the "primitive church" situation of Islam in Arabia where the first caliph, Abu Bakr, did his own shopping in the markets of Madina.

Islam and Christianity were, each in its own way, strongly marked by their early and sustained links with political powers. Christianity became institutionally and ideologically intertwined with empire with results that long shaped Western political thought. Islam followed the path of de facto separation and compartmentalization between state and society, between politics and religion.

Christianity chose to wrestle with the religious problems of political loyalty, of what to render to Caesar and what to God, of who is entitled to speak for Christendom, who decides on religious orthodoxy, and who enforces that orthodoxy. None of these thorny political problems was ever definitively resolved, but Christians—rulers and ruled—kept returning to the task, often provoking in the process schism and conflict.

Islam largely abstained from this effort, clung consistently to the model of the God-ordained early umma, accepted implicitly that later government did not live up to this standard (but largely avoided asking either why or what could be done), and bridged the gap between ideal and reality by accepting the bleak necessity of government however bad (thus the tradition of submission) but at the same time regarding that government as largely irrelevant to the individual believer's task of living according to God's plan (thus the tradition of political cynicism).

The resulting separation between political ideal and political reality from the time Islamic civilization had absorbed the Western Asian imperial tradition to the beginning of modern times can hardly be exaggerated. "It has been well said that in medieval Islam there were never real 'states' but only 'empires' more or less extensive, and that the only political unity was the ideological but powerful concept of the Dar al-Islam, the common homeland of all Muslims."[1]

Much has changed since the distant days of medieval Islam, but the strong similarity with present-day Islam in which most Muslim governments enjoy little legitimacy while the ideal God-ordained Dar al-Islam continues to haunt Muslims points up the old truth that people seldom completely break with their past.

Political structures prove durable in the real world only if they provide a stable and plausible response to their environment. The Western Asian imperial tradition that Islam absorbed had long existed in this region because it did fit well with the environment. In seeking answers to this question one touches upon those seminal ideas of Karl Marx, Max Weber, and several of their disciples. The notion of a distinctive "Asiatic mode of production," of "Oriental Despotism," and of "sultanism" grow out of Western attempts to understand why the "East" seems to be so different.

Such ideas have often been poorly received by scholars and for good reason: they are too crude, too monocausal. They brush over important variations of geography, culture, and history. They are ethnocentric, too prone to evaluate the "other" exclusively by "our" standards. They are the ideological children of a specific time and culture—essentially nineteenth-century Europe—with its emphasis on progress and evolution.

No good purpose would be served in uncritically embracing these Marxist or Weberian ideas, but on the other hand a fastidious refusal to explore such questions at the level of broad cross-cultural comparison is not helpful either. The worldly adjustment of Islam—as civilization and culture—has involved a blending of religion (in the narrow, modern Western sense) with its human and physical environment. The Western Asian matrix of bureaucratic empire is as important to the political expression of Islamic society as the European feudal matrix has been to the political expression of Christendom and its offshoot, the modern West.

A prudent exploration of such bold interpretative theories may well prove useful, especially if they are put to use as working hypotheses, not proven dogma. Marx saw the great difference characterizing the "East" in the virtual absence of private property. He and later writers—especially Karl Wittfogel in his *Oriental Despotism*[2]—emphasized the "Asiatic" need for a strong, centrally controlled imperial state that could insure the distribution of water and the maintenance of canals and dams in the irrigated agricultural regions (as the Tigris-Euphrates and Nile valleys or the elaborate underground *qanats* of Iran). All of this created a special economic/political system dubbed by Wittfogel a "hydraulic society."

Weber saw one line of political/bureaucratic development as moving toward patrimonial bureaucracy, which may, in turn, reach an extreme form in "sultanism": "With the development of a purely personal administrative staff, especially a military force under the control of the chief, traditional authority tends to develop into 'patrimonialism.' Where absolute authority is maximized, it may be called 'sultanism.' "[3]

The common theme uniting the Marxist-Weberian-Wittfogel theories is that the "East" (embracing the core of Islamic civilization but including the Hindu and Chinese as well) offered an ecological system best exploited by central government control, unlike the rich, dry farming regions of Europe that are amenable to decentralized political and economic power—as in feudalism.

Indeed, to bring in the factor of premodern transportation and communication, it might be argued that Europe had vast stretches of good, dry-farming agricultural lands but a climate and topography that made all-weather roads or other means of internal transportation difficult, whereas Western Asia and Northern Africa (the Islamic "heartland") possessed limited clusters of dense urban and agricultural settlement separated by vast seas of sand and water that did provide a maintenance-free transportation and communication network. The European ecological system was not easily controlled from any single center, or even a limited number of centers, whereas the Islamic heartland predisposed a pattern of centralized political and economic control.

Marx summed this up as follows, adding in the process his customary disparagement of the "East":

> Climate and territorial conditions, especially the vast tracts of desert extending from the Sahara through Arabia, Persia, India and Tartary, to the elevated Asiatic highlands, constituted artificial irrigation by canals and waterworks the basis of Oriental agriculture. . . . This prime necessity of an economical and common use of water . . . necessitated in the Orient, where civilization was too low and the territorial extent too vast to call into life voluntary association, the interference of the centralizing power of Government.[4]

This pattern of interpretation seems, in very rough outline, consistent with the broad lines of historical development in the Islamic heartland. Medieval Islam, Gibb observed, had no "real 'states' but only 'empire.' " The theories do fit in with what may be called the "mamlukization" of Islamic politics, or the control of the state apparatus by a legally and culturally distinct group of slave praetorians—a process that began as early as the ninth century under the Abbasids and reached its fullest flowering in the heyday of the Ottoman and Moghul Empires.

Where the theories are perhaps weakest is in their concentration on politics at the top within the framework of an implicit concept of the nation-state as the norm. The result is a tendency to view Islamic government as pure despotism and Islamic society as congeries of discrete groups lacking effective organizational ties among themselves and vulnerable before the arbitrary all-powerful state.

Such an approach thus concentrates on the political weaknesses of Islamic society and slights its societal strengths, with resulting distortion.

Even so, aspects of the Marx-Weber-Wittfogel theories (or, to put it more modestly, insights) can be salvaged simply by moving the perspective from government to society as a whole. A de facto separation between state and society still holds. The "mamlukization" of politics can be accepted. The ecological plausibility of central political and economic control can be acknowledged. The impressive difference between the well-developed urbanism of medieval Islamic civilization as opposed to the much more rural medieval Christendom can be appreciated.[5]

With the focus shifted from government to society, the fairly limited role of the former is properly conveyed, and the tendency toward patrimonialism or even sultanism is placed in its proper context. Arbitrary government existed unchallenged largely because it did not attempt to do too much. Even the extent of direct central government intervention in the economy can be easily exaggerated.

From this viewpoint it might even be argued that the weakness of political ties between rulers and ruled fades before the clear strength of society. This point is often demonstrated throughout Islamic history by the way in which society persevered—at times even flourished—during periods when centralized empires fell apart and political power was decentralized.

For example, after surveying the tortuous politics of post-Umayyad Muslim Spain, E. Levi-Provençal observed that for Spain and without doubt the Maghrib as well "the economic life of the cities suffered in general very little from the political vicissitudes for which the cities might serve as theatre . . . (one has, instead,) the impression of intense commercial and industrial activity."[6]

Equally, the narrowly political history of Mamluk Egypt (1254–1517) offers a dismal series of coups and countercoups, but the cultural history is impressive. Even the casual visitor to Cairo can get a feel for this earlier vitality by visiting the many distinguished architectural remains of the Mamluk period.

In a word, classical Islamic culture adjusted to its environment by producing a powerful but limited government. The very durability and dynamism of the classical Islamic synthesis attests to the strength of the choices made. Nor was this synthesis devoid of ties among groups. It has been persuasively argued that the earlier tradition of Western scholarship on the Muslim world, emphasizing the "mosaic pattern" of different groups (e.g., bedouin, mountaineers, urbanites versus rural folk plus the many distinctions of religion, race, and language), can be pushed too far and thereby obscure the demonstrable cohesiveness and coherence characterizing classical Islamic civilization.[7]

Nevertheless, this classical Islamic synthesis did tend to compartmentalize state and society. This book being about Islam and politics, it is necessary to concentrate on what emerges as one of the less well-developed aspects of an impressive Islamic civilization. Nor is this to be seen as an outsider's attempt to concentrate on a weak spot in Islam's worldly armor. For better or worse, Muslims today are almost oppressively concerned with politics and the state. This, itself, is a measure of the Western impact on the Muslim world in modern times (to be discussed later). One may deplore or applaud this fact. One can hardly ignore it.

Returning to politics—thus narrowly defined—the Marx-Weber-Wittfogel theories are seen as useful but incomplete. Muslims entered the modern age little concerned about the state as a political reality, submissively accepting the need for government in order to avoid anarchy, but pessimistically expecting little else of good from the political process.

The resulting tradition of political quietism as worked out by the Muslim scholars and canon lawyers is to be understood as having both a theological and cultural basis. The tradition proved durable because these theological and cultural factors fit together well.

Epitomizing the mainstream theological tradition is the hadith attributed to the Prophet Muhammad. When asked, "Shouldn't we fight against them (bad rulers)?" Muhammad is said to have responded, "No, not so long as they say their prayers."[8]

Examples of these distinctive Muslim attitudes toward the state will be treated next.

7.

Muslim Attitudes Toward the State: An Impressionist Sketch

A perceptive British diplomat whose long service in the Middle East began early in this century captured the cultural counterpart to the Muslim theological tradition of political quietism in writing:

> The Egyptian man in the street is very quick to recognize the facts of power; he does not have to be blown out of cannons, or even harshly treated to conform. He will support long years of humiliation and, indeed, of ill treatment, buoyed by the golden certainty that somewhere along the road lies a banana-skin on which the object of his dislike is bound one day to put his heel.[1]

Another evocative illustration comes from the great Egyptian nationalist leader, Sa'd Zaghlul (1857–1927), who in a public speech before a huge crowd expressed the hope that the day would come when the Egyptian ceased regarding government the way the bird views the hunter.

The sense of impotence before authority is also well expressed in the story of village notables who had decided to send a delegation to the Ottoman capital requesting the removal of an oppressive governor. When the governor got wind of the plan, he summoned the group to his house, took them to an inner room, pointed out a chest and told them to open it. It was almost filled with coins and precious metals. The governor then said, "When I arrived in this province I brought with me that trunk empty. Now it is almost full. My successor will arrive with his empty trunk." The notables canceled their plans to protest.[2]

Equally, the visual evidence of traditional Muslim residential architecture, which offers the outside world windowless walls at street level, shuttered windows above, and entrances that provide no view of the living quarters within, attests to a turning of one's back to the public world. That such architecture shelters a family—and especially the women—from the curious eyes of outsiders is clearly an important consideration, but it should not be overlooked that such "introverted" architecture serves as well to obscure from the state one's wealth and one's lifestyle.[3]

Lest the image conveyed here appear too much the outsider's view with all the distortions and prejudices that suggests, note the following charge from an important contemporary Arab nationalist:

> The truth of the matter is that we (Arabs) have inherited from the past a feeling that the state is separated from us; that it is imposed upon us; and that we have no influence upon it or interest in it. . . . The simple individual in our Arab society feels that the state is a powerful and distant thing and that he must accept its rulings without hesitation, pay taxes without argument, and not ask anything in return . . . that he has a duty toward it, but no rights forthcoming from it.[4]

Or consider the following:

> Once I tried to find out the meaning of a chant which I had so often shouted in my childhood, whenever I saw an airplane in the sky: "Oh, Almighty God, may disaster take the English" (Ya Azeez, Ya Azeez, Dahiya takhud al-Ingleez). Later, I came to know that that phrase had come down to us from the days of the Mamluks. Our forebears of that day had not used it against the English, but they used a similar one against the Turk: "Oh God, the Self-Revealing, Annihilate the Turk"' (Ya Rabb, Ya Mutajelle, Ahlik al-'Uthmanli). My use of it was but an adaptation of an old form to express a new feeling. The underlying constant continued the same, never changing. Only the name of the oppressor was different.[5]

These words appear in Nasser's *Philosophy of the Revolution*.

The sense that the state was a remote, even alien, body of men best kept at arm's length could easily shade into an adversary relationship. This was most marked among tribesmen remote from the urban-dominated political centers. For example, a French observer of mid-nineteenth-century Tunisia found it odd that tribesmen in that remote area close to the Algerian border unfailingly had a battle with the annual Tunisian tax collectors (who always came as a military expedition). He asked the tribal shaykh why he did not simply pay taxes without a fight. "It is true, the shaykh responded, "that the sum is not much and the kahiya (regional military commander) is a decent man who does not demand too much from us. Still, if we pay without difficulty one year, he may well be tempted to increase the levy the following year. In any case, it would be shameful for mountaineers to pay at the first demand."[6]

Later, French officers serving in Moroccan tribal areas during the days of the French protectorate dubbed the similar ritualized combat there *baroud d'honneur*. Baroud is the Arabic for gunpowder, and by extension the word came to mean any test of arms, especially a skirmish or small battle.

The age-old contest between periphery and center, between the remote hinterland where the ruler's writ ran only intermittently when his troops were physically present on the one hand and the imperial urban center on the other, was perceived by the eminent Muslim thinker Ibn Khaldun (1332–1406) and made the basis of his celebrated philosophy of history.

Ibn Khaldun, it might well be countered, wrote a very long time ago, and efforts to evoke his authority may well tell us more about the ahistorical approach of Western scholars to Muslim history than the dynamics of today's Muslim politics. One is well advised to be on guard against the tenacious tendency of scholars interpreting Islamic history to telescope centuries in an implicit assumption that nothing much changes in the Muslim world. In this case of center-periphery relations, however, well-documented examples of the process so compellingly described by Ibn Khaldun centuries ago are to be found as late as the last century, with echoes of the same geopolitical dynamic even later in time.

The rise of the Wahhabi state first in the eighteenth century and then again under the leadership of the legendary Ibn Saud (creating today's Saudi Arabia) in this century clearly fits the center-periphery thesis. Nor should this and other examples occasion surprise. The geographical constant of urban centers dominating their immediately accessible sedentary agricultural hinterland (the necessary core of states or empires) but surrounded by a vast, elusive human flux of nomads, transhumants, and mountaineers has shaped history in this part of the world since many centuries before Islam and right down to modern times. The resulting political pattern is one of limited government controlling the cities and the sedentary rural areas but more nearly monitoring than actually ruling the remaining countryside.

Modern technology, which greatly increases the potential for states to control even the most remote and forbidding terrain, is modifying this millennial interaction of center and periphery. Still, political patterns with such deep historical roots and based on geographical reality, not all of which technology can change, continue to play a role in shaping developments stimulated by intrusive new forces.

The extent to which this wary attitude toward government pervaded society is illustrated in the oft-cited passage from the work of the Egyptian historian al-Jabarti (1754–1834):

> If the peasants were administered by a compassionate tax farmer, they despised him and his agents, delayed payments of his taxes, called him by feminine names, and hoped for the ending of his tax farm and the appointment of some tyrant without fear of God or mercy for them so as to gain by that means their private ends by the alighting of his violence upon some of their number. Likewise also their shaykhs, if the tax farmer were not an oppressor, were not able in their turn to oppress their peasants, for they gained no profit except when the tax farmer demanded excesses and fines.[7]

Al-Jabarti, although an authentic voice from within Muslim culture, does perhaps exaggerate by unconsciously reflecting the deep-seated urban bias against the countryside and the peasantry, but even this possible exaggeration is additional evidence of the gap separating those close to the culture and politics of the cities from the masses in the countryside.

Here is a more recent perspective as seen from the Syrian countryside:

> In the eyes of the peasants, the government was an evil, encroaching force and its revenue ill gotten. The 'uqqal or Druze sages believed that "the possessions of rulers and emirs are haram (unlawful)." They, therefore, did not "partake of their food or the food of their servants." Alawi Shaykhs shared the same belief. "In my entire life," said Shaykh Ali Salman, the father of Shaykh Salih al-'Ali, the leader of the Alawi upheaval of 1918–1921, "I have not broken bread with a government official for fear that he may have done an injustice to a human being."[8]

The cynicism, based on limited contact between center and periphery, between governors and governed, is also brought out in an incident related by the Tunisian historian Ahmad ibn Abi Diyaf (Bin Diyaf, 1802–1874) of a qadi at the capital who insisted that the people in a certain province were protesting not because the taxes were too high but because the qaids (provincial governors) were extorting additional levies that they then pocketed. The qadi maintained that he could administer the province according to existing tax rates and, in the process, please both the ruling bey and the people. The bey accepted his offer, but after a few years the qadi insisted on resigning even though the province had been restored to prosperity and peace. The qadi, however, had become the target of jibes from other ulama and certain officials. Moreover, the provincial recipients of this good administration had come forward with the following doggerel:

> You are taking a lot of money
> A qadi in the morning and a qaid in the evening.[9]

These stories suggest a comparison with Gogol's *The Inspector General* satirizing the corruption of Russian officialdom while setting out in dramatic fashion the sharp contrast between city and countryside.

This is, moreover, in line with a common theme of traditional bureaucratic empire with its sharp separation between the rulers and the ruled. There is, in short, nothing exclusively "Islamic" about this Muslim attitude toward politics any more than the politics of feudalism or of imperial Russia was distinctly "Christian." It is the political legacy of Muslims, not the theology of Islam, that is under consideration.

The durable pattern presented here as characterizing the traditional Muslim approach to politics is, of course, what Max Weber would call an "ideal type," or a way of generalizing the common features of a much more blurred empirical reality. The traditional Muslim political arrangement schematized as an ideal type was composed of the following:

1. Bureaucratic empire
2. A state apparatus setting out for itself quite limited goals confined essentially to self-maintenance, preservation of public order, and defense.
3. A distinct separation of state and society, both ideologically and institutionally.
4. A pervasive attitude of political pessimism among both rulers and ruled.

This ideal type never existed in pure form (any more than feudalism did). The reality of politics and of attitudes toward politics within the vast Muslim world in premodern times did, however, veer toward this ideal type.

More precisely, the separation between state and society was never absolute (which would be a logical absurdity). There were mediators between governors and governed such as ulama, urban notables, and tribal shaykhs. Moreover, the precise balance of relations between governors and governed, and the role of different mediators between the two, varied over time and place.

Nor was entry into the ruling elite ever quite so regulated and controlled as the ideal type would presuppose. For example, the pioneering study of Ottoman government by A. H. Lybyer is now seen as a classic example of distorted schematization.[10] Lybyer interpreted Ottoman government at its peak of power in the mid-sixteenth century as made up of

1. A "ruling institution" conscripted from periodic levies of Christian youth (the *devshirme*) who broke all ties with family, became legally "slaves of the sultan," received elaborate schooling, and then moved up the military-administrative hierarchy as a distinctive, closed political elite.
2. A "Muslim institution" made up of free-born Muslims who pursued the long schooling leading to ulama status, thereafter becoming qadis and muftis in the Ottoman Empire, serving also as an institutional check on the "ruling institution."

Later research has demonstrated no such neat distinction existed. The ulama were much more integrated into the state administrative system (more than in any previous Muslim bureaucratic empire), there was no clear distinction between "ruling" and "Muslim" institutions, and recruitment into the political class came from a variety of sources.[11]

Similar revisions would be required for a fully adequate presentation of, for example, Mamluk rule in Egypt and Syria, the Moghul Empire in India, or the Safavids in Iran, not to mention the earlier Islamic empires. Moreover, local power elites and virtually autonomous political systems always existed on the fringes of imperial systems. Indeed, this was totally consistent with the classic model of premodern bureaucratic empire. The genius of such long-lived, wideranging empires as the Ottoman or Moghul lay in their political realism and cost effectiveness. Rebels against central authority were not immediately brought to heel, if that proved too expensive. No "search and destroy" mentality governed their military doctrine. Central government saved its resources by awaiting a propitious time when rebel areas could be brought back into the system without undue cost in manpower or money.

The contrast between the politics of traditional bureaucratic empire (Muslim or other) and modern nation-state politics is crisply illustrated in the observations of a singularly perceptive member of the administration in the early years of French rule in Algeria. He realized how the political system of Ottoman Algeria was based on quite limited military force coupled with control of the nodal points of transportation and commerce:

> How many times after having stood up to or even defeated the troops of the bey, have these populations necessarily tributary to the interior markets been obliged to ask pardon and accept the harshest conditions. This state of affairs makes it understandable why the major effort of the Turks was always to achieve a vigorous organization of the agricultural tribes and the intelligent location of the makhzan around the great market areas and the major routes.[12]

The difference between such traditional imperial politics and that of modern concepts of state and warfare is personified in Marshal Bugeaud (1784–1849), the veteran of Napoleon's campaigns who later led the brutal French conquest of Algeria. Bugead stated his modus operandi as follows:

> In Europe we do not just wage war against armies. We wage war against interests. When we have beaten the belligerent armies we seize the centers of population, of commerce, of industry, the customs, the archives, and soon these interests are forced to capitulate. There is only one interest to be seized in Algeria, the agricultural interest. It is more difficult to seize than others for there are neither villages nor farms. I have thought about this for a long time, awake and sleeping. Well, I have not been able to discover any other means of dominating the country than seizing this interest.[13]

This contrast between the military strategy of Ottoman Algeria and French Algeria clarifies what is intended in speaking of "ideal types." Ottoman Algeria often employed force, and very harsh force at that. French Algeria was not simply unrelieved brute military power crushing all native resistance. Many tribal chieftains were actually co-opted into the system. Even so, the contrast, in general, holds, distinguishing a premodern system based on benign neglect, or often malign neglect, but relative neglect in any case from a modern nation-state concept that posits a more complete state penetration into society.[14]

This chapter has introduced a number of characteristics of politics in Islam as compared and contrasted with Judaism and Christianity. In the process we have noted more than once that many of these distinguishing features cannot properly be attributed to Islam, as such, but to the overall cluster of elements in the historical and cultural legacy of Muslims.

Just as feudalism cannot be seen as derived from Christian theology, so too the tradition of bureaucratic empire does not follow from the tenets of Islam. Yet, feudalism helped to shape the existing political traditions of much of the Christian world. The same can be said for the continuing influence of the bureaucratic empire approach to politics in the Muslim world.

We can do justice to our subject of Islam and politics only by avoiding the two methodological extremes of 1. reducing all actions of Muslims to a presumed Islamic stimulus or 2. assuming that the Islamic religious and cultural legacy has little influence on the political thought of modern Muslims. In the process, it is essential to accept that Paul Bowles's fictional protagonist knew he was wrong when he mused that Muslims are "far, far away from us. We haven't an inkling of what motivates them."

Part Two

Convulsions of Modern Times

8.

Islam and Politics in Modern Times:
The Great Transformation

Among the arguments advanced to this point are the following:

1. Islam is a sister religion to Judaism and Christianity. A study of Islam and politics in comparison with what has prevailed in Judaism and Christianity is much more likely to yield both empathy and understanding than an approach viewing Islam as sui generis.

2. Islam and Judaism are similar—and are to be contrasted with Christianity—in the importance placed on religious law (orthopraxy) and in the relatively decentralized, nonhierarchical arrangement of their religious specialists (ulama—rabbinate). There is thus no Muslim (nor Jewish) "church" and nothing quite like the pattern of church-state relations that had such a formative influence on politics and political thought in the West.

   One partial exception is Shi'i Islam since the sixteenth century (essentially in Iran), which has developed more toward an institutionally distinct and hierarchical Muslim "clergy."

3. In terms of politics and state-society relations, however, the Muslim experience has been more like that of the Christian and unlike that of Jews (at least for that over two-millennial span of time between the fall of the Davidic monarchy and the creation of Israel). For centuries most Muslims and most Christians have lived in polities having political leaders of at least nominally the same religious faith.

4. Islamic political thought emphasizes unity and community with correspondingly less valuation placed on the individual and individualism as in Christian (and Western) political thought. One of

the organizing principles to be found throughout Muslim history is the marked aversion to any action or thought that might bring about *fitna* (dissension, civil strife, temptation, etc.)

5. There have been fewer attempts by Muslim political leaders to impose religious doctrine than can be found in Christian history. This is not to say that political leadership has been religiously neutral. A state religion has been the norm, e.g., Hanafi Sunnism in the Ottoman Empire, Twelver Shi'ism in Iran since the sixteenth century, Maliki Sunnism in several pre-Ottoman Maghrib polities, and postcolonial Muslim states specifying Islam as the state religion in their constitutions. Unlike Byzantine emperors or European Reformation-era emperors and kings, however, Muslim rulers have usually avoided deciding issues of creed or practice and have tolerated minority religious communities.

6. Islam does place a significant religious value on living the good life and contributing to the good community in this world. Retreat from the world and denying the importance of this world are reproved. Membership in mystical Sufi brotherhoods, yes; but the members and virtually all the Sufi leaders as well remain concerned with affairs of this world. No monasticism, no celibacy. At the same time, the classical historic posture of Muslims has been politically quietist and pessimistic.

7. Muslim history has been marked by a de facto separation of state and religious community. Political leadership, often autocratic, has usually tempered its authoritarian potential by leaving the ruled free to live their lives demanding only peace (avoidance of fitna) and payment of taxes (which in principle can be manageable since government itself is small and confined to maintaining order). The ruled, in turn, have been satisfied to avoid politics and to accept a fairly distinct separation between rulers and the ruled.

Q

The above very general formulations can be defended by reference to history and to existing historical scholarship. Even though not all specialists would agree, and every specialist—whether of Judaism, Christianity, or Islam, whether of the "East" or the "West"—would insist on modifications, such an interpretation is well within the bounds of the prevailing "received wisdom."

That being the case, it is all the more striking to note that this interpretation of mainstream Islam in its relations to politics offers not just an inadequate but a plainly wrong picture of Muslim thought and action in today's world. Politically quietist? What then about the smoldering civil war in Algeria pitting Muslim religious radicals against a government controlled by the military or the earlier decade-long and ultimately successful Afghan resistance to Soviet domination? Assassination of Egypt's President Sadat or the earlier execution by the Egyptian government of the radical Muslim ideologue Sayyid Qutb?

A de facto separation between state and society in Islamic history? How to explain the Islamic Revolution in Iran that destroyed centuries of government by shahs and ushered in a mullah-controlled Islamic Republic? Or even the very idea of the Muslim state of Pakistan now in existence for over a half century?

Unity, community, and avoidance of fitna? How can one reconcile this with the radical Islamic theories that champion resisting—even taking up arms against—other Muslims now deemed to have lapsed into *kufr* (unbelief, atheism) or *jahiliyya*?[1]

Today Muslims are highly politicized, and the resulting politics is often disruptive and violent. Moreover, the political debate is largely being set by the Islamic radicals as represented by the likes of Ayatullah Khomeini, Abu al-A'la Mawdudi, Sayyid Qutb, Hasan Turabi, and Abbasi Madani. It was not all that many years ago when the political discourse was dominated by quite different persons—Kemal Ataturk, Riza Shah, Sukarno, Habib Bourguiba, Jamal Abd al-Nasir. Even the founder of the Islamic state of Pakistan, Muhammad Ali Jinnah, was notoriously secular in his lifestyle. The story is told that at the time of Pakistani independence Jinnah wanted a celebration with champagne only to be told by embarrassed aides that it was the month of Ramadan during which Muslims fast from sunup to sundown.

Only a few decades ago most Muslim political leaders, and sympathetic outside observers, felt the need to modernize (secularize?) Islamic belief and institutions in order to shake off the presumed dead hand of fatalistic resignation. The situation today in the Muslim world obliges us either to reconsider our interpretation of "classical" Islam or to show how events in modern times have produced such a radical break. It is the latter position that will be argued here.

Why then did this book began with a sketch of classical Islam in its relations to politics? Since the Muslim religio-political radicals are largely dictating the discourse, do these earlier mindsets matter?

Yes, these earlier mindsets do matter. By setting out the past as a frame of reference we are better armed to understand just how innovative and revolutionary many of the ideas now being advanced really are. At the same time, we put ourselves in that ideological past that the present ideologues claim to have recovered. Our sketch of the past enables us to better distinguish the extent to which present-day Islamists are not recovering but rewriting that past.

The temptation at this point to address today's religio-political radicals in the words of the man who dubbed religion the "opiate of the masses" cannot be resisted: "Men make their own history, but they do not make it just as they please. . . . They anxiously conjure up the spirits of the past to their service and borrow from them names, battle slogans and costumes in order to present the new scene of world-history in this time-honored disguise and this borrowed language."[2]

Finally, on this issue, if there is to emerge a more liberal political theory that can appeal to Muslims, it too will draw selectively on a new reading of the Muslim past. Only with past and present both in view are we able to speculate on what approaches such new readings might take.

ﻋ

To interpret the situation of Muslims today it may help to situate roughly the last two centuries within the entire span of Muslim history. This reveals that only in modern times have Muslim political communities faced simultaneously enticing ideological challenges as well as awesome politicomilitary threats from the outside world.

Islam, early on, did face ideological challenges. Its first generation of leaders had created an empire before the details of religious and political institutionalization had been worked out. By contrast, three centuries separated the time of Jesus from the conversion of Constantine. In less than three decades Muslims had extended their sway over virtually all of what we reckon today as the Arab world and Iran, had defeated the Byzantines and the Sassanids,[3] and had created their first imperial dynasty, the Umayyads.

During these early centuries of Islamic history the Muslim political and cultural leadership did confront such challenges as Greek philosophy and science, Byzantine and Sassanid imperial institutions (everything from bureaucracy to taxation to military organization), and the divergent mores and creeds of Christianity as well as other religions. Many of these alien ideas and institutions, conforming to the needs of a still expanding Muslim imperium destined at its peak to extend from Spain to India, were adopted or adapted. They became a part of the emerging Islamic culture, necessarily not the same as that existing during Muhammad's life just as post-Constantine Christianity represented a quite different cultural mix from that of the earliest church fathers.

The resulting classical Muslim cultural synthesis evolved, unlike Christianity, in a consistent climate of Muslim political self-sufficiency if not hegemony. There was no need to accommodate oneself to a threatening neighbor, even less to a non-Muslim political sovereign.

Later Muslim history had its share of politico-military ups and downs, just as was the case in Western Christendom, or what we now call the West. There were even two crushing military defeats inflicted by nomadic warriors from Central Asia—the Mongol sacking of Baghdad and killing the Caliph al-Musta'sim in 1258 and the defeat and capture of Ottoman Sultan Bayazid by Timur (Tamerlane) at the Battle of Ankara in 1402.[4] These two devastating defeats were not, however, accompanied by the imposition, or even the allure, of alien cultural models.[5] The Mongol tide later ebbed, and the Ottomans soon began their recovery capped by the capture of Constantinople (Istanbul) in 1453. Indeed, the heyday of Ottoman strength and influence was yet to come.

Nor is it accurate to assert that Islamic history, in terms of worldly achievement, has been marked by a downward trajectory ever since the earliest centuries. Early Orientalist accounts of Islamic history emphasized the image of a decline from the "golden age" of the early Islamic community. This is hardly surprising, for the decline motif has always figured powerfully in the Muslim collective self-image, especially in what might be called the "high cultural tradition" that early Western scholars tended to concentrate on. Muhammad was God's last messenger bringing the "seal of prophecy," the Qur'an, and in Sunni Islam only the first four caliphs (ruling during the short period from 632 to 661) represented the true caliphate, to be followed by the more worldly period of kingship (*mulk*).[6] In this image the Muslim community has never been so integrated, so pure, and, yes, so powerful as in these early years. This myth of the paradigmatic golden age that must be restored, always important as an organizing theme in Muslim religious and political thought, looms large in present-day religio-political radicalism as well—one reason, among many, why the radicals have been able to dictate the terms of the politico-religious discourse.

If judged by worldly success, however, the pinnacle of Muslim achievement came as late as the sixteenth century when the three Muslim empires of the Ottomans, Safavids, and Moghuls held sway. Nor was this age of latter-day Muslim imperial might lacking in aesthetic and intellectual contributions. In architecture alone these empires nurtured the achievements of the Ottoman architect Sinan Pasha and produced the magnificent Safavid structures that have merited Isfahan being dubbed worth "half the world" (*Isfahan nufs jihan*) as well as the incomparable Taj Mahal built by order of the Moghul Shah Jahan.

The beginning of modern times for the Muslim world was very different, ushering in a traumatizing dual challenge that continues to this day. For the first time in history Muslim societies and states confronted not just raw alien military superiority (as the Mongols or Tamerlane) and not just the broad challenge of alien civilizations that seemed equally attractive and threatening to the true faith. Modern times for Muslims brought a simultaneous military and civilizational challenge—and in an intensity and duration previously unmatched.

Different dates are advanced to mark the beginning of this distinctive and troubled period in Muslim history. For the Indian subcontinent the 1757 Battle of Plassey, in which the British East India Company under Clive defeated the Nawab of Bengal, is often cited as the turning point. A century later the last remaining trace of the Moghul Empire was swept away when the British government put Emperor Bahadur on trial for complicity in the Sepoy Rebellion and sent him into exile.[7]

In Iran the Safavid Empire had split asunder early in the eighteenth century, well before European penetration became the dominant theme. There the beginning of European domination is better situated in the early nineteenth century. Two treaties (Gulistan in 1812 and Turkmanchay in 1828)[8] ending wars with Russia marked by considerable territorial losses and other onerous terms left Iran thereafer a catspaw of Russia to the north and of the British who controlled India and the Persian Gulf.

The most appropriate turning point for the Ottoman Empire is 1774. That year ended a disastrous war with Russia and the signing of the Treaty of Kuchuk Kaynarja.[9] For the first time the Ottomans surrendered to infidel control territory occupied overwhelmingly by Muslims (the Crimea). This war, provoked by Catherine the Great, delivered a clear message to the Ottomans that was quickly picked up in the chancelleries of Europe as well: the Ottoman Empire, with territorial holdings that had for centuries extended deep into Southeastern Europe and whose armies had twice beseiged Vienna (1529 and 1683), was no longer a match for the European Great Powers. This introduced the age of the "Eastern Question" or Europe's efforts to dismember the once mighty Ottoman Empire without risking intra-European warfare.[10] It was to last until the early 1920s.[11]

The British and Dutch East India Companies had begun to penetrate

Southeast Asia even earlier, in the seventeenth century, and by the next century the principal question of power was simply whether the British or Dutch would exercise hegemony there. By the Treaty of Paris in 1783 (which also recognized American independence) Dutch primary control there was recognized. European colonial penetration of Africa, both the Islamic and the non-Islamic areas, belongs to nineteenth-century history.

All in all, the last two centuries have witnessed a radical change in power relations between the West and the entire Muslim world. Viewing the present-day Muslim situation (and the Muslim perception of that situation) in the context of all Muslim history underscores the distinctiveness of these last two centuries. The Muslim concept of a worldly *umma*, a *Dar al-Islam* that was self-sufficient, superior, and secure from any outside threat had struck deep roots, and for good reason. It was built on and sustained by historical reality, not just the reality of the early Muslim community but centuries thereafter until, as we have seen, roughly the eighteenth century. All the more rude would be the ensuing shock to the many ideas and institutions that had been refined by the reality of previous centuries.

That something of the same plight has faced most of the world in modern times as the West increasingly imposed its will has not made the problem facing the Muslim world any less difficult. Even though the task of taking the measure of Western hegemony has been perhaps the dominant organizing theme of modern history for all peoples, a case can be made that the challenge to Muslims has been the most sustained and the most severe. Japan, China, and the states of Southeast Asia have emerged today as dynamic economic or political powers, if not both.[12] Latin America as well as Russia and Eastern Europe are in the ambivalent position of being either West or non-West depending on the criteria (whether subjective or objective) employed. In any case, the same sense of being dominated by an alien religion and culture does not pertain. India, not lacking its own problems, has at least less difficulty in selectively assimilating much that came with Western domination in the form of the long-lived British raj if only because Hinduism as a religion and civilization is much more malleable and syncretist than the sister Semitic religions Islam, Judaism, and Christianity.

Generally speaking, the situation in non-Muslim Africa today after about two centuries of Western domination is discouraging, but in continuing the comparison with the Muslim world the following nuances can be recorded: all of Northern Africa have Muslim majorities and many of the states south of the Sahara have either Muslim majorities or significant Muslim populations. They thus share the Muslim reality and perception being considered. That major point aside, in considering Africa south of the

Sahara as an entity it can be noted that Westernization in stimulating Christianization removed to some extent the alienness of the change taking place. Also, although states and civilizations did exist in non-Muslim Africa before Western domination, they were less extensive in time and space than were the Muslims empires. The intrusive Western ways could more readily replace or modify the traditional religio-legal institutions, since the Western impact produced larger and stronger political units that the postcolonial elites sought to keep. Accordingly (again the important Muslim element in Africa to be classified with the rest of Dar al-Islam), there has been at least the potential for a less agonizing confrontation between indigenous and exogenous, between the presumed golden age of the past and the threatening present.

Only Islam of the world religions and regions presents an uninterrupted history of confrontation (and, all too often, conflict) with the West. During most of that long period those living within the Muslim world more than held their own against their Christian/Western neighbors and rivals. Living for roughly twelve centuries in such self-sufficiency and security gave the Muslim world a rich span of time to develop institutions and ideologies governing all aspects of government and society. Islamic civilization was in control of the terms under which alien ways were accepted or rejected. Then, beginning some two centuries ago, their world began to turn upside down. The very deep-rootedness and coherence of Islamic civilization before the advent of modern times gave added severity to the multiform challenge brought by Western domination. Islam and the West, it can be argued, is a special case.

9.

Meeting the Western Challenge:
The Early Establishment Response

To present the Muslim confrontation with the West as the principal organizing theme for interpreting modern times in the entire *Dar al-Islam* is not to embrace the simplication of an unchanging East stirred up by a dynamic West. No, the different parts of the Muslim world had not opted out of history until the West arrived and, depending on your politics, (a) disrupted a society whose many different peoples had formed a coherent organism or (b) played the role of the prince whose kiss awakened the long sleeping princess.

Major changes were taking place within various parts of the Muslim world before the Western presence and peril became predominant. Major changes continued within the Muslim world thereafter unrelated or only remotely related to the Western factor. To mention only a few, it was as long ago as the sixteenth century when the great Indian Muslim reformer, Shaykh Ahmad Sirhindi (1564–1624) resisted the efforts of the enigmatic Moghul emperor Akbar (1542–1605, r. 1556–1605) to synthesize Islam, Hinduism, Christianity, and Zoroastrianism into a unified state religion.[1] The same century witnessed significant advances in the Islamization of Indonesia with a concomitant partial de-Hinduization of its peoples and cultures.

Even in the eighteenth century, which brought what soon became massive Western intrusions, many developments bespoke a dynamism that was both ushering new converts into the Islamic *umma* and intensifying the absorption into mainstream Islamic culture of those already nominally Muslim. The broad-ranging activities of the Naqshbandiyya brotherhood or the early Wahhabiyya in Arabia are examples.

Yet all such developments did usually converge, sooner or later, with the dominant motif of the Western challenge. The Moghul vacillations in religious policy can be seen, in retrospect, as having eased the task of the British East Indian Company in conquering India. The Wahhabiyya, not to mention other Muslim revivalist tendencies, contributed to developments that served either to question existing political authority or to change it. Then, as Western penetration proceeded, these indigenous stirrings blended into the emerging pattern of Muslim peoples facing this dual threat—material and ideological—imposed by the alien infidel.

Confrontations of cultures occur in a context of power disequilibrium. One side is more powerful than the other, sometimes very much so, sometimes only slightly. One side (often but not always the most powerful) is better able to change, to adapt, to innovate. The politically and militarily weaker may be stronger economically or, for that matter, in cultural achievement (however difficult that may be to measure). Or one side in the confrontation may have assembled an awesome combination of strengths virtually across the board. Moreover, the several different power indices are ever shifting even while the process of acculturation proceeds. It is never simply a dynamic dominator and an inert dominated.

All players to the game, the weak as well as the strong, are choosing their strategies—always, of course, with incomplete knowledge of what is going on. Earlier generations did not, could not, see events with the clarity (or presumed clarity) we enjoy in hindsight. The image of the Western potter molding the Muslim clay is a poor parody of reality. All are simultaneously acting and reacting with constantly evolving images of self and other.

Rudyard Kipling, thus, offers a good epitome of Western images of the non-West in the heyday of colonialism but a poor picture of third world reality in writing:

> Now it is not good for the Christian's health to hustle
> the Aryan brown,
> For the Christian riles, and the Aryan smiles, and it
> weareth the Christian down;
> And the end of the fight is a tombstone white with the
> name of the late deceased,
> And an epitaph drear: "A fool lies here who tried to
> hustle the East."

Rather, for the Muslim world as for others, tactics changed over time. Passive resistance sometimes, active resistance at other times. Emulation at times, total resistance to even the most neutral aspect of the alien's culture at other times.

Even a summary sketch of Muslim history during roughly the past two centuries would be a disproportionate digression from the broader purposes of this book.[2] Instead, a schematic presentation of the modes and moments of the Muslim response will be presented.

Since the new age aborning in the Muslim world was being created by a powerful alien threat coming from the West, the governments and the political elites of the Muslim world were the first to be in danger and the first to respond.

The rest of Muslim society—whether ulama, artisans, merchants, or peasants—became fully aware of the radical changes being imposed on their way of life only later. Such was the case, at least, where states survived the first shocks of the Western impact. Where, on the contrary, the states fell apart early in the process—as in Algeria whose three-centuries-old Ottoman Turkish government was destroyed in the early days of the French conquest or in India where the Moghuls were a spent force before the end of the eighteenth century—the pattern was that of adjusting to direct alien rule.[3] Even in these cases the first response came largely from the existing indigenous political elite.

Muslim political leaders were usually the first to wrestle with these new problems because the stark reality of Western military superiority soon dictated the rules of the game even if Western hegemony often began with seemingly peaceful trade. Hilaire Belloc's lines written at the end of the century sum up the new age:

> Whatever happens, we have got
> The Maxim gun, and they have not.

In Northern Africa, for example, three decisive defeats frame the beginning, middle and end of the nineteenth century rather better than precise chronological dates: 1798: Napoleon's routing of the Mamluks at the Battle of the Pyramids; 1844: the French defeat of the Moroccan forces at the Battle of Isly; 1898: British victory over the Mahdist forces in the Battle of Omdurman. At other times and in other places Muslim leaders came to realize the radical change in the power balance between Muslim lands and the old enemy, Europe, not so much after a cataclysmic battle but rather in response to incremental changes. An incident in the beylik of Tunis in the early 1800s illustrates the point. Reacting to a dispute with Sardinia, Husayn Bey wanted to go to war, but an old Mamluk serving the bey put the case poignantly: "Sardinia and Genoa are not what we used to know. They have advanced in prosperity and power just as we have declined."[4] Even the lesser European states could henceforth threaten the Muslim states.

The Muslim political leadership faced limited choices. The crushing defeats of 1798, 1844, and 1898 inflicted on Arab Africa demonstrated the futility of military confrontation. Major defeats elsewhere could be added to the roster: Plassey in India as early as 1757, the naval battle of Navarino in 1827, and the Russian victories over Persia in 1812 and 1826. Seemingly, a more promising strategy for Muslim rulers was to enter into alliance with one or another European power against the more immediately threatening European power. Thus Muslim rulers sought to play off the British and French contending for control of India or the British and the Dutch in the East Indies. They jockeyed between the British and the Russians facing off in that vast area from Anatolia to Afghanistan in the celebrated nineteenth-century equivalent of the twentieth-century cold war that the British dubbed the "great game."[5] Beleaguered Muslim rulers in the Mediterranean area tried as best they could to take advantage of the multipower Eastern Question diplomatic confrontations among the several European powers.

Along with this strategy of divide to avoid being ruled[6] there grew up among a few prescient members of the Muslim elite the will to study the institutions and ideas that seemed to undergird Western strength with an eye to adapting them to their own societies. Thus arose, beginning some two centuries ago, the pattern of seeking to play "catch-up" with a neighboring and threatening state system. The heirs to this tradition of "Westernization" and "defensive modernization" remain in power in most Muslim states to this day.[7] They are, in the eyes of Islamic radicals or fundamentalists who oppose them, at best foolish fellows smitten with "Westoxication"; at worst they have so abandoned the true faith of Islam as to be deemed not just infidels but apostates deserving death. This pejorative appraisal of the Westernizers is, however, a parody of reality. In fact, both the so-called secularists (or, a more benign label, the Muslim Erastians) and the Islamic radicals (or fundamentalists) have embraced a number of ideas and actions traceable to the West. Both groups are also aware, indeed, oppressively aware, of the still intrusive Western "Other." Both are trying in their quite diverse ways to reconstitute a self-sufficiency that began to slip away from Muslims in the modern era. Many things have changed in the past two centuries, not the least important being the vastly widened circle of those involved in politics, but the core challenge of defensive modernization still confronts them all.

The struggle within the Islamic world since the Western impact became predominant may be schematized as being between those prepared to adjust to the world as it is versus those insisting on making the world adjust to their image of what the world should be. The former risk eventually losing important aspects of their religious tradition through piecemeal accommodation to alien ways. The latter risk losing all in one cataclysmic defeat, somewhat like the fate of the Jewish Zealots in confronting Rome. The former may well succeed in achieving a workable new synthesis that maintains the core religious values while being in line with the world they are fated to live in. The latter by their inflexible resistance may manage to do the same by challenging overly latitudinarian ways. Neither accommodationist nor rejectionist is always correct or more "religious" than the other. Specific historical circumstances govern each case. The opportunists and the sincere are to be found in both camps.

Another way to classify the two approaches that have developed in response to the intrusive West is as establishment versus antiestablishment groupings. The former, having a stake threatened by but not yet totally lost to the alien challenge (such as ruling an existing state with its army, bureaucracy, and other institutions) have usually tended to adopt some combination of accommodationist, play-for-time strategies. The latter, with little or less to lose, are more inclined to radical measures.

The accommodationists/establishment forces were not only first in the field against the Western challenge. They have also been more important than the resisters/antiestablishment forces in terms of political power wielded. They continue to be so even today, although the cumulative weight of the Islamic radical forces may yet swing the balance to a degree unmatched during the past two centuries. More on that later.

Sketching the Middle Eastern and North African response to the Western threat may illustrate the above interpretation. This important segment of the larger Muslim world offers the example of several long-established states confronting the Western state system. Largest and most important by far was the Ottoman Empire. This long-lived state had two autonomous provinces that can be counted as de facto states, Egypt and Tunisia (Algeria would have been another but for the French occupation beginning in 1830). To the east and west of the Ottoman lands were two other Muslims states, Iran and Morocco. These five—the central Ottoman Empire, Egypt, Tunisia, Iran, and Morocco—went through a strikingly similar development during the nineteenth century. The pattern may be presented schematically as follows:

1. Military defeats by Western forces.
2. Efforts to catch up by adopting Western military procedures and technology.
3. Leading to new schooling for the military, student missions to Europe, Western military advisers recruited to serve in the host countries, and construction of factories to produce needed military supplies and thus attain military autonomy.
4. Increasing contacts with Western ideas and institutions produced by the above brought forth a small but slowly growing number of Muslims seeking to substitute more "constitutional" forms of rule for the centuries-old autocracy. These "Westernizers" often came from the existing political and bureaucratic class bent on consolidating their gains within existing governmental structures.
5. Efforts to adopt Western-style conscript armies and a state supported military-industrial complex (however puny by twentieth-century standards) greatly increased the level of state expenditures. This occurred at a time when Western commerical penetration sapped the vitality of indigenous industry and thereby weakened the available tax base.
6. The gap between state expenditures and revenues was later covered by state loans at extremely unfavorable terms in the European money markets. Since most of the loans went to current expenses and not capital development, it was only a matter of time before each state could not longer meet its debt obligations.
7. This led to increased European intervention (formal European financial control and debt collection established in three cases: the Ottoman Empire, Egypt, and Tunisia).
8. In three of five cases (Tunisia, Egypt, and Morocco) the fiscal crisis plus the loss of state legitimacy in the wake of the failed efforts to "catch up" with the West led to an internal time of troubles that gave Europe the opportunity to establish direct colonial rule— French protectorate in Tunisia, British occupation of Egypt, and French and Spanish protectorates in Morocco. The Ottoman Empire and Iran escaped this fate largely because the European states could not agree on which of them should get these spoils.

In other parts of the Muslim world either the state crumbled much earlier (as the Moghul Empire in India) or the states, being less bureaucratic and more local, were in no position to follow the sequence of steps outlined above. Such, grosso modo, was the case, for example, in Afghanistan and the East Indies. Still other Muslim entities succumbed early on to outright Western control. Examples include the steady Russian advance into the Caucasus and Central Asia and the French conquest of Algeria.

For all these varieties of power relationship with the West one significant consistency characterized the Muslim world. Here and there throughout the vast and diverse Muslim umma a few individuals came forward to offer a similar answer to the combined politico-military and ideological threat posed by the West. That answer came down to variations on the following: We can't beat them. We don't want to join them. We must try to learn from them.

Three individuals from three different parts of the Muslim world illustrate the early Muslim accommodationist and modernizing responses to the Western challenge. They are Khayr al-Din al-Tunisi (1810/1820?–1879), Sir Sayyid Ahmad Khan (1817–1898), and Shaykh Muhammad Abduh (1849–1905).

Khayr al-Din was a Circassian mamluk who spent most of his active life in the service of the beys of Tunis and then capped his career with a brief (alas, inglorious) year as grand vizier in Istanbul. His long and active political life gave him extensive contact with European culture (he became fluent in French) and convinced him that the Muslim world could catch up with Europe only by openly adopting many of Europe's ways. During a period of political exile in the 1860s, he wrote a political treatise, *Aqwam al-Masalik fi Ma'rifat Ahwal al-Mamalik* (The Surest Path to Knowledge Concerning the Conditions of Countries).[8] Soon translated into Turkish and French, this small work was an appeal to Europe on the one hand and to the conservatives (especially the ulama) in the Muslim world on the other.[9] Khayr al-Din asked Europe to join hands in supporting the Muslim modernizers (he specifically mentioned, and himself identified with, the reformist Ottoman Tanzimat statesmen).

Then, in appealing to conservatives at home, Khayr al-Din set forth a number of themes thereafter often used by Muslim accommodationists justifying massive borrowing of alien ways. These include:

Learning from others is not only permissible but is enjoined. Did not the Prophet Muhammad accept the good advice of Salman the Persian in adopting appropriate battle tactics? This was the celebrated Battle of the Trench, so called because Salman the Persian had advised the digging of a trench in order to hold off the forces from Mecca seeking to crush the early Muslim community. Failure of the seige was a turning point leading later to reconciliation with the Meccans and the victory of Islam in Arabia.

European progress is not because these are Christian nations. The Vatican is the most backward state in Europe.

The decline of Muslim countries is not due to Islam. Rather it stems from Muslims having abandoned the rules governing life in this world as set out in the time of the Prophet and the early Muslim community.

Europe's progress is to be explained in part by its people's having earlier had the good sense to borrow from the Muslims their great advances in philosophy, mathematics, and the other sciences. It would be ironic if we Muslims are not equally open now to borrowing what is useful from others.

Reason and Revelation are in accord that good government is based on justice and security. There must be fixed rules that men can count on. Thus, autocracy is both unreasonable and un-Islamic. No one can ensure that the good ruler today will be good tomorrow or that his successor will be good. Non-Muslims can establish the rules of good government using reason. Muslims, using reason, and sustained as well by divine revelation, should be able to do even better.

Khayr al-Din, given the opportunity to serve as chief minister in Tunisia from 1873 to 1877 (when he was arbitrarily dismissed by the bey responding to the intrigues of a court favorite and foreign consuls), sought to put into practice his ideas concerning openness to alien ideas and institutions and government based on fixed justice and security. The most influential and long-lived of his reforms was the creation of the Westernizing Sadiqi College in 1875.[10]

Sir Sayyid Ahmad Khan (knighted by the British in 1888) had family connections with the Moghul court but opted, early in his career and against the wishes of his family, to work with the British East Indian Company.[11] Seeing the 1857–1858 Indian Mutiny as futile, he remained loyal and was instrumental in saving many Europeans.

Thereafter, he set out to accomplish the dual goal of 1. convincing the British that the Muslims of India could be loyal and useful subjects and 2. urging Muslims to adopt modern Western ways. In seeking to implement this latter goal he too (just like Khayr Al-Din and Muhammad Abduh) maintained that Islam, properly understood and interpreted, was perfectly compatible with modernity. In order to establish that point he rejected *taqlid* (imitation, i.e., of the decisions worked out by earlier theologians) and welcomed *ijtihad* (independent judgment, use of one's own reasoning). Sayyid

Ahmad Khan was even not prepared to accept the traditions of Sunni Islam as hammered out by earlier generations of ulama. In a manner reminiscent of Protestant theology based on the Bible (*sola Scriptura*), he offered a Muslim interpretation that relied almost exclusively on the Qur'an. Although not trained as an *'alim*, he nevertheless undertook to write in Urdu a commentary on the Qur'an that he was unable to complete before his death.

Sayyid Ahmad Khan was, however, the very opposite of a scriptural literalist in any fundamentalist sense. Islam, he insisted, was completely compatible with reason and with "nature" (a key concept in his thought, which al-Afghani—discussed later—singled out for attack). This meant that any supernatural events in religion, even in the Qur'an, could properly be interpreted either allegorically or psychologically. In short, he was very much a nineteenth-century advocate of science and positivism. His regard for Britain—one could even say his loyalty to Britain—was not just tactical. He truly admired what he saw as British accomplishments. A high point in his life was his trip to Britain in 1869–1870. This unfeigned admiration was matched by a sense of shame concerning the state of his Indian compatriots. Writing from England in 1869, he observed: "Without flattering the English I can truly say that the natives of India, high and low, merchants and petty shopkeepers, educated and literate, when contrasted with the English in education, manners, and uprightness, are as like them as a dirty animal is to an able and handsome man."[12] Still, like several other modernists of his generation (and, indeed, later too) his sense of the failings of his own community evolved not into a rejection of his roots but rather an intensified concern to make the Muslims of India worthy of Islam as a religion and a culture.

Convinced that Muslims must adopt Western ways, he involved himself in getting English works translated into Urdu, writing numerous tracts presenting his reformist ideas, and establishing schools. His crowning achievement was the creation in 1877 of the Westernizing Muslim Anglo-Oriental College at Aligarh, now the Aligarh Muslim University.

Shaykh Muhammad Abduh is the only one of our three Westernizing examples who came from the ranks of the ulama. He was also younger than the other two, and his active contributions came a generation or more later. This conforms to the pattern of first responses to the West usually coming from within the political elite with the ulama joining in later.[13]

For a time he was a disciple of Jamal al-Din al-Afghani (al-Asadabadi),[14] the mercurial and peripatetic champion of Muslim unity and resistance to Western (especially British) imperialism. Al-Afghani, a thorough activist prepared to consider armed resistance, clandestine cabals, assassination, or whatever tactic might seem to offer immediate result, personified the adamant resister scorning the strategy of the accommodationists.[15] Abduh's association with al-Afghani brought him banishment from his native Egypt following the 'Urabi Pasha revolt and the ensuing British occupation, but in exile Abduh's more meliorist mindset won out. Permitted to return to Egypt in 1888, Abduh accepted the British occupation, even becoming a personal friend of Lord Cromer whose later support won him in 1899 the lofty post of mufti of Egypt. He held this post until his death in 1905.

Abduh's message was that Islam, properly understood and implemented, was easily compatible with the requisites of modern times and thus of Westernization. All the general points mentioned above in summarizing Khayr al-Din's ideology could be found, with no more than slight stylistic modification, in Abduh's as well. Islam, he insisted, imposed upon believers the obligation to use their God-given reasoning powers in adapting the basic principles set out in the *Shari'ah* to changing conditions of life in each generation. In Muslim technical terminology the pious Muslim must use ijtihad and not taqlid. Abduh's attacks on what he saw as the excesses of Sufi mysticism were of a piece with his emphasis on reason and ijtihad. It was a major step away from a premodern mindset in which the world was seen as beyond man's comprehension and requiring otherworldly intervention mediated by holy men or amulets or what have you.

The world, to Abduh, not only made sense. It was given full religious significance. Thus, the hadith of the Prophet Muhammad "Work for this world as if you would live forever, work for the world to come as if you would die tomorrow" became an oft-cited slogan of Abduh and his followers in the movement that took the name of Salafiyya. Abduh

> made popular a hopeful attitude toward politics, a belief that human action, based on rational and scientific principles, could ameliorate the human condition. He felt that the intellectual, by denouncing superstitions and propagating science and philosophy, held the key to political and social progress. Needless to say, such an attitude is a radical departure from the attitude of the traditional intellectual leaders of Islam, whether they were in the mainstream of orthodoxy or were philosophers transmitting a corpus of esoteric knowledge deeply suspect to orthodoxy.[16]

The name *Salafiyya*, from the Arabic *salaf*, plural *aslaf*, meaning "predecessors" or "ancestors," refers to the Prophet Muhammad and the early Muslim community. Just as the Protestant reformers spoke of eliminating the presumed deviations brought by the intervening centuries, so too did Abduh and his disciples challenge the existing societal synthesis as having badly deviated from the true religion. Abduh's message presented as well the Muslim equivalent of the priesthood of all believers. All Muslims were able—indeed, were enjoined—to understand the Islamic precepts governing life in this world and to adjust their lives accordingly. Such an orientation downgraded the standing not just of the Sufi shaykhs but of the ulama as well. Nor did the imperial presumption of the ruler as the "shadow of God on earth" coupled with the idea that submission to political authority is required to avoid disorder (*fitna*) escape scrutiny. Political leadership has to pass the test of reason or, in a word, efficacy. Moreover, the Salafiyya movement highlighted the concept of *shura* (consultation) to argue for representative government.[17]

Emphasis on the golden age of early Islam as the paradigm for later ages did, however, risk undercutting the case made by Abduh and his followers for massive borrowing from the infidel. The more traditionally minded could readily heed only half the argument and seek to restore a distant past, ignoring the call for openness to new circumstances. This is why much of the later conservative as well as liberal Muslim political thought stems from the Salafiyya.

Another characteristic, now generally seen as a weakness, was that Abduh and his school were so eager to assert Islam's compatibility with modern times that they often slipped into measuring Islam by prevailing modern Western ideals. To the extent that Western ideals changed, the Salafiyya case would appear anachronistic or even ridiculous. Yes, Islam favored, or prefigured, democracy or capitalism or socialism or women's liberation ... The touching search for Western spokesmen, past or present, who had a good word for Islam betrayed a tendency to let the intrusive Other set the rules.

The ideologies and political programs epitomized in the lives of Khayr al-Din al-Tunisi, Sir Sayyid Ahmad Khan, and Shaykh Muhammad Abduh did not completely win over the political elites, and the extent to which they penetrated into the larger Muslim society was even more limited. Such leaders have long been highlighted in historical scholarship largely because from the twentieth-century perspective they seemed to represent the dominant motif of future developments. In recent years, with the rise to prominence of Islamic radicalism, second thoughts are being expressed.[18] This much, however, survives even the most adamant historical revisionism: these Westernizing liberals addressed the existing political class. To the extent that they gained the ear of existing political leadership—which they did, not consistently but often—they possessed an influence out of all proportion to their numbers.[19] Their influence also reached alien political leadership. Thus, Sayyid Ahmad Khan or Shaykh Muhammad Abduh could influence the policy of their colonial overlords just as Khayr al-Din al-Tunisi or the men of the Tanzimat could, working with still independent governments, have some impact on the European powers.

Moreover, they initiated a major ideological shift in Muslim political thought by rejecting political quietism and giving religious value to this-worldly concerns. That orientation is still very much in play and has become part of the cultural heritage of intellectuals and political leaders throughout today's Muslim world.

10.

The Early Antiestablishment Response to the Western Challenge

What then of the opposition to acccommodationists and the pro-establishmentarians? First, it must be emphasized that the Muslim world never lacked individuals with the courage and the conviction to resist alien domination by force of arms. Abd al-Qadir's sustained and heroic resistance to the French in Algeria (1832–1847), the Mujahidin movement in Muslim India led by Sayyid Ahmad Brelvi and Shah Ismail Shahid in the 1830s, the Indian Mutiny of 1857–1858,[1] the rising of the Sudanese Mahdi and the creation of the Mahdist state (1881–1898), the Urabi Pasha revolt in Egypt (1879–1882), the two nineteenth-century British-Afghan wars and early twentieth-century resistance to imperial pressures by the Somali leader Muhammad Abdullah Hasan (dubbed the "mad mullah" by the British) are only the more important or better-known examples. Others, great and small, could be cited.

Even established governments, although obliged by bitter experience to accept that diplomacy might gain more (or lose less) than war, never completely abandoned the military option. This was shown in the Ottoman actions leading to and during the Crimean War and the "Eastern Crisis" of the 1870s ending in war against Russia.

On balance, however, the military options could not change the strategic configuration based on Europe's overwhelming military and technological dominance. That many of the sustained and, for a time, successful military actions against Western imperialism took place in remote hinterland areas less inviting to Western economic interests and more conducive to guerrilla tactics puts limits on their significance in the larger tableau of developments.

All of the examples of outright armed resistance to European domination were undergirded by a strong Muslim religious message, and in most cases one or more individuals from the ranks of the ulama or the Sufi brotherhood leadership can be pinpointed. A striking example was the early nineteenth-century fatwa of one Shah Abdul Aziz ruling that India under British rule was *Dar al-Harb*. Accordingly, Muslims must either drive the British out (jihad) or emigrate to Muslim territory (hijra). This call was picked up by Sayyid Ahmad Brelvi and Shah Ismail Shahid, whose movement bore the significant name of Mujahidin.

What then about the role of the Muslim "clergy" in other forms of resistance to the Westernizers and the accommodationists? One general theme to be noted is that even the more politically quietist ulama began to perceive the threat to their interests as the Westernizers made serious inroads into their virtual monopoly over formal education. The ulama response tended to take the form of holding out for the autonomy of their own educational institutions even if they could not stem the tide of new, essentially Westernizing, schools growing up around them. The Westernizers, in turn, often found it expedient to found new institutions circumventing thereby the old religious establishment. For example, the ulama's resistance to "reform" at al-Azhar led to the creation in 1872 of the Dar al-'Ulum as a teachers college to train those bound for service in the governmental schools. With a teaching college, a national library (founded the same year, 1872), a network of governmental schools, plus other such institutions as the first secular law school (1886) the Egyptian government was simply bypassing those ulama who dug in their heels against change.[2] An equivalent tactic was used in Istanbul.

The Ottomans paid lip service to the ulama and championed Islam but continued to create Westernizing, government-controlled educational institutions. By 1847, for example, the Ottoman government had a separate ministry for education. This grew out of the 1845 Council of Public Instruction, the announcement of which included the following pious statement: "The first of the necessities of this life is to know the duties and obligations which religion imposes on man." These comforting words for the ulama papered over a continuing reduction of their educational role. The ulama in this period also became clearly distinguished in dress from other Ottoman officials, being permitted to keep to their robes and turban after all others were obliged to don the European-style Nizami uniforms.[3]

The ulama potential for encouraging or at least legitimating political protest remained, however, intact. Two prominent examples in the period before the First World War took place in Iran. The national boycott against the shah's having granted a British subject monopoly control over the production and sale of tobacco throughout the country was largely sparked and sustained by ulama leadership. A more nuanced example of ulama political leadership came during the 1906–1909 period when a number of eminent ulama joined ranks with secular leaders in pushing for a constitutional monarchy. Certain of the ulama were, however, lined up in favor of absolutism, and others who had been constitutionalists later had second thoughts.

Two incidents elsewhere illustrate the extent of ulama involvement in politics. In 1913 the municipal council in Kanpur (Cawnpore), India sought to demolish the ablutions area of a mosque to make room for a new road. The local ulama countered with a fatwa stating that destroying the ablutions area was tantamount to destroying the mosque itself. In a scenario duplicated often in modern times in various parts of the Muslim world, crowd protests at the mosque became a riot put down by police with loss of life. The incident was only brought to an end by the decisive action of the British viceroy, Lord Hardinge, who personally went to Kanpur and reversed the municipality decision.[4]

Earlier in Tunisia in 1857 Muhammad Bey had been forced by European pressure to issue the *'Ahd al-Aman* (Fundamental Pact), providing for European-style legal guarantees similar to those the Ottoman sultan had earlier introduced in 1839. The ulama, asked to give their legal opinion, produced fatwas that made no effort to reconcile the 'Ahd al-Aman with Islamic law. Instead, they hewed strictly to the most literal interpretations of Islamic law, which meant, in effect, a categorical rejection of these Westernizing reforms. At the same time, however, the ulama passed the buck back to the bey, concluding that he had the right to decide as he saw fit.[5]

These two incidents separated by more than a half-century in time and roughly four thousand miles in space epitomize ulama involvement in the political arena. With very few exceptions the ulama opposed the alien borrowings from Europe and expressed that opposition when it seemed safe to do so. Yet, their age-old fear of *fitna* and reluctance to confront government usually induced them to hold back whenever that seemed prudent. They would speak out to protect narrowly Islamic interests (e.g., the integrity of mosques or of the *Shari'ah*, even if the latter was increasingly marginalized by state-made law.) They were disinclined to challenge political leadership directly. Indeed, many cases of such apparent confrontations involved, on examination, little more than ulama post facto legitimation of actions taken by those within the political and military classes. This was essentially the case in the fatwa deposing the reformist Sultan Selim III in 1807 and in the events leading to the deposition within a year of his successor, Mustafa IV, to be replaced by Sultan Mahmud II. The most important ulama supported the deposition of Selim III, but it was military action by the Janissary auxiliaries that made the difference. The quite formal role of ulama in such political struggles was well indicated when the successful rebel against Sultan Mustafa IV, Bayrakdar, summoned the *Shaykh al-Islam* and leading ulama, obliged them to support the restitution of Selim III, and sent the Shaykh al-Islam to work this out with Sultan Mustafa IV. Mustafa IV then had Selim III assassinated and tried to do the same with the young Mahmud (for then Mustafa expected to be secure as the only surviving male in the Ottoman line), who escaped just in time.[6]

Much the same can be said for the deposition of Sultan Abdulhamid II 102 years later in 1909. A fatwa was obtained, even though most of the ulama and certainly the many students in the religious schools supported Abdulhamid II. Indeed, the religious students had been instrumental in Sultan Abdulhamid II's short-lived regaining of autocratic power in 1908–1909.

That the ulama were honored to the extent that they remained "above politics" is illustrated by the famous Bakri family, which had provided the principal imams of the Zaytuna Mosque in Tunis for over 190 year and presided as well over a famous Tunisian *zawiyya*. One Abu al-Ghaith al-Bakri, however, forsook a religious career and became a governmental concessions farmer. He received the following rebuke from the chief minister, "We used to rise to greet you out of respect for your ancestors, but since you were not satisfied to follow in their way preferring instead governmental positions you must become as other men of government . . . without any other distinction."[7]

This, at least, was the general situation governing the political participation of those ulama in the capital cities or those areas under effective government control. In the hinterland, where governmental writ could be quietly circumvented, ignored, or even resisted, a less inhibited Muslim leadership could be found not just from the ulama but from Sufi leaders or, for that matter, individuals with no Islamic religious specialization. There, the centuries-old pattern of religio-political challenges from the periphery against the political center, as Ibn Khaldun had highlighted centuries earlier, prevailed. Such movements long predated the modern age of Western domination (the earliest go back to the early years of Islam in the seventh century, e.g., the Kharijites) and could be found at one place of another throughout the vast Muslim world in every century thereafter. Interesting modern examples in Islamic Africa taking place before the period of outright

Western colonial rule are the establishment of the Sokoto caliphate by Uthman dan Fodio (1754–1817) and the jihad movement of Hajj Umar Tal (1794–1865). Other movements important in shaping later Muslim thought and action that arose before the West had assumed its hegemonic role were the Wahhabiyya in eighteenth-century Arabia and even the earlier Naqshbandiyya Sufi order arising in the eastern reaches of Islam. It would be anachronistic to views such movements as responding to alien infidel intrusions.

Other opposition movements, however, were clearly resisting the alien West. These would include several in what was in the process of becoming British India:

- Sayyid Ahmad Barelwi (1786–1831) led the Pathan resistance to the British until he was killed in battle.
- One Titu Mir (1782–1831), a Calcutta wrestler—and thus an interesting example of a leader with no specialized religious training, emerged to lead a movement whose followers wore distinctive dress and ate only with other members of the brotherhood. Titu Mir had been influenced by Barelwi and he, too, died fighting in an uprising.
- Hajj Shari'at Allah (1764–1840, an alternative birthdate of 1781 is given) founded the Fara'idi movement of Bengal. Continued by his even more militant son, Dudu Miyan (1819–1862), this movement emphasized that India under British rule was no longer a Muslim land but was *Dar al-Harb*. This movement declined after the British authorities arrested Dudu Miyan in 1847.

In what is now Indonesia three very serious armed religious movements challenged Dutch rule:

- In Sumatra at the beginning of the nineteenth century three scholars returning from pilgrimage to Mecca began a campaign of preaching puritanical religious reform. Known as the Padri movement (the *kaum puteh,* or "those in white," since the followers wore white robes as in Arabia) this movement opposing what was seen as unorthodox Islamic practice held out against the Dutch, in cooperation with some of the local political elite, until 1837.
- In Java the son of a local sultan, Dipa Negara, led a resistance movement, supported by the ulama, against the Dutch for five years, from 1825 to 1830.
- Much later in the century the Dutch attempt to establish direct control over the sultanate of Atjeh (Acheh) provoked an extended war

lasting from 1873 until 1908 in which resistance to colonialism was led by the ulama.

In Central Asia and Northern Africa resistance to foreign control was often led by different Sufi orders. Pride of place in opposing Russian colonialist incursions into the Muslim regions of Asia go to the Naqshbandiyya order and especially to a certain Imam Shamil who led a three-decade-long resistance to the Russians until his final defeat in 1859. Undergirding this movement was a disciplined and puritanical religious calling. Another Sufi order of importance in this area was the Qadriyya. Later, the Naqshbandiyya and the Qadriyya together provided the backbone of one more great revolt against Russian rule in the years 1877–1879. Other revolts broke out from time to time, one as late as during the First World War, but before that time there had begun to emerge a more accommodationist tendency personified in the career of Ismail Gasprinski (1851–1914), who championed a program of introducing modern techniques and thought to the Muslims of Russia while seeking to achieve sociopolitical strength through unity. Thus, the term *Jadidism* (from the Arabic for "new") to label this movement.

In North Africa Algeria's Abd al-Qadir, who held off the French from 1832 until his surrender in 1847, was from a family of Qadriyya brotherhood leaders. Muhammad b. Ali al-Sanusi (1787–1859) founded the Sanusiyya brotherhood that provided a matrix for both sociopolitical strengthening and a deepening of Islamization in North and Central Africa. Later, as European penetration into these areas grew, the Sanusiyya brotherhood often was involved in resistance to the invader. This was especially the case in what is now modern Libya. Following the Italian invasion beginning in 1911 the Sanusiyya brotherhood led resistance in Cyrenaica (the eastern region of Libya) for more than two decades until finally subjugated by Mussolini's Fascist regime.

The Sudan in the last two decades of the nineteenth century offered a major example of short-term success in rolling back foreign intervention and establishing an indigenous state and government free of outside control. This was the work of the radical religio-political movement created by Muhammad Ahmad al-Mahdi (1848–1885). He, too, had Sufi roots. In fact, an important step in his personal religious itinerary was his bitter disappointment in discovering that his chosen Sufi shaykh was too lax. He later claimed to have received a special mandate from God and, acting on that claim, sought to create a renewed holy community.

Muhammad Ahmad exemplifies that figure found throughout the centuries in Muslim history—a mahdi, or leader of a messianic movement with apocalyptic overtones.[8] After Muhammad Ahmad's death following his crowning success in capturing Khartoum, his successor presided over the Mahdist state until it went down in defeat before the armies of the Anglo-Egyptian reconquest, culminating in the famous 1898 Battle of Omdurman.[9]

Such millenarian movements that presume to add to existing scriptures and prophethood are viewed with extreme caution if not downright disapproval by the religiously orthodox in all three sister Semitic religions, and none more so than Islam with its doctrines of the Qur'an as the literal word of God and Muhammad as the "seal of prophecy." Accordingly, when the millenarian forces do not win their Armageddon and the world does not come to an end such movements try to work their way back toward orthodoxy. Within a generation after the Mahdist state had been overthrown and the Anglo-Egyptian Condominium established the Ansar (as the Mahdi's followers were called) were on their way to becoming, in effect, yet another brotherhood in a plurality of Sufi orders.

These many movements of resistance to the foreign infidel—whether led by mahdis, puritanical preachers, sufi leaders, ulama, or even the religiously unlearned—can be fitted into the following schema:

- Several were quite localized. Others extended over significant area (as the Sanusiyya in Africa or the Naqshbandiyya in Asia). All, however, either met ultimate defeat in battle or survived only by accepting the fait accompli of colonial domination. Indeed, the entire Muslim world eventually fell under outright European colonial rule with only the following exceptions: Iran and the Anatolian portion of the Ottoman Empire that became the Republic of Turkey escaped being taken over by a single European power largely because the deadlocked power balances within the European state system preserved their tenuous independence. Even so, Iran was twice in this century divided up and partially occupied by British and Russian forces—from 1907 through the period of the First World War and then again during World War II. Only remote Afghanistan and much, but not all, of the Arabian Peninsula can be added to this small list of Muslim lands escaping outright European colonial rule. All other Muslim peoples lost their independence to the alien infidel.
- As the different efforts at physical resistance failed throughout the Muslim world, the stock of those Muslim leaders preaching accommodation with the outsider intruders and learning their ways rose.

The idea that Muslims were being colonized because they were "colonizable" (the expression adopted years later by Algeria's Malek Bennabi) came to the fore. Muslims, it was argued, needed to put their own house in order, get back to the basic values of their religion, accept the painful task of learning from the arrogant dominator, and work for the day when Islamic society could again stand on its own.

- Yet the allure of outright resistance here and now never died out. Appeals to prudence, preparation, and long-term planning could be seen to make sense, but the Muslim heart was stirred by bolder action. Accordingly, any hand raised against infidel domination was assured of at least quiet, unspoken approval, and if that resistance showed signs of achieving success this subdued support could be swiftly activated into a powerful mass movement throughout the Muslim world. Thereafter, the dying embers of overt resistance to the infidel so quickly kindled by signs of success would just as quickly subside when the armed resistance proved to be yet another disappointing mirage.[10]

These developments in the vast Muslim world from Morocco to the Indies were not taking place in isolation and must be integrated into ongoing global history. Among the changes affecting Muslim peoples, just as the rest of the world, were the creation of stronger, more centralized states and the steady spread of the made-in-Europe concept of nationalism. Added to these were the many inventions and technological improvements that made all parts of the world more accessible and eroded the possibility for certain peoples to opt out of global politics.

And the nineteenth century brought increased literacy. The literacy rate remained quite modest throughout the "third world" (to use today's term) in comparison with the explosion of schooling and rising literacy rates during the last half of the twentieth century), but it was sufficient to challenge the old monopoly of knowledge held by religious elites and government officials. Hand in hand with increased literacy and Western-style schooling emerged a radically different image of language and literature. The older concept of a "higher" language used by the religious and governing elite alongside a value-less patois spoken by the common people began to fade. In its place evolved the idea of a language purified of foreign words, stripped of obfuscating tropes, and made representative of the robust genius of the people.

All these factors moved Muslims, just as the rest of the world, in the direction of increased politicization. More people were becoming politically involved. Different categories of people were becoming politically involved.

It is at this very point that the distinction between establishment and anti-establishments forces dissolves. The efforts of both, however diametrically different in other respects, fostered and favored increased politicization. The blurring of distinction between the two groups is well represented in a movement that appealed to Muslims and caused concern to the West from roughly the 1870s until the First World War. This was Pan-Islam, a movement personified in the career of a quintessentially antiestablishment figure, Jamal al-Din al-Afghani, but given political muscle when adopted as a program by the principal establishment leader in the late nineteenth-century Muslim world, Ottoman sultan Abdulhamid II. Not confined to a single country, Pan-Islam reached across state borders to impact on all parts of the Muslim world. In a way, Pan-Islam prefigured the internationalized political Islam characterizing today's world.

Jamal al-Din al-Afghani (1839–1897) was a very complex man who deliberately veiled his activities in mystery and misrepresentation. Born in Iran and raised as a Shi'i Muslim, he claimed to be a Sunni of Afghan origin (thus, al-Afghani) in order to better reach the Sunni Muslim majority in preaching Muslim political unity against Western imperialism. His activities either took him to or heavily involved him with politics in the Ottoman Empire, Iran, British India, Egypt, the Sudan, and Afghanistan, and the influence of his writings—his mystique—extended to all Muslim countries. Appraisals of him to this day vary wildly. To some he was a charlatan. To others he was an inspired diagnostician of the Muslim plight who prescribed the needed strong medicine of unity and political activism.[11] A good way, perhaps, to take the measure of the man is to see him as a Muslim Ernesto (Che) Guevera (1928–1967). Both were intellectuals and writers while being very much political activists. Both ranged over a vast cultural area (Latin America for Che, the Muslim world for al-Afghani) well beyond their homeland (Argentina and Iran). Both had great charisma enhanced during and after their lives by a continuing mystery concerning the mundane details of their activities. Both became virtual cult figures. This comparison serves also to underscore the extent to which al-Afghani was a very modern man working in an increasingly politicized Muslim world. Indeed, a major part of his legacy has been to activate ever greater numbers of Muslims hitherto inclined to eschew government and politics. "One reason Jamal ad-Din al-Afghani, the leading ideologist of Pan-Islam, has had such a continuing vogue in the Muslim world is that he drew not only upon traditional Islamic loyalties, but also on nascent anti-imperialist and protonationalist sentiments that have not lost their pertinence even today."[12]

Pan-Islam was not, however, the creation of one man. It can most readily be placed in context if we return to the idea of an ongoing dialectic between those Muslims advocating accommodation with the West as opposed to other Muslims pushing for resistance. It has been suggested that each failure of Muslim armed resistance to Western penetration made the less "heroic" tactic of buying time through accommodation in order to learn from the West seem more realistic. This process, however, was cylical, not linear. Accommodationism could also be discredited when governments following that tactic faced nothing but setbacks.

No Muslim state had worked longer to accommodate the European state system and use the time bought to Westernize fundamental political institutions than the Ottoman Empire. The last third of the nineteenth century, however, brought the Ottomans nothing but grief. The peace that Russia imposed on the Ottomans after the 1877–1878 war entailed major losses both in the Balkans and the eastern reaches of the empire, giving up an estimated one-fifth of its total population, roughly half of whom were Muslims.[13] Another blow at this time was Britain's gaining de facto control over the island of Cyprus. This was the condition that Britain, hitherto the principal supporter of the Ottoman Empire, imposed in return for diplomatic support at the 1878 Congress of Berlin. An even more shocking setback was the British occupation of Egypt (still juridically part of the Ottoman Empire) in 1882. That loss had followed hard on the previous year's French conquest of Tunisia.

Somewhat earlier, Russian conquests deep into Muslim Central Asia in the 1860s and 1870s left a vulnerable corridor of Muslim governments (Ottoman Empire, Iran, and Afghanistan) confronting these two expanding European empires, Russia and Britain.

This fateful epoch from the early 1860s to the early 1880s thus added several million Muslims to the number already living under alien rule. At the same time, losses in the largely Christian Balkans gave the Ottoman Empire an overwhelming Muslim majority, and the loyalty of the remaining Christian subjects was suspect. Under such circumstances the ideology of Ottomanism or a political loyalty to the Ottoman state linking together those of different religions, languages, and ethnicity appeared increasingly irrelevant. Since the alien infidel was bent on both "liberating" all non-Muslims and dominating all Muslims, then clearly the overarching existential reality was a common Muslimness.

Such in essence was the ideology that al-Afghani and others advanced. It remained only for Sultan Abdulhamid to make it state policy. Appeals to the Ottoman sultan for help from Muslims as far away as India and the Indies indicated the possibilities for such a policy. Also at hand was the title of

Abdulhamid as caliph—that most venerable of Islamic political offices. Little matter that the title had had slight political relevance for centuries. Indeed, to many of the learned Sunni Muslims the true caliphate had been confined to the original four rightly guided caliphs who succeeded the Prophet Muhammad. Thereafer, leadership was believed to have degenerated into *mulk*, or kingship.

A hectoring Europe had actually managed to stimulate the idea that the Ottoman sultan, in his capacity of caliph, exercised a certain religous leadership over Muslims wherever they might live. A critical development leading to this end is seen to have been the 1774 Treaty of Kuchuk Kaynarja ending the decisive Russian defeat of the Ottomans. Its terms granted Russia the right to intervene in support of Orthodox Christians who were Ottoman subjects. At the same time, the Muslims of the northern Black Sea area, having been wrested from Ottoman control, were deemed independent, but they were to remain somehow linked to the Ottoman sultan "in his capacity of Grand Caliph."[14]

Thus, the Ottoman sultan, as caliph, was to be seen as Muslim pope or patriarch with transnational responsibilities. Such was the implication of these vaguely written treaty articles. The idea was given substance thereafter throughout the nineteenth century as European powers competed to support their Christian compatriots (did not the Crimean War grow out of a European dispute over the control of the Christian holy places in Bethlehem and Jerusalem?). Simple logic demanded that the "right" of European states to intervene on behalf of Christians beyond their borders meant that a Muslim ruler, especially one claiming the title of caliph, should have a similar right.

Given this context and the pleas for Muslim unity advanced not just by Afghani but also many others, including the Young Ottomans and beleagured Muslims in India and the Indies, it is understandable that Sultan Abdulhamid would come forward to champion Pan-Islam. Even the internal situation in the Ottoman Empire predisposed him so to act. Pan-Islam offered an effective way to outflank those latter-day men of the Tanzimat— those liberal constitutionalist Westernizers within the governmental elite.[15] He could, instead, build his autocracy on a solid foundaton of religious legitimacy.

The tit-for-tat logic of a Muslim ruler supporting Muslims wherever they be just as Christian rulers support Christians is unanswerable. Indeed, the Ottoman sultan as caliph (and thus the Muslim equivalent of pope or patriarch in European eyes) would seem to have an even stronger case for intervention beyond his borders in support of Muslims than a Russian tsar,

Austro-Hungarian emperor, or, certainly, a French president. Perhaps Queen Victoria as "Defender of the Faith" and head of the Anglican Church might claim equivalent status,[16] but the number of Anglicans or even all Protestants then living in Muslim lands was small in any case. Neither logic nor religious office made a difference. No Muslim ruler, including the strongest—Sultan Abdulhamid—had adequate power to intervene in support of Muslims elsewhere. Rulers of several European states did have the power to intervene in support of Christians, and they continued to do so.

Even so, the threat of Muslim unity disturbed those European powers—Britain, France, Holland, and Russia—exercising imperial control over millions of Muslims in Africa and Asia. They watched warily as Sultan Abdulhamid, in a brilliant political stroke, initiated the building of the Hijaz Railway starting at Damascus and planned to reach the holy cities of Mecca and Madina. That Pan-Islam would have found favor among Muslims is readily understandable, but in the absence of effective countervailing power to stem Europe's steady encroachment such support would remain largely one of sentiment, not active political commitment. When the Young Turk regime rashly brought the Ottoman Empire into the First World War on the side of the Central Powers, the sultan acting as caliph declared a jihad. The impact on Muslims in general or, more important, on Muslim troops serving in Allied colonial armies was virtually nil. Muslims would understandably wish to see the last important independent Muslim state survive and thrive, but they could discern as well that, under the circumstances, a wait-and-see attitude made more sense.

11.

From World War I to the 1960s: The Years
of Muted Islamist Politics

The First World War marks a major watershed in history. Restricting our attention to the Muslim world, and treating that vast area with only the broadest of brush strokes, the second decade of this century produced the following developments:

- The last great Muslim empire, that of the Ottoman state, went out of existence. Juridically speaking, this took place in 1923, but in fact the only question following the Ottoman defeat in the First World War was whether there would be a truncated Ottoman remnant or, as turned out to be the case, a nation-state in Anatolia, the Republic of Turkey, with all remaining Ottoman territories parceled out as separate political entities.
- Europe completed its division of the colonialist spoils in Africa and Asia with the British mandates in Palestine (and Transjordan) and Iraq and the French mandates in Syria and Lebanon plus several mandates in Africa, largely a reshuffling of former German holdings. The League of Nations mandates, however, presupposed ultimate independence for the mandated states. The mandates system itself represented a step away from confident colonialism as had existed in the nineteenth century (and in previous centuries) and toward the European acceptance of decolonization such as took place in the post–World War II period.
- The Western concept of "natural" nations and of nationalism as the normal legitimate policy of any people (the idea of easily distinguishable "peoples" being assumed) was henceforth the dominant

operational framework for political action throughout the Muslim world. Early stirrings in this direction over roughly the previous half-century can be traced, but this second decade of the twentieth century brought a giant step forward. Woodrow Wilson's championing of the self-determination of nations served to establish the dominant rhetoric (but not yet the reality) in both the West and the non-West. Nor was there any confusion concerning the presumed applicability of self-determination to Muslim lands. The twelfth point of Wilson's celebrated fourteen points, given in his address to Congress on January 8, 1918, read in part: "The Turkish portions of the present Ottoman Empire should be assured a secure sovereignty, but the other nationalities which are now under Turkish rule should be assured an undoubted security of life and an absolutely unmolested opportunity of autonomous development."

Accordingly, the political history of the Muslim world from this time can be interpreted in terms of would-be "nations" seeking to become states and of existing states seeking to legitimate their existence on nationalist principles. Both the reality and the ideal of a multilingual, multiethnic, and, yes, multireligious empire led by a Muslim ruler was eclipsed. The dominant political paradigm that had existed virtually unchallenged in theory and was usually present in practice since the rise of Islam was giving way to the quite different notion of cohesive, coherent nation states.

The question not so readily answered, however, was what should be the basis of these presumably natural nation states. Who were "we" and who "they" in these nation-building exercises? The answers throughout the Muslim world—just as in the West where nationalism developed—were multiple and contradictory.

Ethnolinguistic nationalism characterized Turkey and the Arab world, but for both there were problems and choices to be made, not always consistent with the emerging nationalist ideology. Pan-Turanism (or the concept of a common Turkicness extending into Central Asia) was abandoned in favor of an Anatolian Turkish nationalism. Arabism emerged at first as an ideology binding together the Arabs of Asia (Fertile Crescent and Arabian Peninsula). Only later in the interwar period did Arabism expand to embrace the Arabic-speakers of Egypt, Sudan, and the Maghrib. In any case, several different Arab countries had a long history of statehood. These included Egypt, Morocco, Oman, and Tunisia. With a somewhat looser definition of "state" one might well add Algeria,[1] Kuwait, Lebanon (at least the Mount Lebanon core), Sudan, and Yemen. In all these a potential for nationalism based on existing cultural and territorial borders was present.

Other Arab countries had significant segments of their population with strong antipathy to being absorbed into a larger Arab political unity of any kind. This would include the Maronite Christians of Lebanon, the large non-Muslim and non-Arabic speaking population of Sudan, and the Kurds of Iraq.[2]

Moving eastward, Iran, like Egypt in the Arab world, looked back on centuries of political existence, even long predating Islam. Religion (Shi'a Islam), territory, and history fit together as the matrix for an Iranian nationalism that continues to this day. Even so, the presence within Iran's borders of appreciable non-Shi'a Muslims and also non-Persian speakers added complications.

Neighboring Afghanistan, although a cluster of different tribes and ethnic groups, was ruled in 1919 by a dynasty with roots going back to the early eighteenth century, Moreover, the cement of Sunni Islam (some 90 percent of the population), the land as a mountainous bastion, and the shared history of either resisting invasion or bursting out to found dynasties in neighboring lands provided elements on which to built an Afghan nationalism.[3]

In the Indian subcontinent Muslims faced hard choices. Indian nationalism as organized by the Indian National Congress was receptive to Muslim participation and many Muslims joined this movement. Still, even though Congress leader such as Gandhi made a real effort to make Muslims feel that they belonged, there was no getting around the harsh demographic fact that Muslims, for all their millions, would be a minority alongside the Hindu majority. Of course, Hindus and Muslims (plus even smaller numbers of Sikhs, Parsees, Christians, and others) had lived together for centuries, but in a distinctively imperial form of communal autonomy. Nationalism presupposed a breaking down of such caste and community barriers in order to realize a shared Indian patriotism. This move toward a unified "national" culture would be, many Muslims understandably feared, overwhelmingly Hindu in character.

In addition, the protean nature of Hinduism, capable of absorbing other gods into its pantheon, was so different from the scripturalist, monotheistic, and transcendent Islam that all-Indian togetherness must have struck quite a few pious Muslims as likely to erode the very foundation of their religion. Accordingly, many but not all Muslim secularists who feared minority political status found common ground with many but not all pious Muslims who feared loss of religious autonomy to create the idea of a separate Muslim state—a Pakistan—in the Indian subcontinent.[4]

Southeast Asia, then divided into British and Dutch colonial domains and with a Muslim majority of roughly the same proportion as existed in the

Arab world, presented a somewhat similar majority-minority situation. In both regions the non-Muslim minorities were more urban, more economically successful, and better positioned to influence the colonialist overlords. The Southeast Asian equivalent of the Christian and Jewish minorities in the Arab world were the Chinese and, to a much lesser extent, the Indians. In both regions a more Islamist political stance could thus appeal to peasants and petty merchants as well as traditional elites, both religious and secular. On the other hand, Islamist politics risked strengthening the more traditional forces, weakening modernizing efforts, and dividing forces in the ongoing struggle against European colonial rule.

The Islamic culture of the two regions—Arab world and Southeast Asia—was, however, sharply different. It is often maintained that Southeast Asia was much less Islamicized than was the Middle Eastern heartland. That approach is prejudicial, implying a Middle Eastern norm against which all other parts of the Muslim world are necessarily to be measured. By such logic Western Christianity would be described as less authentic than Orthodox Christianity, with its roots remaining in the Holy Land. What can be said, however, is that the Islam of the Malay cultural area had integrated much more of Javanese and Hindu mores, embraced a more pantheistic approach to religion, and gave less authority to the scripturalist and legalist aspects as championed by the ulama.

At the same time, many Muslims from Indonesia and Malaya were becoming converted to Islamic reformism (inspired by either the Wahhabiyya or—even more—the Salafiyya of Shaykh Muhammad Abduh and his school) through their pilgrimages to Mecca and their studies in Arabia or Cairo's al-Azhar. This produced an struggle within the Muslim population between would-be reformers and their traditionalist opponents. It was the *kaum muda* (young group) against the *kaum tua* (old group).[5]

Muslims of what was soon to become the Soviet Union experienced the turbulent post–World War I years of civil war and outside intervention before being yoked to harsh Communist rule.

As for the Muslims of Africa living south of the Arabic-speaking belt, all were under colonial rule. The Somali Muhammad b. Abdullah was to die in 1920, bringing to an end his long jihad against not just European rule but Somali clans, opposing Sufi brotherhoods and neighboring Ethiopia.[6] The Somalis were thereafter brought into some semblance of alien controlled order, divided between British, French, and Italian overlords. Elsewhere, as in Nigeria and the Cameroons, nationalism was in its infancy as the struggle within the Muslim communities between would-be modernizers and the traditional alignments got under way. European colonial rule, generally, tended to side with the traditional forces, devolving considerable authority, for example, to selected Sufi brotherhoods or manning the colonial armies and security forces with many Muslims. This nod toward "indirect rule"—which was even picked up by the French, usually so prone to centralized control—shored up the traditional forces in the short run but provided nationalists an additional incentive to take on both colonialism and the indigenous old guard.

Not all that clear a picture from one end of the vast Muslim world to the other, it is true. Even so, two broad generalizations apply in most cases: 1. The principal locus of political action and thought was within existing state units, whether independent or colonized, and 2. the many different nationalist movements frequently sought a political ideology that included non-Muslims and transcended Islam to include other organizing principles such as common language, culture, and history.

A significant exception to the second generalization was the movement for the creation of Pakistan, which aspired to create an Islamic state. Even this movement, however, conformed to the first, the struggle to create Pakistan being fought out within the confines of British India. Put differently, creation of a state and not Pan-Islam was the goal.

A partial or apparent exception to the first generalization was Arab nationalism, which corresponded to no existing territorial unit. Indeed, the projected borders of that would-be state were nebulous and also expanded over time. Yet, Arab nationalism was very much in line with the second generalization. From its origins Arab nationalism sought to transcend religious communalism. Christian Arabs played a role out of all proportion to their numbers in the rise and development of Arab nationalism. Moreover, although Arabism struck a responsive cord across state borders—especially in the Fertile Crescent—the day-to-day political activities in the colonial period and even beyond are most readily tracked along existing state lines.

What then of transnational Muslim political unity? Pan-Islam as preached by al-Afghani and practiced by Sultan Abdulhamid II came to grief during this period. It will be recalled that after the Ottoman Empire entered the First World War on the side of the Central Powers the Young Turk rulers prevailed upon the sultan, in his capacity as caliph, to declare a jihad against the allies. This call for holy war had, however, slight impact on the outcome. Overwhelmingly, the many millions of Muslims under allied colonial rule remained if not loyal to their overlords at least acquiescent, and a not inconsiderable number of Muslims fought for the allies in the several different colonial armies. Ottoman-sponsored Pan-Islam at this testing appeared to be more sound that substance.

Then, after the war, the question of whether Islamic unity could be a cohesive force in world politics was again put to the test. The Ottoman general, Mustafa Kemal, who later adopted the name Kemal Ataturk (or father of the Turks) dismantled what remained of the dying Ottoman Empire and put in its place a nation-state—the Republic of Turkey. This was done in quick stages. First, he abolished the office of sultan (November 1922) but left the last ruler in the centuries-old Ottoman line with the title of caliph.[7] Less than a year later, in October 1923, the Turkish Republic was proclaimed. The Ottoman Empire was no more. The caliph remained a ruler without a state, without even a tiny autonomous territory such as the pope's Vatican City. This residual anomaly was dispatched the following March when Ataturk abolished the office of caliph and sent all members of the Ottoman family into exile.

Ataturk had acted with such dramatic decisiveness because efforts both to give the caliphate some measure of political power in Turkey as well as authority over all Muslims wherever they lived threatened his plans for a sovereign nation-state. As he later insisted in his celebrated 1927 six-day speech, "I explained to the nation that for the sake of the utopia of establishing a world-wide Islamic state, the Turkish state and its handful of people cannot be subjugated to the service of a Caliph."[8]

That reference to the "utopia of . . . a worldwide Islamic state" pointed at not only religious opposition within Turkey but also developments such as the mass Khilafat movement that had sprung up in British India under the leadership of the two brothers, Muhammad and Shaukat Ali. Muslims in India over the previous two decades or more had become increasingly disaffected with British rule and were turning away from the policy of loyalty to the British raj as championed by Sayyid Ahmad Khan. A more confrontational Muslim leadership was seeking to organize the disparate Muslims of the subcontinent into a unified political force. This latter goal was probably more important to the Indian Muslim leaders than that of defending the Ottoman Empire and the caliphate.[9] Even so, the symbolic appeal of the caliphate to Indian Muslims, with their strongly felt need to see themselves as part of a larger entity and not just a minority in a Hindu world, can not be discounted.[10]

Ataturk's bold stroke of abolishing the caliphate outright forced the issue. It was no longer the simple question of whether to maintain an existing institution. Now answers were needed about whether to revive the caliphate, how to do so, and who should be the caliph.

The Khilafat movement, launched five years earlier in 1919 and, for a brief time, a genuinely mass movement, was the largest organized body to weigh in on the caliphate, but many others from virtually every Muslim country became involved. Even those Muslim leaders who had other, more pressing concerns felt obliged to address the issue. The question of the caliphate after March 1924 became more complex—and more political.

A clear example of the problems involved in continuing the caliphate in one form or other, in one place or another, predated Ataturk's abolition of the office. The incident even helped Ataturk gain support for his action. In November 1923 two Indian Muslim leaders, Ameer Ali and the Agha Khan, entered the fray by writing to the Turkish government underlining how important the caliphate was to Sunni Muslims and urging "the imminent necessity for maintaining the religious and moral solidarity of Islam by placing the Caliph-Imamate on a basis which would command the confidence and esteem of the Muslim nations."[11] Since both of these Indian Muslim notables were not Sunnis but Shi'is, who, moreover, had supported Britain during the First World War and were thought to have played an important role in countering the Ottoman sultan/caliph's 1914 declaration of a jihad,[12] Ataturk and his followers had a field day attacking this injudicious intervention.

Ataturk was thus able to disentangle his new Republic of Turkey from the caliphate, but many Muslims throughout the world were not yet ready to let this venerable office go out of existence. Nor were candidates lacking. There were Sharif Husayn, for a short time king of the Hijaz (until ousted by Ibn Saud) and thus in control of the Holy Cities of Mecca and Madina. There was King Fuad of Egypt. Moreover, the deposed Ottoman caliph wrapped himself in the mantle of caliphal legitimacy. That is, having received the required *bay'ah* (oath of loyalty), he could not legitimately be deposed by a secular ruler, even less by one bent on destroying the very institution of the caliphate.

A small group of Sharif Husayn's followers actually met in Palestine to proclaim him caliph on March 5, 1924, just two days after the bill in Turkey abolishing the caliphate became law. The response throughout the Muslim world was negative, if not often derisory. Attempting to shore up a rickety cause, Sharif Husayn called a conference in Mecca during the pilgrim season (July 1924). It was not representative of the vast Muslim world. Most were Arabs with a strong Palestinian representation. Even so, Sharif Husayn failed to get conference approval of his appointment as caliph. In fact, the brief charter adopted by the conference did not even mention the caliphate.[13]

Efforts in support of Egypt's King Fuad fared no better. In May 1926 a "Caliphate Congress," largely organized by Egyptian ulama backing Fuad's aspirations, met in Cairo. Those in attendance represented more of the Muslim world but were heavily weighted toward Egyptian and Palestinian delegates. The Egyptian organizers acted with circumspection, but their efforts at saving appearances fooled no one. The Indian Khilafat movement even refused to send delegates, fearing that the Congress was designed to advance the Egyptian king's caliphal claims.[14]

In any case, those who did attend represented so many conflicting political orientations that the congress, while able to agree on the importance (indeed, the necessity) of the caliphate, proposed no precise steps for his selection. A motion was passed to meet the following year in Cairo, but no further action ensued.

Two later international meetings of Muslims fared no better on the caliphal issue. Neither the Muslim congress in Mecca (in June-July 1926, thus only weeks after that in Cairo) nor the 1931 General Islamic Congress in Jerusalem even put the matter of the caliphate on the agenda. In the former Ibn Saud, recently victorious in ousting Sharif Husayn and the Hashimites from the Hijaz, was seeking international support for Wahhabi control of the holy cities—with only limited success. In the latter the Palestinian leader, Amin al Husayni, looking to gain worldwide Muslim support for the Palestinians resisting Zionism and British mandatory rule, was eager to avoid the divisive issue of the caliphate.[15]

By this latter year the last Ottoman caliph, Abdulmajid, was living removed from *Dar al-Islam* in Nice, and the only announced claimant to the office, Sharif Husayn, had just died in Amman after having spent all but the final dying months of his exile years in Cyprus.[16]

Instead, the political history of the half-century following the First World War is more adequately told in terms of nationalist parties, state building, and secular political leaders. A representative list of those major Muslim political leaders around whose ideas and exploits so much of modern history has been framed would include Egypt's Sa'd Zaghlul and Gamal Abd al-Nasir, Habib Bourguiba of Tunisia, Sultan Muhammad V of Morocco, Sukarno in Indonesia, Riza Shah and his son Muhammad Riza Shah plus Muhammad Musaddiq all in Iran, Afghanistan's King Amanullah, Ibn Saud the founder of Saudi Arabia, and Muhammad Ali Jinnah the principal founder of Pakistan plus Ahmad Ben Bella and Ferhat Abbas in Algeria. Not a one of these political leaders was religiously trained, but this in itself hardly distinguishes them from non-Muslim politicians. Very few nationalist leaders or presidents or kings have been seminarians.

Many in the above list of leaders wore their Muslim religion lightly, did not strictly observe all the tenets of Islam, and even violated a few. Again, they were very much like most non-Muslim political figures. They were also prepared to observe the public pieties and resisted the ulama or religious leaders only when they stood in the way of their political programs. This, too, is in line with what political leaders tend to do everywhere. All were working in a nation-state political context, and even those few interested in modifying the existing state thought in terms other than of unifying all Muslims. Arab unity, for example, and not Islamic unity was the only significant ideology transcending a single existing state advanced by Arabs.

Perhaps the various ideas of Fertile Crescent unity should not be so summarily dismissed, but they, too, strengthen the argument that Islam did not provide the political matrix during these years. All the many variations on the theme of Fertile Crescent unity posited a regional, cultural, and multireligious political ideal.[17] Pakistan, again, is the partial exception that tests the rule, but even there the goal sought and obtained was the creation of a nation-state. Further, the relative success of independent India under Nehru in gaining Arab diplomatic support and countering Pakistani diplomacy in that region reveals the limitations of employing a shared religion as an instrument of international politics. Moreover, a shared Islam did not provide the social cement needed to prevent the breakup of Pakistan and the creation of Bangladesh in 1971.

In short, politics in Muslim countries in the half-century from 1918 to the late 1960s is best understood in terms applicable to other parts of the world. The efforts of political leaders in these years and the institutions and ideologies they adopted were directed toward achieving independent nation-states led by strong centralized governments.

These leaders can be seen as twentieth-century heirs of the nineteenth-century modernizing Muslim monarchs (themselves Islamic equivalents of the European enlightened despots) such as Ottoman sultans Selim III or Mahmud II, Egypt's Muhammad Ali and Ismail, Tunisia's Ahmad Bey. The twentieth-century group, like their predecessors, were men of government. To the extent that the Muslim religious apparatus (ulama, Sufi brotherhoods, the traditional Qur'anic schools, *Shari'ah* courts, the institution of *waqf*, etc.) fostered, or at least did not hamper, these modernizing programs, they were tolerated. Otherwise, they were resisted.

The extreme case was Ataturk's Turkey, which became an avowedly secular state, and Islam was, to use a Western term not inappropriately, disestablished. Riza Shah, a contemporary in neighboring Iran, was hardly less adamant in taking on the religious establishment. Clerics were soon relegated to subordinate roles, even in their traditional power bases, the judiciary and education. Moreover, the move to modernization in education, although imposed with an iron hand, was welcomed by its student constituents. The response of the young has been neatly captured by a scholar who grew up in Iran during Riza Shah's reign:

> A new, relatively secure, and respectable professional class, admirably placed for furthering the national goals of the regime, was created, and a corresponding change in social attitudes came about. . . . Nowhere was this attitude more striking than in the classroom, where the young bow-tied teacher of physics commanded the close attention and respect of the students and often fulfilled their hero-image, while the calligraphy and Arabic classes of famous old craftsmen and scholars were scenes of mayhem and cruel practical jokes played on the teachers.[18]

Many symbolic changes were pushed through, intended to create "new Iranians," e.g., outlawing the wearing of the veil, replacing the Islamic lunar year with the pre-Islamic Iranian solar year, while also replacing the Arabic and Turkish names for months with "old Persian equivalents."[19]

Riza Shah's son and successor, while circumspect during the early years of his reign, was no less forceful when he deemed himself to be secure against domestic opposition. The shah's effort to reconstruct a twentieth-century adaptation of ancient Persian empires was most strikingly demonstrated in the huge celebration of the twenty-five hundredth anniversary of the Persian monarchy at Persepolis in 1971.[20] It was the most grandiose official celebration that the Middle East had seen since Khedive Ismail presided over the opening of the Suez Canal in 1869. These two sumptuous celebrations also augured the beginning of the end for both monarchs.

Sukarno, the nationalist who emerged as leader of independent Indonesia, is remembered for his five principles (Pantja Sila), which were 1. nationalism, 2. humanitarianism, 3. democracy, 4. social justice, and 5. belief in Almighty God. For a country that is almost 90 percent Muslim, religion figured last, and no religion was mentioned by name. Sukarno did not worship "the God of Islam. . . . God was for him the all-powerful being who animated the world, the essence of all being and of every religion."[21] His aim, embraced by those who rallied to his cause, was to create a modern nation-state (a polity of "all for all" or "one for all, all for one" as he once put it) that went out of its way to include the tiny Christian, Hindu, and Buddhist minorities.

Habib Bourguiba, less than five months after Tunisian independence, pushed through a radical legal reform (August 1956) that outlawed polygamy and made judgment for divorce a prerogative of the court, withdrawing the husband's exclusive right to divorce his wife. Although fourteen Tunisian ulama issued a fatwa denouncing the new law, it was received with considerable enthusiasm by the modernists and met with no appreciable resistance. Bourguiba had taken on the Muslim official class and bested them. Modernization and secularization of education followed, including the downgrading of the venerable Zaytuna Mosque-University. It became simply a *faculté* of religious studies in the University of Tunis.

Algeria's Ferhat Abbas was the very personification of the modernizing and thoroughly Westernized leader. He was so fully infused with things French—not just language but culture and political ideology—that he appeared (as many commentators noted) more like a Third Republic Radical Socialist than a Muslim nationalist. If French colonialism in Algeria had not been so deep-rooted, broken only by a brutal six-year war for independence, the educated Francophone likes of Ferhat Abbas would have led their country to independence in negotiated steps with only limited violence employed on either side (such as took place in Tunisia and, for that matter, in most former European colonies).

In Algeria, however, independence was won by the National Liberation Front (FLN) with a more proletarian leadership. Ahmad Ben Bella, for example, had been a sergeant in the French army. The FLN had split from the movement organized back in the mid-1920s (largely in France among Algerian workers living there) by Messali Hadj, who created a leadership style blending the mores of an activist Sufi shaykh with those of a leftist ideologue and organizer. The break with Messali, however, came not along the religion-secular divide but against what those who created the FLN saw as his autocracy and ineffectualness.

The long, bitter Algerian struggle for independence was infused with Islamic symbolism—the very pronounced French tendency during most of the long period of *Algerie française* to depict Islam and the Muslim as the unassimilable "other" dictated as much—but this was clearly a movement seeking to create an Algerian nation-state. The nationalist rhetoric called for restoration of Algeria's lost independence.

As for Egypt, Sa'd Zaghlul's Wafd Party had a strong record in favor of religious toleration. Zaghlul's first cabinet contained two Copts and one Jew. The president of the legislative chamber was also Christian.[22] Nasser and the Free Officers had had ties with the Muslim Brethren (about which more later), but the Egyptian regime began a pitiless crackdown on this early, and continuing, example of radical religious fundamentalism beginning in 1954, after a Muslim Brother had attempted to assassinated Nasser.

Such were the leaders throughout the Muslim world who during roughly the first seven decades of the twentieth century appeared to have taken at flood that tide in the affairs of men leading to fortune. They were the modernizers, the nationalists, the state builders. They and the movements they developed were the future. The Islamists (even that usage was not known, not used until later) were anachronisms. Yes, they could still cause trouble here and there, but they were an ebbing force.

Then the situation began to change. No one event can be singled out as the turning point for the entire Muslim population, but it would not be far off the mark to situate the turning of the tide in the mid to late 1960s.

Those heretofore deemed at the cutting edge of modernizing nationalism came to be seen as discredited spent forces. One began to hear of Muslim fundamentalists, Islamists, political Islam. Such terms as ayatullah and *jahiliyya* and such medieval Muslim theologians as Ibn Taimiyya became no longer cloistered in the vocabulary of specialists. They appeared in the popular media.

Why this change? That will be considered in the next chapter.

12.

The Return of Islam?

When and why did this change toward Islamist politics occur throughout the Muslim world? Many Arabs and Middle East specialists opt for June 1967 as the turning point. During those six days in June Israeli forces routed the combined forces of Egypt, Syria, and Jordan and occupied the entire Sinai Peninsula, Golan Heights, and all of what had been Mandate Palestine up to the Jordan River. It was a body blow not only to Nasserist Pan-Arabism but to existing regimes throughout the Arab world. As a traumatic event bringing into focus the failures of previous decades of ideology and institution building the Six Day War of 1967 can hardly be exaggerated.

Yet, although the June War undoubtedly had a decisive effect on subsequent events in the region, Islamist politics would probably have emerged even if this very surprising and avoidable war had not occurred.[1] Nasserist Pan-Arabism was already in decline. The idea that a larger Arab political entity was the wave of the future had been jolted six years earlier, in 1961. That year brought the breakup of the Egyptian-Syrian union that had created the United Arab Republic only three years earlier, in 1958.

Moreover, the June War did not necessarily discredit territorial nationalism throughout the Arab world. This crushing Arab defeat actually strengthened one important nationalist movement, that of the Palestinians. Observers with an eye for irony were wont to insist that the only victors of the June War had been Israel and the Palestine Liberation Organization (PLO). The latter under Yasir Arafat's leadership became thereafter less a creature of the Egyptian-dominated Arab League and more a nationalist movement (a would-be state) beholden to its own self-defined interests.

In any case, Arabs make up only about one-fifth of the world's Muslims. However shocking this 1967 war was to Arabs (and it certainly was that), it was less so to the millions of Muslims concerned with events closer to home.[2] To cite a few critical events in other Muslim countries, the 1965 army coup in Indonesia toppled Sukarno with resulting disturbances that brought the massacre of some 750,000 Indonesians (a conservative estimate). Nigeria in 1966 had coups and countercoups pitting the largely Christian Ibos against the predominantly Muslim Hausa. The Ibos then in 1967 seceded from Nigeria creating Biafra only to be defeated in a long, bitter civil war lasting until 1970. In Pakistan 1969 marked the resignation of Ayub Khan discredited after a decade-long rule only to be replaced by another general. Worse was to come in 1971 when East Pakistan seceded and became the independent state of Bangladesh. India, supporting Bangladesh, then intervened in December 1971 and soundly defeated Pakistan in a two-week war. The sixties in Turkey opened and closed with military interventions: in 1960 and 1970. The year of 1963 in Iran brought a confrontation between the shah's regime and the opposition led by one Ayatullah Khomeini, then little-known outside of Iran. Ayatullah Khomeini was sent into exile, and the shah's ambitious programs of reform from the top seemed on the road to some success. It would take events of the following decade to demonstrate the depth of Iranian opposition and the fragility of Pahlavi autocracy.

In short, no one event signals the move of Islamism from the wings to center stage in the vast and diverse Muslim world. Setting the June 1967 war alongside the several other crises taking place throughout the Muslim world does, however, reveal a significant temporal concordance: various regime- and system-challenging confrontations did take place within roughly one decade. This is perhaps as accurate an answer to the question "when" as can be provided.

But why? Just as no single event pinpoints the timing, no monocausal explanation offers an adequate answer. That the existing political leadership had scant popularity is generally true, with rare (and then only limited) exceptions. All too many regimes, in spite of their populist rhetoric, relied on army, police, and intelligence forces to stay in power. This answer, however, demands yet another question. Why did these many regimes command such limited loyalty? The existing political leaders throughout most of the Muslim world were of the generation that had won independence from Western colonial rule. One might have thought that this aura of achievement would continue to offer these rulers some margin of maneuver. It appears that just the opposite was the case. Most of these regimes were seen by their people as having fallen far short of the expectations with which the newly independent years were ushered in.

Such a blanket appraisal needs further refinement. The governing elites of the many different Muslim countries add up to such a mixed bag—military juntas, traditional monarchs, single-party regimes and ranging from radical left to reactionary right on the political spectrum—that lumping them all together as having limited political legitimacy offers scant explanatory power. Why was this generalized religio-political malaise directed against these many and diverse establishment structures? There are, in fact, a number of factors that transcend the distinctiveness of individual regimes. These factors also bring us back to aspects of the historical developments traced in earlier chapters.

The many different modernizers and Westernizers of the Muslim world, going back to the latter years of the eighteenth century and thereafter, with fits and starts, generation after generation, had achieved one significant change: people were much more caught up in and engaged with the state. Politics was less confined to the local levels of tribe, village, or quarter. The political quietism that earlier rulers could count on to get them through difficult times was much less in evidence even though it was by no means totally dissipated. European colonialism played a role here, for alien rule had centralized power. States had become more capable of influencing the daily lives of all inhabitants. The one consistent legacy of independence was an enlarged and strengthened public arena. European pressure and example had stimulated the same result in those states, e.g., Iran and Turkey, that had escaped outright colonial rule.

Nationalist and populist ideologies had so permeated society that even autocrats, both the traditional and the parvenus, employed a terminology loaded with references to democracy, equality, brotherhood, and "the people." The ideological climate fostered not only a sense of belonging to the larger community but also great expectations. People whose ancestors had expected nothing but fiscal and physical burdens from government were being exposed to the quite different ideas of government as both representative and servant of this larger community that made up the nation. Such perceptions were, of course, still offset by deeply ingrained pessimism regarding arbitrary government. Even so, these nationalist and populist ideologies had imposed a new and dangerously high level of expectation upon government. That most governments fell short of these high standards is hardly surprising.

Major social changes undergirded these nationalist ideologies. The last several decades have witnessed a massive rural to urban migration throughout the Muslim world. In the short span of forty years the estimated urban percentage of the total populations in selected Muslim countries has increased as follows:

Table 12.1

	1950	1960	1970	1991
Egypt	31.9%	45%	42%	47%
Indonesia	n.a.	15%	17%	31%
Iran	20%	34%	42%	57%
Nigeria	n.a.	13%	20%	36%
Pakistan	10.4%	22%	25%	33%
Tunisia	25.9%	36%	44%	55%
Turkey	21.3%	30%	38%	63%

Sources: United Nations, *Demographic Yearbook 1960* and World Bank, *World Development Report* 1984, 1993, and 1994.

In two of these countries (Iran and Pakistan) the urban proportion of the total population more than doubled from 1950 to 1970. The shift in Tunisia and Turkey was only slightly less. Indonesia and Nigeria accomplished the awesome population shift of more than doubling the urban proportion in the period 1970–1991.

This massive population transfer to the cities becomes even more imposing when set alongside the overall population increase during these years. For the same countries the population estimates for the decades from 1950 to 1990 are as follows:

Table 12.2

	Total Estimated Populations (millions)				
	1950	1960	1970	1980	1990
Egypt	20.40	25.33	33.30	42.30	53.15
Indonesia	73.50	92.60	121.20	148.03	179.30
Iran	18.70	20.68	28.66	37.45	54.61
Nigeria	24.00	35.09	55.07	77.08	108.54
Pakistan	75.04	93.73	114.19	82.14[3]	112.05
Tunisia	3.47	4.17	5.14	6.37	8.07
Turkey	20.9	27.8	35.23	44.92	58.69

Sources: United Nations Yearbooks for 1951, 1961, 1971, 1981, and 1991.

Millions of people throughout the Muslim world have thus been obliged to adopt the changing lifestyles imposed by the move from rural to urban areas—all within a decade or so. Even if, as urbanists have pointed out, these rural folk of yesteryear often clustered together and managed to "ruralize" the cities as much they were urbanized by their new environment, the change of territorial location and the unavoidable accommodation to radically different spatial arrangements necessarily brought a major physical and psychological uprooting.

This same time period has also witnessed an equally imposing quantitative change in school attendance, and since this increase has been carried out by the state it has been accordingly uniform and "national" in its impact. Since the 1950s all Muslim countries have registered impressive increases in education to such extent that most have achieved, or come very close to, universal primary school education for both boys and girls. Available figures for selected countries for the decades 1960–1990 reveal the following:

Table 12.3

	Number Enrolled in Primary School as Percentage of Age Group							
	T = Total percentage				F = Total percentage of females			
	1960		1970		1980		1990	
	T	F	T	F	T	F	T	F
Bangladesh	47%	26%	54%	35%	62%	47%	73%	68%
Egypt	66	52	72	57	76	52	98	90
Indonesia	71	58	80	73	98	91	117	114
Iran	65	27	72	52	101	80	106	102
Morocco	47	27	52	36	76	58	68	55
Nigeria	36	27	37	27	98	—	72	63
Pakistan	30	13	40	22	57	30	37	26
Saudi Arabia	12	2	42	29	64	51	78	72
Tunisia	66	43	100	79	103	88	116	109
Turkey	75	58	110	94	101	93	110	105

Note: Gross enrollment ratios may exceed 100 percent because some pupils are younger or older than the country's standard primary school age.

Beginning the statistical table as late as 1960 actually minimizes the extent of increased school attendance, for in several Muslim states the great increase in school attendance started a decade or so earlier. Tunisia, for example, in 1945 had only 9.5 percent of the primary school age population in school, and that figure had risen to 27 percent a decade later.[4] In Egypt the 1950 primary school enrollment took in only about 30 percent of the school age population,[5] not a bad record compared with most Muslim or, for that matter, third world countries at that time. That percentage had been more than doubled by the end of the decade.

The numbers enrolled in secondary education, while much smaller, are no less impressive in terms of the increases achieved in recent decades:

Table 12.4

	Number Enrolled in Primary School as Percentage of Age Group							
	T = Total percentage				F = Total percentage of females			
	1960		1970		1980		1990	
	T	F	T	F	T	F	T	F
Bangladesh	—	8%	—	—	15%	—	17%	11%
Egypt	16	5	35	23	52	—	82	17
Indonesia	6	—	16	11	28	—	45	41
Iran	12	—	27	18	44	—	56	47
Morocco	5	—	13	7	24	—	36	30
Nigeria	4	—	4	3	15	—	20	17
Pakistan	11	—	13	5	15	—	22	13
Saudi Arabia	2	—	12	5	51	—	48	41
Tunisia	12	—	23	13	27	—	45	40
Turkey	14	—	27	15	37	—	54	42

Sources for this and the table above: World Bank, *World Development Report,* 1983, 1984, and 1993.

The picture in higher education is especially important, for it is largely from the ranks of this group that the leaders and cadres of the several Islamist movements have come. The percentages become proportionally less as one moves from primary through secondary to higher education, but—again—the sharp rate of net increase in all levels stands out.

Table 12.5

	Number Enrolled in Higher Education as Percentage of Age Group[6]			
	1960	1970	1980	1990
Bangladesh	1%	3%	3%	3%
Egypt	5	18	18	19
Indonesia	1	4	4	10
Iran	1	4	4	6
Morocco	1	6	6	10
Nigeria	—	2	3	3
Pakistan	1	—	2	3
Saudi Arabia	—	7	7	14
Tunisia	1	5	5	9
Turkey	3	6	6	14

Percentages may well leave an overly bland impression. Perhaps citing a few figures will help: it has been estimated that the total number of students in higher education throughout the entire Arab world in 1945 was 20,000. By 1979 that number had increased to 1,000,000. The corresponding figures for Turkey are under 20,000 in 1945 and 270,000 in 1979.[7] University College at Ibadan in Nigeria was established in 1948, with 210 students in residence during its first year; today roughly 336,000 Nigerians are students in higher education.[8]

This vast national investment in education throughout the Muslim world was, consistent with the dominant nationalist ideologies prevailing in those years, designed to train modern productive citizens (not subjects). It was, accordingly, a state-directed Kulturkampf fought on two fronts— against foreign domination and also against any indigenous traditions or institutions that were believed to hamper national unity and strength. Of course, these dual aims were burdened with a built-in ambiguity if not downright contradiction. The nationalist leaders were rejecting alien Western culture even while adopting in large measure that same alien Western educational curriculum. They were vaunting indigenous culture but doing so selectively, weeding out elements that impeded national unity and strength.

Parts of the national heritage destined to be passed over in silence, if not, indeed, obliterated, included much of the traditional centuries-old synthesis of the Muslim religion in its relation to the state. The curriculum was to be set by the state, not the ulama. The teachers also were to be trained in state schools, not educational institutions manned by the ulama. There was to be a single unified national legal system controlled by the state, not by the ulama serving as qadis. Sufi brotherhoods were viewed as obscurantist. They were also seen as representing so many disparate pockets of particularism and thus were obstacles to national unity. Where states had significant numbers of non-Muslims a high priority was given to developing a political community of citizens with equal rights and obligations regardless of religion.

The political leadership in certain Muslim states openly championed these nationalist goals. Leaders in other states were more circumspect, but essentially the same goals were implicit in the actions taken. One example of the former approach in education was Tunisia under the leadership of Habib Bourguiba and the Neo-Destour Party. The stated educational purpose was to create "new Tunisians" and, in the process, do away with societal norms associated with the "old turbans." In 1947 a Tunisian professor at the Institute des Hautes Etudes (created only two years earlier, in 1945, and the matrix of what was to become the University of Tunis) insisted that "education is social integration. If the society is a living reality, one and indivisible, the culture will be so as well, and the pedagogical system must be a harmonious whole. . . . To ignore the principle of cultural unity is . . . to sow the seeds of discord."[9] That same professor, appointed minister of education in 1958, two years after independence, put his ideas to practice with a vengeance. This meant that the religious primary and secondary schools as well as the venerable mosque-university of Zaytuna were quickly absorbed into the single integrated national educational system.

There was no time to lose. A major Tunisian policy statement insisted that "reduced or only slowly increasing school attendance implies a choice of underdevelopment or at least a resigned attitude toward a permanent protraction of economic and social underdevelopment." The policy of accelerated schooling keyed to national goals would, on the contrary, support "any plan of transforming the economic and social structure of the nation."[10]

Islamic studies took a backseat to those subjects in the secular and modern curriculum in terms of the number of hours taught, and the idea of what constituted Islamic thought was presented in an early official statement of the different secondary curricular options as follows:

> The methods to be relied upon in teaching Islamic thought should be those employed in what is today called the study of religious thought from the sociological point of view. This is the method which attempts to go beyond the investigation of any given mindset ['Aqliyya in

Arabic] in order to discover the substantive factors which determined its various viewpoints just as they determined the solutions and the problems arising out of that very mindset in any given age. This method, in short, calls not for simply receiving and believing but for thought, investigation and criticism.[11]

This is a bold statement. One might well ask if it would pass muster with the typical American school board reviewing secondary school curricula. Similar boldness characterized other Tunisian reforms in those heady early years after independence was gained in 1956. The radical Personal Status Law of 1956 that, among other things, gave women rights equal to men in matters of marriage and divorce exemplified the trend. Only Ataturk's earlier reforms in Turkey are comparable in secularizing revolutionary zeal.

Most states were more cautious in taking on the entrenched religious establishment or challenging the traditional views that most members of the community had long accepted as normal, if not, indeed, God-given. Nor did these revolutionary reforms that characterized Bourguiba's Tunisia or Ataturk's Turkey immediately penetrate all levels of society. A recurring pattern in modern Muslim history is that of reformers, in a hurry to catch up with the dominant—and domineering—West, imposing reforms from the top and coming up against those resistant to the changes being ordered. Sometimes the partisans of modernization have had the upper hand, sometimes their opponents.

Seen in this light, the bold reformist program of a Tunisia and the more cautious acts of other states merge to establish an important general trend: the decades of the 1950s and 1960s represented the heyday of secularizing, centralizing, nationalizing Muslim states.

Then, what happened? A few maxims popularized by social science research on the third world since the 1950s point to the answer: "the passing of traditional society," the presumed "take-off" stage of economic growth, the "revolution of rising expectations," "relative deprivation," etc.[12] The secularizing, centralizing, nationalizing political leaders were in power, but their support was thin. They would be able to deepen and institutionalize their position if their performance appeared positive on balance. That was to be a very difficult assignment.

Almost all these Muslim states adopted, with greater or lesser intensity and persistence, the planning strategy of a "command economy" (taking their guidance from either Western developmental economic thought or the Communist model). What, after all, was more in line with the basic ideology of secularizing, modernizing, centralizing nationalism than an economy planned and controlled by the state? At the same time, millions of the young poured into the national educational institutions, from primary schools to universities. The intellectual old guard in these countries might well deplore the resulting decline of educational standards, and they would surely be right to some extent. That plaint, however, overlooked the more important point that virtually the entire rising generations were being socialized to the canons of, again, secularizing, modernizing, centralizing nationalism. In the process they were being dislodged from the mindset and mores of their elders.[13] They were also being shown new, more attractive, roles in these would-be societies abuilding. All the while that everpresent egalitarian populist rhetoric seemed to offer careers and lifestyles beyond the dreams of their elders.

Reality did not live up to expectations. Too many of those graduates spilling out of the newly created schools and universities could not find the jobs they had come to expect, could not even find jobs at all. Democratization, which is to say the implementation of the populist egalitarian ethos so long preached, foundered, and that earlier buzzword *guided democracy* could not paper over the reality of de facto autocracy, whether led by military cliques, single party elites, shahs, sultans, kings, or presidents for life. Centralized state planning had created swollen bureaucracies but sluggish economic performance.

The military performance of Muslim states could only add to this sense of beleaguered impotence: the last half-century has been marked by six Arab-Israeli wars and six Arab losses,[14] plus three wars between India and Pakistan.[15] Added to this bleak legacy have been the several intra-Muslim wars, the most devastating being the Iraq-Iran war (1980–1988), but others less costly in lives and resources highlighted divisions within the Muslim *umma*. These have included the border disputes between Morocco and Algeria, Egyptian intervention in the Yemen Civil War in the early and mid 1960s, and the 1991 Gulf War beginning with one Arab state (Iraq) overrunning and annexing another (Kuwait) and followed by the liberation of Kuwait in which several Arab states joined the U.S.-led coalition against Iraq.

Ironically, the two Muslim states that achieved some success against outside military forces, Afghanistan and Somalia, drew their military prowess from traditional tribalism.[16] As such, they were the very antithesis of centralized and modernized nation-states. Their victory was to that extent yet another reproach to the secularizing, centralizing, modernizing nationalists.

Compounding all of the troubles confronting established political leadership was the stark demographic dimension: population growth and population transfer (rural to urban but also the millions of Muslims seeking their economic Eldorado in the oil-rich Arabian Peninsula or in Europe) during these years reached unprecedented intensities. The millions of people coming into the Muslim world, the millions moving about the Muslim world increased exponentially the magnitude of all problems to be tackled. These massive physical, mental, and psychic changes taking place at an ever increasing rate produced a systemic overload so extreme as to threaten complete breakdown. No, reality did not live up to expectations. It could not.

13.

The Radical Muslim Discourse

The previous chapter sought to explain the shift throughout the Muslim world toward religio-political radicalism by presenting quantifiable data (such as population increase and mobility, education, shortfalls in economic performance, and military defeats) as well as insights incapable of measurement (such as massive disorientation, a search for certainties, and a sense of vulnerability in facing hostile forces). That chapter set out the underlying factors preparing the ground for the religio-political movements thriving today throughout the Muslim world. It did not, however, address why Islamist movements emerged instead of other alternatives, secular or religious. Nor did it introduce the ideas and ideologues of today's Islamist surge. Adopting two broad-ranging comparative approaches may serve to establish a larger context for studying the question.

First, the case of Muslim fundamentalism in today's world is not all that distinctive. The economic, political, military, and social factors set out in the previous chapter have not been confined to Muslim states. This litany of woes sounds familiar for most of the Third World. Religio-political radicalism is a global phenomenon. Movements strikingly similar to those found in Muslim countries exist among Christians, Jews, Hindus, Sikhs, and Buddhists.

From this many observers embrace the idea of a generic fundamentalism characterizing today's world. Such, for example, is the thrust of the multi-volume fundamentalism project directed by Martin E. Marty and R. Scott Appleby. "Religious fundamentalisms," they write, thrive in the twentieth century when and where masses of people living in formerly traditional societies experience profound personal and social dislocations as a result of rapid modernization and in the absence of mediating institutions capable of meeting the human needs created by these dislocations. Occasioned by mass migration from rural to urban areas, by unsynchronized social, economic, and cultural transformations and uneven schemes of development, by failures in educational and social welfare systems, and ultimately by the collapse of long-held assumptions about the meaning and purpose of human existence, the experience of dislocation fosters a climate of crisis. In this situation people are needy in a special way. Their hunger for material goods is matched by a thirst for spiritual reassurance and fulfillment. If these needs are integrated and integral, so must be the power offering fulfillment. Religion presented as an encompassing way of life suggests itself as the bearer of that power.[1]

Yet this perceptive statement, emerging from an in-depth group research project involving scores of specialists, is not beyond challenge. Do the rubrics "formerly traditional societies" or "hunger for material goods" explain, say, Christian fundamentalism in the United States or Jewish fundamentalism in Israel? These American and Israeli exceptions suggest that explaining fundamentalisms too much in material terms may be faulty.

Other observers have favored the idea that the problem is essentially spiritual, that "man does not live by bread alone." Certainly, the spiritual message has always dominated the discourse of those fundamentalist movements we seek to understand. While it is necessary to look beyond what people claim to be doing, it is important to take seriously what they are, in fact, saying.

Perhaps a satisfactory overall explanation of fundamentalism as a global phenomenon could transcend the material-spiritual dichotomy by, first, identifying a people persuaded that their lives and their societies are marked by disorientation, uprootedness, lack of purpose, and (deliberately choosing an old-fashioned word that belongs in any serious study of this subject) sin. Then, one could move on to uncover in each particular case a different mix of quantifiable material factors plus factors not reducible to such quantification.

In this pattern of proceeding it can be shown that Muslim fundamentalisms do seem to fit into the larger category of third world fundamentalisms. The very intensity of quantifiable material changes and of severe expectation shortfalls, as set out in earlier pages, can explain the rise of system-challenging religio-political movements. At the same time, the existence of fundamentalist movements among peoples not experiencing such severe economic or political challenges and not being wrenched from radically different "traditional societies" to a disturbing modernity indicates that material factors are contributing but not determining causes. Put differently, radical religious movements exist today in the Muslim world, the United States, India, Israel, and elsewhere. All may be seen as efforts to give ultimate meaning to life in a context in which peoples feel adrift. To that extent, these movements grow up in the soil of material conditions but are germinated by the seeds of distinctive religious messages. The material and the message are both important.

The messages of different religious fundamentalism may well also share similarities, and this brings us to a second broad comparison. In this case the linkage to be suggested is not a synchronic contemporary comparison of the Muslim experience with that of, say, Christians or Jews or Hindus . . . It is, instead, across time, a diachronic comparison spanning the centuries—today's Islamist ideologues measured alongside the thought and action of Reformation leaders.[2]

Such a perspective has the advantage of shifting attention to individual men and to ideas, balancing thereby the previous chapter's concentration on anonymous social forces. Even the most Marxist interpretation of the Reformation must take the measure of Luther,[3] Calvin, Zwingli, Knox, and other flesh-and-blood human actors writing treatises and tracts, organizing churches and defying—or at times supporting—established political authority. Surely the likes of Hasan al-Banna, Abu al-A'la Mawdudi, Sayyid Qutb, and Ayatullah Khomeini deserve no less attention.

Moreover, many today, and not just Protestants, are inclined to evaluate the long-term impact of the Reformation in positive terms. Even Catholic historiography tends to view the dialectic process of the Reformation/Counter-Reformation (to use the conventional rubrics) as bringing into being a strengthened Church and better societies. That the Reformation period in Europe is often classified in our simplified historical imagination as having been a "good thing" enhances the utility of comparing it to present-day Islamism, for the latter certainly has a "bad press" in the West and, for that matter, among many throughout the Muslim world. The suggestion that we are witnessing a Muslim "Reformation" may ensure a more judicious reading of these different leaders of today's Islamist movements.[4]

Although at first blush the comparison may seem strained, an impressive number of common themes binds together the Reformation and today's Islamism. Both emerge in a period bringing into existence powerful, centralizing nation-states with a concomitant fading away of broader imperial regimes (the Holy Roman Empire for Europe and, for the Muslim world, the Ottoman Empire plus the alien European colonial empires—all alongside the lingering ideal of a common *Dar al-Islam*).

Both are marked by rapidly increasing literacy—Gutenberg and printing in Europe, the exponential rise in the numbers of students in state-directed educational institutions throughout the Muslim world.

This, in turn, for both sixteenth- and seventeenth-century Europe and today's Muslim world has shattered the centuries-old division between a small literate elite and the great mass of the population having scant contact or discourse with that literate minority. In Europe the Bible became more readily available in the several vernacular languages, e.g., Luther's German translation or Tyndale's English translation.[5] This, in turn, served to make "the priesthood of all believers" a meaningful concept.

Vernacular translations of the Qur'an had, of course, existed long before the 1960s, and the classical Arabic of the Qur'an, instead of being understood by declining numbers of Muslims (as is the case with Hebrew, Latin, and Greek among Christians), is being read and understood by more Muslims than ever before. This increase is to be accounted for largely in the Arab world where rapidly rising literacy has made it feasible for Arabic-speaking Muslims not so much to memorize the sacred texts without always comprehending them (as in past centuries) but to read and understand.[6] Rising literacy and schooling in other parts of the Muslim world may well have produced a slight increase in those capable of reading the Qur'an or other texts in the original Arabic, but the quantum jump making possible a Muslim equivalent of the "priesthood of all believers" has been not so much the enhanced availability of the scriptures in the vernacular languages as the general increases in literacy, schooling, and all media.

Broadened and intensified communication breaking down both the elite-mass dichotomy and the small-scale particularism characteristic of premodern agrarian society marked both the Reformation and today's Islamism, but the latter would appear to be exposed to even more vertiginous convulsions. Underlying the changes in Reformation Europe were increased literacy, the rise of printing, and the early stirring of exploration and entrepreneurship that would lead to capitalism. A case can be made that the Muslim world today is seized with the equivalent of all such factors plus more. Not only are the increases in literacy, publications, rural to urban migration, and economic interdependence greater for today's Muslims than for Europeans of the Reformation period. Not only is the time involved squeezed down for today's Muslims to a few decades as opposed to at least a century and a half, if not more, for Reformation Europe.[7]

In addition to all this, the present age of radio, television, cybermedia, and even such simple artifacts as tape recordings (which played a major role in the overthrow of the shah in Iran) has fostered a breadth and intensity of communication beyond the control of any political authority, however arbitrary.

Surely, the most important characteristic shared by the Reformation and today's Islamism is the basic thrust of their religio-political doctrines. Both are scripturalists. The scripture (Bible or Qur'an) is God's program for mankind. Its meaning is transparent and can be understood by all believers, without the need of intervening religious specialists or institutions.

Both adopt, to borrow Max Weber's classification, a stance of "inner-worldly asceticism."[8] They preach the moral obligation not only to make one's individual life conform to God's plan but to achieve that ideal for all, to bring into existence the divinely ordained society here and now. Both stress the omnipotent sovereignty of God. To both, government is necessary in order to control and guide the community in accordance with God's plan, but obedience is due only to those leaders who do not violate God's ordinances.

Both posit a golden age that stands as a reproach to and weapon against existing establishment doctrines and institutions.

Admittedly, there is an important difference between the two golden ages. That of the Islamists is squarely in the historical past: the time of Muhammad and those who knew him. For the Reformation leaders that golden age is more ahistorical, more paradigmatic: the "New Jerusalem." The difference is, of course, to be explained by the different historical development of the two religious traditions.

It can be argued, rightly, that none of the above is absent from the Christian heritage before the Reformation or the Islamic heritage before present-day Islamists. The scripture as God's word, the ineffable sovereignty of God, mankind's need for government, but government led by those who will heed God's divine plan, the historic age when God's message was, as it were, finalized, being exemplary for all time—these tenets are not new. What is distinctive, however, is that both Reformation Protestants and today's Islamists preach and practice with an oppressive rigor, a total commitment, and a Manichaean certitude that leave little latitude for morally neutral areas of human conduct.

These men and women of the Reformation and the Islamist movements see themselves as revolutionary saints.[9] They have enlisted in militant religious movements bent on changing the world. Their core ideology positions them to challenge existing established structures across the board.

This comparison between the Reformation and Islamism today reminds us of the force militant religious messages have brought to bear throughout history. One more ingredient is required: the message must resonate with those receiving it. The messenger must be, if not charismatic, at least credible. The Reformation had its messengers. Who are the Luthers and Calvins of today's Islamism?

Today's Islamist movements have to some extent transcended the divide separating Sunnis from Shi'is. Sunni Muslims were stirred by the Islamic Revolution in Iran and read attentively the writings of Ayatullah Khomeini, especially his famous treatise *Islamic Government*. Shi'is have studied the writings of Sunni theorists, perhaps especially those of Sayyid Qutb. Examples can be cited, as well, of governments cooperating across the Sunni-Shi'i divide, e.g., the Islamist government of Sunni Sudan and Iran of Khomeini and his successors.[10] Even so, the ideological roots of present-day Islamist movements are best traced by considering the Sunni and Shi'i cases separately. The Sunni case will be sketched here and in the following chapter. Chapter 15 will then treat Shi'i Islamism as demonstrated in the thought and actions of Ayatullah Khomeini.

Sunni Islamist doctrines are customarily seen as both growing out of and in reaction to the earlier ideological climate subsumed under the name of Islamic modernism. The best-known school of Islamic modernism was that of the Salafiyya, based on the teachings of Shaykh Muhammad Abduh as continued by his disciples, especially Rashid Rida. Abduh, as noted in chapter 9, represented the effort to establish the claim that Islam, properly understood, was completely in accord with the demands of modern life. Using one's God-given intellectual capacity was not just permissible. It was enjoined. Islam gave religious significance to both this world and the world to come. This world was not simply a vale of tears. One had a religious duty to make this world better for its inhabitants. Islam stressed the equality of all believers. It required governors to consult and, by extension, rule in accordance with the wishes of those ruled. Islam was tolerant, protected non-Muslims, and eschewed forced conversions. These tenets were then employed to accept scientific discoveries, economic activism and entrepreneurship, representative government, and an implicit acknowledgment of the world's diversity (i.e., Islam as one religion alongside others).

Abduh himself was building on the ideas and efforts of those Muslims who, since roughly the latter years of the eighteenth century, had witnessed their vulnerability to European incursions and had sought to borrow from this threatening but tempting Europe in order to "catch up." He was thus in tune with a spectrum of statesmen and scholars—such as Khayr al-Din al-Tunisi or Sir Sayyid Ahmad Khan or the "Men of the Tanzimat"—who sought to reconcile their society and their religion to the world they confronted.

These intellectual exertions of Abduh and others provided an Islamic ideological justification for the effort at "Westernization," or "modernization," that has been a dominant theme in Muslim history these past two centuries. All told, it was an impressive performance. Still, just as with any ideology—and, even more, any theology—not all questions were satisfactorily answered. The efforts of Abduh and others were most effective in undercutting what might be dubbed Muslim scholasticism, which turned a blind eye to changing circumstances and embraced uncritically the traditional Muslim canon. To this extent, the Salafiyya may rightly be seen as setting in motion a Muslim "Reformation."

Two weaknesses, however, characterized the ideology of Islamic modernism. First, it was too much an effort to justify Islam to modernity. The presumed values of modernity (à la européenne) were implicitly taken as the standard against which Islam was to be measured. As the ideas of what constituted modernity changed, Islamic modernism had to adjust to this fluctuating alien standard. To insist, for example, at one time or another that Islam was compatible with—if not, indeed, mandated—capitalism or socialism or communism, exposed the defensive and derivitive nature of the Islamic modernist discourse.

Second, the Salafiyya movement argued that Muslims over the centuries had deviated from God's divine plan as transmitted to his chosen prophet, Muhammad, and as practiced by the early Muslim community. The solution, they maintained, was to use that earlier golden age as the needed model. This gave the modernists a powerful rhetorical weapon against established authority, whether religious or political (leaders of the Protestant Reformation, for that matter, enjoyed a similar advantage).

Yet, since their basic aim was to justify rejecting blind traditionalism and embracing new—and alien—answers to society's problems, the Islamic modernists could be outflanked by the scriptural literalists. If everything Muslims need to know and need to do is to be found in the Qur'an, the Sunna, and the actions of the early Muslim community, then why concern oneself with borrowing from the West?

Even the supporting argument—often used by the Muslim modernists—

that Muslims would only be borrowing back what the West, centuries earlier, had borrowed from the Islamic world could be turned to fundamentalist purposes. The modernists might well argue that the West's present strength was based in considerable measure on earlier European borrowings from their Muslim neighbors in the fields of science, philosophy, and technology. Modernists would advance this argument to justify empirical research and openness to new ideas, methods, and institutions. Fundamentalists, however, with equal logic, could retort that Muslims attained worldly superiority when they followed God's divine plan. Neighboring Europe, lacking—or rejecting—God's plan, could only be helped by borrowing from a superior (because God-guided) Islamic civilization, and Muslims could regain ground lost by getting back to their divine-inspired roots, not by seeking answers beyond the orbit that God has drawn.

It was these two characteristics (perhaps it is unreasonable to dub them weaknesses) that largely shaped the legacy of Islamic modernism. The argument that Islam, properly understood, not only was consonant with modernity but required acceptance of modernity provided a program for the Westernizers. The argument that to right their present plight Muslims needed only to get back to that golden age when God gave Muslims the comprehensive unchanging pattern for individual and communal living (valid everywhere and for all time—*li kull makan wa zaman*, in Arabic) was tailor-made for the scriptural literalists.

Accordingly, scholars have tended to see a bifurcated legacy left by the Salafiyya. On the one hand, they served to justify moves toward a de facto secularism in politics and government and a concomitant privatization of religion. On the other, they advanced the goals of a Muslim fundamentalist Reformation by emphasizing that all believers should rely on the scriptures, not on a Muslim "church" establishment of ulama who were often, to make matters worse, subservient to irreligious political authority. Even less should they heed secular authority that would make religion a private concern.

That second legacy leading to today's Islamists is best illustrated in the writings and actions of two Egyptians and one Indian Muslim who became a Pakistani after partition. They are Hasan al-Banna, Sayyid Qutb, and Abu al-A'la Mawdudi. Many others could be mentioned, but these three have been the most influential. Moreover, in large measure the ideas and programs of other Sunni Islamists can be seen as glosses on the basic doctrines advanced by al-Banna, Qutb, and Mawdudi.

All three were sons of this century. Al Banna, born in 1906, was assassinated in 1949. Qutb, born also in 1906, was executed by the Nasser regime in 1966. Thus, both Egyptians met a violent death at the hands of state authority (for the Egyptian secret police were involved in al-Banna's assassination). Only Mawdudi, born in 1903, died a natural death in 1979, but his life—like that of Qutb—was marked by imprisonment. These three, in short, were not closeted academic thinkers. They were—like Luther, Zwingli (who died in battle), Calvin, and others of the Reformation—political activists.

Al-Banna, founder of the Muslim Brethren in 1928, was more nearly the charismatic leader and organizer. Mawdudi and Qutb left more writings and provided a more comprehensive and coherent body of doctrine. The ideological influence concerning these two ran largely from Mawdudi to Qutb, not the other way round, even though they were essentially contemporaries (Mawdudi born only three years before Qutb). This was because Qutb came to his radical Islamism only in the late 1940s, abandoning an earlier modernist orientation that included a passion for English literature. Al-Banna and Mawdudi, by contrast, had both been deeply involved in Islamist thought and activities from their earliest years. All three were from reasonably well-established but traditional families, examples of those most vulnerable to losing the limited social standing that traditional society gave them. The onslaught of modern, alien ideas and institutions challenged and, indeed, dismantled their way of life. All three responded with a Manichaean image of the divinely inspired in-group confronting the godless other.

Chapter 14 discusses these three principal ideologues of Sunni radicalism. Then, chapter 15 will treat Ayatullah Khomeini in the context of Shi'i Islamism.

14.

Al-Banna, Mawdudi, and Qutb

Hasan al-Banna was born in a small provincial town, Mahmudiyya, some 90 miles northwest of Cairo in October 1906.[1] He was the eldest of five sons. Much of his early religious training came from his father, the imam and teacher at the local mosque who supplemented his income as a watch repairman. Another formative influence was his Qur'anic school (*kuttab*) teacher. At the age of twelve he moved from the kuttab to the local primary school. During these years he also became involved with the local chapter of the Hasafiyya Sufi brotherhood as well as other religious organizations. The next step, in the early 1920s, was enrollment in the Primary Teachers' Training School in Damanhur, also in the Delta, 13 miles from his hometown.

At age sixteen he entered Dar al-'Ulum, a higher-level teacher training institution that had been founded in 1873 to offer the modern (i.e., Western) curriculum that al-Azhar had resisted adopting. Graduating from Dar al-'Ulum in 1927 at the age of twenty-one, al-Banna accepted his first post as a primary school teacher of Arabic in Isma'iliyya.

Located on the Suez Canal, Isma'iliyya in those years was replete with the signs of alien military, economic, and cultural domination. British military bases,[2] the foreign officialdom of the Suez Canal Company, foreign economic domination of all major businesses and public utilities, even street signs in English brought home to al-Banna the colonized status of his fellow Muslims. It was in this environment that he organized his Muslim Brethren, the first members being, significantly, six Egyptian workers from the British military camp. The earliest recruits and activities were in the canal zone, but when al-Banna succeeded in getting transfered to a teaching post in Cairo (1932) he was ready to make the organization a national force.

The continued British control, the uprootedness following on the accelerating exodus from countryside to city, and the added hardships brought by the depression years of the 1930s produced an Egyptian population longing for security, fellowship, a sense of personal worth, simple and clear answers to what was needed plus equally simple and clear answers to what must be opposed. That all this could be presented as getting back to the clear moral imperative demanded by Islam made the call even more attractive. Al-Banna's charismatic personality and good organizing skills did the rest. The Muslim Brethren experienced explosive growth. Mitchell's careful study offers the following estimate: "Four branches in 1929; 5 in 1930; 10 in 1931; 15 in 1932; 300 in 1938; 500 in 1940; 2,000 in 1949." And the peak membership is estimated to have been perhaps a half million active members with at least an equal number of sympathizers.[3]

Thus, by the late 1930s and throughout the 1940s the Muslim Brethren had become a political force in Egypt. The organization expanded as well beyond Egypt's border, into Syria by the mid-1930s, among the Palestinians and in Transjordan somewhat later, and south to the Sudan in the mid-1940s, plus a not inconsiderable impact throughout other parts of the Muslim world.

Organizationally, the Muslim Brethren may be seen as a hybrid of traditional Sufi orders and modern totalitarian parties.[4] The traditional Sufi brotherhood has its several different local branches (*zawiyas*) linked in an overall fraternal network by a common ritual and led by a master (shaykh). One became a full-fledged member by passing through staged tests. The radical mobilization movements of fascism and Communism (but especially the latter) have had their cells, their careful testing and indoctrination of members, and the strictly hierarchical principle of "democratic centralism" requiring adherence to the party line and a dismissal (or worse) of all deviants.

The Muslim Brethren also had their hierarchy, starting from small groups of "families" (*'usrahs*) of no more than five and later ten members, right up through several organizational levels culminating in the "general guide" (*al-murshid al-'amm*), with a consultative assembly and a general headquarters.[5] Potential members went through a probationary stage before being accepted as "active" (*'amil*), but even thereafter members were enjoined to repeat their oath of allegiance (*bay'ah*) at each meeting, and backsliders could be disciplined or even ejected from membership. There was also a group known as the "rovers" (*jawwala*), clearly patterned on the Boy Scout movement. More ominous was the secret apparatus (*al-jihaz al sirri*), also known as the "special organization" (*al-nizam al-khass*) for carrying out its underground and often violent activities.

And the brethren did get involved in acts of violence against the British in the Canal Zone, in support of the Palestinians against the Zionists, and in attacking Egptian politicians seen as frustrating their goals. It was the assassination of Egyptian prime minister Nuqrashi Pasha on December 28, 1948, by a Muslim Brother that led to the government-instigated assassination of Hasan al-Banna less than two months later, on February 12, 1949.

Thereafter, the brotherhood went through a period of divided orientations. On the one hand, there was an effort to present a more moderate face and to gain at least grudging acceptance by the Egyptian regime. Symbolizing this tendency was the appointment in 1951 of Hasan al-Hudaybi, an Egyptian judge known for his moderate politics, to fill al-Banna's shoes. There were, however, others within the brotherhood who drew the opposite lesson from the violence and assassinations of the forties. Only resistance to the existing political establishment, they believed, would work.

The late 1940s and early 1950s brought many clandestine contacts between various brotherhood members and those Egyptian Free Officers who seized power in July 1952. For a time thereafter it looked as if the Muslim Brethren would be able to play an organizationally and ideologically dominant role in the new Egyptian regime being constructed by Jamal Abd al-Nasir and his fellow officers. All political parties had been banned, but the Muslim Brethren, not deemed a political party, was permitted a legal existence—for a time.

The brotherhood, however, was soon on collision course with the Free Officers, and this for a number of reasons. Nasser and his fellow officers, having in general a much more modernist and nationalist orientation, were not all that attuned to the brotherhood's fundamentalism. The one thing both the Free Officers and the Muslim Brethren shared was a keen sense that Egypt and Egyptians were being dominated and manipulated by outside forces, the British in particular. The Free Officers, however, did manage in 1954 to reach an agreement with that old oppressor, Britain, providing a conditional evacuation of British troops from the Suez Canal area and plans for determining the status of the Sudan (whether it would be united with Egypt or—as happened by 1956—opt for independence). The more radical elements of the Muslim Brethren opposed the agreement, and their opposition turned violent. When in October 1954 a Muslim Brother attempted to assassinate Nasser,[6] the stage was set for a governmental crackdown on the brotherhood.

The subsequent history of this organization, impressive in its size, organization, and fervor, that al-Banna had started from ever so modest beginnings in 1928 can be told in terms of its famous leader, Sayyid Qutb, who will be considered later. For now, what can be said about al-Banna as an ideologue?

Most observers see al-Banna as not nearly so logically coherent or comprehensive as either Mawdudi or Qutb—or, for that matter, Khomeini. Al-Banna, his critics and his partisans would probably agree, was more nearly a charismatic orator/preacher and a gifted organizer than a creative and consistent thinker.

Perhaps, al-Banna was, for this very reason, all the more effective. Scholars, usually somewhat removed from the hurly-burly of politics, often give too much weight to ideological clarity. In the real world, however, people rally around powerfully delivered messages that may well be incomplete, inconsistent, and even illogical.

An often cited statement by al-Banna was his description of the Muslim Brethren as "a Salafi movement, an orthodox way, a Sufi reality, a political body, an athletic group, a scientific and cultural society, an economic company and a social idea." Such a protean definition—"all things to all men"[7]—is in line with al-Banna's own vacillation concerning whether the brotherhood should claim to be above divisive politics or act as one of many political parties in Egypt's pluralistic polity. When it seemed that the brotherhood could thereby gain in strength, al-Banna was not averse to playing by the prevailing political rules.

Even so, al-Banna's essential conception of the brotherhood was clear. It was an all-embracing organization transcending political parties, indeed, making them unnecessary. He envisaged an Islamic utopia with no political parties, no class antagonism, and no legitimate differences of personal or group interests: the Islamist equivalent of the utopian Marxist classless society. In the case of the brotherhood, however, the utopia to be achieved in the future was based on restoring the utopia deemed to have existed in the past, at the time of the Prophet Muhammad and the rightly guided Caliphs.

Al-Banna's Islamic utopia also is in large measure a version of classic Muslim political thought (e.g., the good ruler ruling well, the "circle of equity," the *Shari'ah* as a comprehensive code of conduct valid for all time and place) adapted to modern times and terms.

Such an ideology, in effect, worked out in a more simplified fashion the basic tenets of the reformist Salafiyya school founded by Muhammad Abduh and continued by Abduh's principal disciple, Rashid Rida (1865–1935). The young al-Banna had been in contact with the followers and the ideas of Rida. Al-Banna represents the more restrictive fundamentalist branch of thought and action growing out of the Salafiyya, just as secularizing nationalism reflects the more liberal tendency.

If Abduh may be said to have gone to great lengths to reconcile Islam to a liberal, democratic, and—yes—even individualist political stance, al-Banna advanced a more rigorously constraining pattern of group conduct that was to be, moreover, controlled by the state—provided, of course, that state had rulers who were properly Muslim as al-Banna understood the term. The end result to be achieved would produce a state controlling education and using it to instill the proper Muslim values, a state whose officials passed muster as both pious and religiously informed, a state that would implement social justice and also enforce a strict code of conduct on one and all. Not surprisingly, al-Banna favored the ultimate restoration of the caliphate, but he was realistic enough to accept—indeed, approve—the existence of separate Muslim states. Nor was nationalist sentiment to be deplored. Within appropriate bounds, nationalism, al-Banna held, was consistent with Islam.

Al-Banna's ideology was thoroughly, and sincerely, populist. He railed against Egypt's gaping economic inequalities. He was eloquent in citing the plight of millions of landless peasants or in calling for a greater social responsibility on the part of the "haves." Anyone with even a rudimentary idea of al-Banna's Egypt, with its stark contrast between pashas and peasants, its grinding poverty alongside luxurious villas, its widespread socioeconomic dislocation exacerbated by the demographic explosion and the massive rural-to-urban migration would surely understand the attraction of al-Banna's ideology.

Yet to many observers the Muslim Brethren became a dangerous group that deserved the label fascist. That it did develop into a movement boasting a secret organization bent on advancing its goals by any and all means, including assassination, is well documented. That it did not scruple to consider appropriate any available measures to come to power is also clear. There was little regard for the rules of liberal democracy in al-Banna's doctrines. How could there be, convinced as he was that God had provided His plan regulating all aspects of worldly life and that this plan could be readily understood by all?

Even so, to dub al-Banna's ideology and the organization it spawned fascism will not do. Structurally, a number of similarities link the Muslim Brethren to fascism, but the ideologies are quite different. Fascism offers a promethean vaunting of worldly heroism, places nationalism above all values, worships the leader, and is ambivalent toward—if not dismissing of—

scriptural religion. Al-Banna was not *il duce*. There was no equivalent of the Nazi leadership principle in his thought—quite the contrary. Yes, the Muslim Brethren placed a decided religious value on this-worldy affairs, but it was linked to the religious notion of the hereafter. Al-Banna accepted nationalism but only as a part of God's greater community—the *umma*. Totalitarian it was in ideology, if by totalitarian is meant covering all aspects of social and political life, but it was not totalitarian nationalism. The Muslim Brethren was a religious movement that embraced but transcended nationalism, not the other way round. Perhaps Hasan al-Banna's Muslim Brethren is best labeled an Islamist totalitarian movement.[8] As such it cultivated "true believers" with a mindset dividing the world into the good and the bad, the saved and the damned. Given this orientation, it was easy to sanctify any means, including violence, used to advance God's plan and to oppose God's enemies. As such, it was the prototype of many later Islamist movements.

Abu al-A'la Mawdudi, born in 1906, numbered among his ancestors those who had served the Moghul dynasty and, even earlier in time, had been connected with the Chishti Sufi order that had played a significant role in spreading Islam in the subcontinent. Sometime after the 1857 Indian Mutiny, members from both the paternal and maternal side of the family were to be found in service to the Muslim princely dynasty (the Nizams) ruling in Hyderabad, the last sizeable and somewhat autonomous Muslim polity under the British raj. The Nizams, however, ruled over a considerable Hindu majority, and the princely state of Hyderabad could be seen as a ghostly survivor, a Moghul Empire writ small.

Mawdudi grew up in a family context of nostalgia for past Muslim political glory, a distaste for infidel British rule, and a tenacious hanging on to what remained of traditional Muslim mores. In what might have seemed to be a step toward a different orientation, Mawdudi's father actually enrolled him in that very symbol of Islamic modernism and accommodation to the British raj—the Muslim Anglo-Oriental College at Aligarh founded by Sir Sayyid Ahmad Khan. It is, perhaps, more telling that Mawdudi did not stay long at Aligarh but completed his education in law at Allahabad.[9]

Mawdudi's father, an ardent Sufi and traditionalist, attended to the education of his sons in their first years. It was only at age eleven that Mawdudi, enrolled in a school at Aurangabad, was first introduced to modern subjects. When his father died five years later, Mawdudi dropped out of school and began while still in his teens a prodigious career in journalism. Indeed, during the years 1921–1924 he edited the party newspapers of the Jami'at-i Ulama-i Hind (Society of Indian Ulama).

It is sometimes suggested that Mawdudi, just like al-Banna, Qutb, and—in fact—most of the present-day Islamist leaders, never received the traditional education of the ulama class. This is not quite true. Tutors selected by his pious and puritanical father had introduced the young Mawdudi to what can properly be called a classical education in Islamic high culture. This included the study of Arabic and Persian, in addition to Urdu. Mawdudi relates in his memoirs that at the age of fourteen he translated Qasim Amin's *Al-Mar'a al-Jadida* (The New Woman) from Arabic to Urdu—no mean feat at any age.[10]

Then, while associated with the Society of Indian Ulama, he studied with an eminent religious scholar and later at a renown mosque/seminary in Delhi, earning in 1926 the certificate that entitled him to be numbered among the ulama. Yet, Mawdudi always identified himself as a journalist and was silent on his formal scholarly training, preferring to present himself as an autodidact.[11]

Mawdudi's formal education is, in fact, more properly distinguised from that of most other Sunni Islamists in the relatively slight exposure he had to modern studies, including English (which he later learned on his own) or any Western language.

In these early years the young Mawdudi was very much the Indian nationalist, having even written essays in praise of Congress Party leaders, including Gandhi. Moreover, before taking his editorial position with the Society of Indian Ulama he had worked for a pro-Congress Party paper. He was also caught up in the Khilafat movement, which, it will be recalled, was supported by Gandhi and the Congress Party.

By the mid-1920s the Khilafat movement was sinking into irrelevance, and Mawdudi was souring on nationalism. Then in 1925 came an incident that seemed to shape the Islamist orientation that he would maintain, and refine, during the remainder of his long life. In that year a Muslim killed a Hindu who had been agitating for the reconversion to Hinduism of low-caste Muslims. The tragic incident spawned a spate of publicity alleging the intolerance and rigidity of Islam and including the old canard about paradise being assured to any Muslim killing an infidel.[12]

In response Mawdudi wrote a series of newspaper articles later collected into a book on the subject of jihad in Islam. These articles were well received, and the still young Mawdudi was embarked on his mission of providing an Islamist ideology to Muslims, and especially to the millions of Muslims in the subcontinent who, in spite of their numbers, were a vulnerable minority living amidst the Hindu majority.

Since Mawdudi rejected the idea of a nationalism that would unite Hindus and Muslims, one might have expected him to have joined the camp of those pressing for a Muslim nation-state, a Pakistan. It was not to be. Mawdudi fervently and consistently spoke out against nationalism, Muslim or otherwise. Indeed, when Mawdudi gathered some seventy-five followers to create the Jama'at-i Islami in 1941, he was challenging the nationalist Muslim League's celebrated Lahore Resolution of the previous year calling for a separate Muslim state.

Mawdudi's thinking in this matter was, as always with him, logical but quite idealistic in the sense of rejecting any compromise in principle. He was never to accept the notion that politics was the art of the possible. The Muslims of India, in his view, were not a nation to be defined by ethnicity or language or culture or even by a formal adherence to Islam. Muslims were a community to be distinguished from others only to the extent that they heeded and implemented God's divine plan as set out in the Qur'an and Sunna. Consistent with this manner of thinking, Mawdudi would resolve the plight of Indian Muslims by having a committed vanguard instruct and discipline others and thus eventually bring into existence a righteous community, a *salih jama'at*.[13] Muslims were in disarray and vulnerable not so much because of external factors such as British imperialism or a Hindu majority in India but rather because they had strayed from the straight path God had ordained for believers.

Better, in other words, to postpone independence indefinitely than to achieve an independent state based on other than truly Islamic principles. Mawdudi believed that the followers of Jinnah and the Muslim League were more nearly embarked on nationalizing Islam than creating an Islamic nation. He wanted none of it. Neither the overwhelmingly Hindu Congress Party seeking a single India that would embrace all religions nor the Muslim League attemping to construct a nation of Muslims (but not, by Mawdudi's stern logic, an Islamic nation) offered an acceptable choice.

The much more popular and powerful Muslim League viewed the Jama'at-i Islami as weakening Muslim ranks at a time when all should rally around the goal of an independent Pakistan. To opt out of the campaign for a Pakistan was, in their eyes, to play into the hands of the Congress Party. Mawdudi's response amounted to insisting that the task was to Islamicize first, then create a Muslim state.

With partition and the emergence of India and Pakistan as separate independent states in 1947, the dispute dividing the Jama'at-i Islami and the Muslim League became moot. The Jama'at split into two groups—those Muslims in what was now Pakistan and those left in India. Mawdudi had for several years before 1947 been living in what became Pakistan, and without hesitation he chose to remain there. Not having been able to cleanse, as he saw it, the Muslim League leadership of its secular nationalist orientation he now worked to transform the Pakistan they had created into a proper Islamic polity.

The Westernizing, secularist Muslim elite ruling Pakistan made much of Mawdudi's footdragging in the fight to create the state, but Mawdudi saw himself as being completely consistent. Since he had not succeeded in creating a *salih jama'at* first and thereafter a truly Islamic state, he would henceforth seek to Islamicize Pakistan.

The Jama'at was a designedly small party of the truly dedicated, not a coalition assembled by means of bargaining and compromise in order to win elections. Such has been the case both during the long period of Mawdudi's presidency (1941–1972) and thereafter. The Jama'at never became a mass political party and has over the years elected only small numbers of representatives at either the provincial or national level.

Yet, given Pakistan's pluralistic politics, the Jama'at has been able to act effectively as a single-issue lobby. Moreover, the single issue championed by the Jama'at has been difficult to challenge head on. How can a Pakistani politician be against an Islamic state? That is what everyone must want if the concept of a Pakistan makes any sense. And those who would reject Mawdudi's very strict definition of an Islamic state risk appearing less dedicated to that end.

Since unswerving consistency was always a hallmark of Mawdudi's ideology, his opponents could not readily label him manipulative or opportunistic. On the contrary, he could often catch out the ruling elite's inconsistent use of Islamic symbolism. A striking example was Mawdudi's stand in 1948 that the Pakistani government could not declare the fight against Indian rule in Kashmir to be a jihad while observing an Indian-Pakistani cease-fire. Pakistan could properly speak of a jihad only after declaring war against India (which would have been, of course, disastrous). Nothing popular about this argument at the time, but Mawdudi was absolutely correct in terms of Islamic law, and he managed to drive home the point in maintaining that a jihad could not be declared in circumstances of "hypocrisy."[14]

Mawdudi demonstrated the same consistency in an issue that scandalized liberal Muslims and non-Muslims alike. This was the deplorable campaign to declare the Ahmadiyyah sect to be non-Muslims. Actions against this tiny minority that was, however, well represented in the educated elite (including the then Pakistani foreign minister) wreaked such havoc that martial law had to be imposed in 1953. Mawdudi, without approving the violence, did support the idea that the Ahmadiyyah could not be considered Muslims. The Ahmadiyyah saw one Hazrat Mirza Ghulam Ahmad (thus the name, Ahmadiyyah) as the promised messiah, and this to Mawdudi was an unacceptable theological error, for Muhammad was the last divinely inspired person. The Prophet Muhammad was the "seal of prophecy."

Brought to trial before a military court for his role in the anti-Ahmadiyyah agitation, Mawdudi was sentenced to death, but this draconian judgment brought such a public protest that it was commuted to fourteen years in prison. He was actually released after having served twenty months.[15]

Unlike many Islamic modernists, Mawdudi never tried to tone down or reinterpret the literalist readings of scripture that would be most jarring to modern sensitivities. The argument, for example, that the non-Muslim *dhimmi* in Mawdudi's Muslim state becomes a second-class citizen does not faze him. The dhimmis, he would counter, are protected, permitted to follow their own religious practices, and released from certain duties such as serving in the armed forces. This compensates for disabilities such as being barred from many public offices, paying a tax imposed on non-Muslims (*jizya*), and having subordinate standing vis-à-vis Muslims in litigation. Dhimmis, according to his logic, who wanted to be full-fledged citizens of the Muslim state could convert, but the Muslim state will not pressure them. "There is no compulsion in (the Islamic) religion" (Quran 2:256). Those who do not convert wish only to be protected and left in peace. Thus, to Mawdudi, the circle of logic is completed.

Such is the continuing influence of Mawdudi that his ideology has become the norm for all Sunni Islamists, the principal themes of which may be outlined as follows:

1. The ineffable and undisputed sovereignty of God.
2. The vice-regency (the term is *khalifa*—caliph) of all believers.
3. These Muslim "caliphs"—that is, all pious, practicing Muslims— confine themselves to determining God's will as set out in the Qur'an and Sunna. There is no legislative function as such but only the duty of discovering and implementing the divine plan. The resulting system is a "theodemocracy" or a "democratic caliphate."[16]

4. Consultation (*shura*) is enjoined. The Muslim ruler must consult, but the concept of a government and an opposition or of different political parties is ruled out. In a properly constituted Islamic state, interests and needs are reconciled. This, in turn, downgrades the necessity for elections or changes in administrations. The ideal Muslim state and community, once realized, brings, seemingly, an "end of history." The lion lies down with the lamb.

5. In this idealized government political leaders and administrators must be not only competent but pious. Nor should they eagerly seek political office. Indeed, those who seek office are to be disqualified.[17]

6. Islam is comprehensive, embracing both public and private life. The idea that there could be religiously neutral social or political institutions is ruled out.

7. To the extent that government or public life falls short of this Islamist idea, it lapses into *jahiliyya*. This "age of ignorance" is not just a historic era coming to an end with the arrival of God's message to mankind through His prophet Muhammad. Jahiliyya exists in any time or any place in which the divinely ordained ideal community has not be realized. In Mawdudi's worldview many of the serious shortcomings that make for jahiliyya can be attributed to Western ideas and institutions.

Most of these basic ideas have been advanced in one form or another by other Muslim thinkers, past and present, but Mawdudi occupies a special niche in having produced a richer corpus of writings that in their consistency and coherence have been of great influence to others, including our third major Sunni Islamist, Sayyid Qutb.

Sayyid Qutb was born in an Upper Egyptian village in 1906, the son of a moderately prosperous farmer. His early schooling included the traditional Qur'anic school (kuttab), and he had memorized the Qur'an by the age of ten. While still in his early teens he moved to Cairo and completed his education at Dar al-'Ulum. The parallels with the life of Hasan al-Banna are striking. Born in the same year, provincials from families with good standing in their villages, they both received a traditional Islamic rote education in their earlier years and completed their training in Cairo, but not at al-Azhar. Neither of these two leading figures in twentieth-century

Islamist thought and action was a seminarian. Both chose careers in education.

Qutb's intellectual development, however, took a different tack from that of Banna until the late 1940s. Whereas al-Banna remained consistently within an Islamist mode throughout his life, Qutb during the 1920s and 1930s carved out a modest niche for himself as a writer and critic. He is believed to have been especially influenced by the eminent modernist writer/critic Abbas Mahmud al-'Aqqad.[18] Qutb's literary output in these years consisted of poetry, short stories, and criticism, and he was much taken with English literature, eagerly devouring all he could lay his hands on in Arabic translation. Not surprisingly, later in life, as a convinced Islamist, he expressed regret in having wasted time with such literary interests.

Yet his was not so much a sharp break from a belles-lettrist past to an adamant Islamist position as it was a natural development for this intense, subjective, and highly moralistic man. For that matter, al-'Aqqad, his early literary mentor, and others of the modernist school all began to elaborate upon Islamic themes in their writings from the late 1930s on.[19]

Another milestone in Qutb's intellectual odyssey to radical Islamism was the two years (1949–1950) he spent in the United States. Qutb, then an official of the Egyptian Ministry of Education, was sent to study educational administration. Soon after his return he joined the Muslim Brethren and from that time until his execution in 1966 Qutb had his mission: to formulate in writing and implement in action what he believed to be God's plan for mankind.

From one perspective, Qutb's visit to the U.S. was yet another link in the long chain of influential Egyptian intellectuals whose views had been shaped by having lived for a time in that attractive/repulsive West. The chain may be considered as having started with Shaykh Rifa'a Rafi' al-Tahtawi, whom Muhammad Ali posted to Paris in the 1820s to serve as "chaplain" of the Egyptian student mission. It continued right down to Qutb's older contemporaries and the literary lions of his day: Taha Husayn (1889–1973), Muhammad Husayn Haykal (1889–1956), and Tawfiq al-Hakim (1899–1987), who had all been students in Paris. Just such contacts contributed in no small measure to the broad spectrum of Westernizing influences on modern Egypt, ranging from liberal nationalism to Islamic modernism.

Not so for Sayyid Qutb. He was jolted by American racial prejudice (Qutb was swarthy) and by what he saw as America's anti-Arab and pro-Israel posture (he had arrived in the U.S. one year after the birth of Israel and the first Arab-Israeli war). His letters from America as well as the short articles written in 1951 convey his antipathy.[20] Americans might smile smugly when reading of the American mores that evoked Qutb's displeasure. They included such details as dancing at church parties or the sexual innuendo of the popular song "Baby, It's Cold Outside." A closer reading, however, when set within the context of his many other writings, reveals a coherent perspective of the "Other" that provided a foil for better explicating Qutb's own religious program. Americans, to Qutb, were powerful and wealthy but emotionally primitive, too materialist and licentious. Most of all, Americans and the people of the West in general were racist and imperialist. "The white man is our primary enemy," Qutb maintained.[21]

Qutb's American experience probably sharpened his sense of a clash of civilizations—beleagured Islam against threatening West, and to that extent it may have accelerated his intellectual journey to Islamist radicalism. Still, a more rounded look at his entire life indicates that he would have reached the same goal even without that time in the United States. One of his most famous works, *Social Justice in Islam*, first published in 1949, was written before his visit to America. *Social Justice* reveals Qutb as much more than just a religious nationalist bent on defending Egyptians and Muslims everywhere from the intrusive Other. He was also, and perhaps even more, a populist condemning the harsh lot of the common folk and scoring the Egyptian establishment, including the official ulama, for their inattention to the plight of most Egyptians.

Qutb in *Social Justice* even offered indirect praise of American "social justice" when insisting that it was acceptable for the American president to live in the luxurious White House since the American worker has his automobile and the wherewithal to take vacations with his family, but such was not the case in Eygpt. Qutb added:

> When there are millions who cannot afford the simplest dwelling, who in the twentieth century have to take tin cans and reed huts as their houses; when there are those who cannot even find rags to cover their bodies, it is an impossible luxury that a mosque should cost a hundred thousand guineas, or that the Ka'bah should be covered with a ceremonial robe, embroidered with gold.[22]

Qutb, moreover, followed the line of many leftists, including Communists, in singling out Abu Dharr al-Ghifari, a companion of the Prophet Muhammad and champion of the poor, for special praise.

There is, however, one more twist to the story. The favorable reference to the American worker and the following lines cited above were deleted from all editions of *Social Justice* (there were many, as well as several translations, too) after 1954.[23] Did Qutb's populist orientation diminish in his later writings? Perhaps it is more accurate to see this theme as having been somewhat muted as he moved toward a larger conceptualization of three major forces in the world—Communism, capitalism, and Islam. In Qutb's evolving theory it was axiomatic that neither Communism nor capitalism but only Islam offered the solution needed.[24] To suggest that America or any other part of the non-Muslim world did rather well in providing at least material benefit to workers would have weakened Qutb's case. Better to emphasize Communist atheism, Western imperial aggressiveness, and the toadying of the Egyptian establishment to such outside forces. Qutb thus regarded all— the alien non-Muslims and the indigenous nominal Muslims—as living in a state of jahiliyya.

Here Qutb built on Mawdudi's ingenious reinterpretation of a venerable Muslim term—*jahiliyya*, or the time of "ignorance" before God's message to Muhammad—to make it describe not a historical period but a condition that can exist at any time. In the Mawdudi/Qutb formulation, even professed Muslims who do not live up to God's comprehensive plan for human life in this world and the world to come are living in a state of jahiliyya. Nor is the true Muslim who follows God's plan to the letter permitted simply to suffer in silence the wickedness of others, including those who claim to be Muslim. No, God alone possesses sovereignty (*hakimiyya*), and God alone is to be obeyed. Any individual and certainly any ruler who seeks to impose other than what God has mandated is to be resisted, for "governance belongs to God" (Qur'an 12:40). "Those who do not rule in accordance with what God has revealed are unbelievers" (Qur'an 5:47).[25] And resistance takes the form of jihad.

Accordingly, Qutb's mature political theory as worked out in his many writing throughout the 1950s and 1960s, including his six-volume Qur'anic commentary,[26] may be seen as a rigorously logical and consistent working out of the implications of his three concepts: jahiliyya, hakimiyya, and jihad. In simplest terms it comes down to this: God's sovereignty (hakimiyya) is exclusive. Men are to obey God alone. Men are to obey only rulers who obey God. A ruler who obeys God faithfully follows God's mandate. That mandate is clear and comprehensive. It is available for mankind's guidance in the Shari'ah. To set aside that clear and comprehensible divine mandate is to lapse into jahiliyya. Rulers who so act are to be resisted. Resistance under these circumstances is a legitimate act of jihad. The ruler's claim to being a Muslim ruling a Muslim state is null and void.

It cannot be stressed too often just how much Qutb's hardline interpretation departs from the main current of Islamic political thought throughout the centuries. Yes, it does evoke the memory of the early Kharijite movement, with their all-or-nothing approach to politics (*la hukma ila lillah*, "judgment only to God"), but in the eyes of the great majority of Muslims, both scholars and "laity," *Kharijite* was a term of abuse. They were seen as having brought strife and anarchy (*fitna*) to the early Muslim community by resisting Muhammad's son-in-law and fourth caliph, Ali, who is venerated by both Sunnis and the Shi'a. It was a Kharijite who later assassinated Ali. Thus, when Egypt's President Sadat dubbed the Islamists of his day "Kharijites" he was placing them outside the acceptable boundaries of Muslim orthodoxy. His description, sadly for him, soon became even more appropriate. Sadat's assassins came from the ranks of these radical Islamists, implementing Qutb's ideology. It was Kharijism redux fourteen centuries later.

Qutb also buttressed his hardline jihadist ideology by reference to Ibn Taimiyya (1268–1328), who justified a jihad against the Mongols. Why? The Mongol rulers had embraced Islam but did not apply the Shari'ah. Therefore, they should be resisted. This was just the legal finding that the Mamluk opponents of the Mongols were looking for. The Mamluks themselves were hardly paragons of Islamic virtue, but they did cater rather better to the interests and concerns of the ulama. In a word, the precise historical case Ibn Taimiyya judged was less an issue of black versus white than of gray versus less gray. The legal principle that he asserted, however, emerged in a more categorical form: even nominal Muslim rulers not living up to the high standards of Muslim orthodoxy should be resisted. They would rightly become the object of a jihad. This, of course, explains why Ibn Taimiyya has become the champion of modern-day Islamists.

Ibn Taimiyya has the deserved reputation as one of the most powerful Muslim thinkers. He was no minor figure known only to specialists until discovered and dusted off by present-day Islamists. In fact, Ibn Taimiyya greatly influenced Muhammad ibn Abd al-Wahhab, founder of the strict official Wahhabi doctrine followed in Saudi Arabia. Indeed, at the tactical level of resisting governmental censorship the Islamists could rest assured that governments might ban Qutb's works but not the works of a master of the tradition Muslim canon such as Ibn Taimiyya. Even so, all things considered, Ibn Taimiyya's ideas on this issue are not in the mainstream of Muslim political thought. The case for this assertion was presented in part 1, where it was argued that the dominant Muslim political tradition tilted toward quietism and acceptance of any political authority provided it did not impede individuals believers in carrying out their religious duties. That rulers should *impose* religious orthodoxy or orthopraxy was very much a minority view. The predominant Muslim position throughout the ages was that those who made the profession of faith were deemed to be Muslims. The question of how faithfully the Muslim implemented the divinely ordained plan was a matter between each believer and God. It was not for Muslims to "excommunicate" other Muslims. Thus, the notion of professed Muslims lapsing into jahiliyya and becoming legitimate targets of a jihad represents a bold reworking of Islamic political thought.

Such ideas were political dynamite. They had been during the 1930s and 1940s, in the years of Hasan al-Banna's active leadership of the Muslim Brethren. They were no less so from 1950 on, when Sayyid Qutb, after returning from America, embarked on his explicitly Islamist years brough to an end sixteen years later by his trial and execution in 1966.

It is not certain exactly when Qutb joined the Muslim Brethren. It may have been as late as 1952. In any case, his writings had given him a standing that placed him quite soon in charge of the brethren's publishing and pros-elytizing activities.[27]

That same year, 1952, brought the Free Officers' coup and the advent of what became the Nasser era. Since many of those Free Officers (including Sadat) had developed close ties with the Muslim Brethren during their years of clandestine preparation, it appeared that the brethren were destined to play a major role after 1952. That brief honeymoon between the Free Officers and the Muslim Brethren, as noted earlier in discussing al-Banna, lasted less than two years, to be followed by harsh repressive actions through the remainder of the Nasser era.

Qutb himself experienced a dramatic rise and fall in his relations with the Nasserists. For roughly the first six months after the July 1952 Free Officers coup he was viewed as having "eaten, slept, and voted on matters of policy with the (Free) Officers trying to influence their plans for the country."[28] It has even been suggested that Nasser contacted Qutb with the idea that he become secretary general of the Liberation Rally.[29] Whatever the precise nature of Qutb's ties with the Free Officers, it was short-lived, following if not even slightly preceding the rapid decline of ties between the Revolutionary Command Council and the Muslim Brethren. Within a year of the July 1952 coup the Free Officers were bent on bringing the Muslim Brethren to heel. The ups and downs of this struggle, involving as well the Nasserist split with the older officer recruited to represent the new govern-ment in those early days, General Muhammad Naguib, offer a fascinating case study in postrevolutionary consolidation of power. For present purpos-es, however, it will suffice to note that Qutb was arrested and detained for a short time in early 1954, in the first and incomplete showdown with the

Muslim Brethren. He was again arrested in the massive arrests that followed the failed attempt of a Muslim Brother to assassinate Nasser in October 1954.

Qutb was destined to spend the next ten years of his life in prison. Struggling against poor health and harsh treatment, he nevertheless managed to produce an impressive corpus of writings during those years of confinement.

He was released in May 1964, the official reason for commuting the remaining five years of his fifteen-year prison term being his poor health, but it is generally accepted that none other than Iraqi president Abd al-Salam Arif, then on a state visit to Egypt, interceded to get him freed. He was to enjoy only somewhat more than a year of freedom before being arrested with many other Muslim Brothers accused of planning, yet again, assassination of Nasser and the seizure of power. Tried by a special military tribunal beginning in April 1966, he and others were sentenced to death. Sayyid Qutb was hanged on August 29, 1966.

The Nasserist military tribunal sought to make it a show trial that would expose the un-Islamic extremism of Qutb and his followers. The prosecution produced experts in Islamic law and tradition to question and challenge Sayyid Qutb, drawing on the texts of his copious writings and especially his most famous book, penned in prison, *Ma'alim fi al-Tariq* (Signposts on the Way). The trial actually gave Qutb one final forum to present his ideology in severe and uncompromising fashion. Those many Muslims (surely a majority) who just as in past centuries deplore acts of fitna and cringe at the idea of calling a fellow Muslim an infidel would not have felt at ease with Qutb's views as aired in these proceedings. Still, hanging a man for his writings (and Qutb's involvement in an alleged assassination and coup conspiracy was not effectively established) did not sit well with liberal opinion. The manifestly stacked nature of the trial, leading to a preordained conclusion,[30] was hardly designed to educate the public concerning the justice of the government's case.

As for those many Muslims in Egypt and elsewhere inclined toward radical fundamentalism, the trial and hanging of Sayyid Qutb provided yet another martyr, an Islamic *shahid*.

Three Sunni Islamist leaders, all born in the first decade of the twentieth century. All learned in Islamic studies but not members of the religious establishment, the ulama. The only one whose formal studies entitled such a standing, Mawdudi, deliberately avoided the title. All found themselves struging against existing government (two killed by their rulers) but not so much to claim the individual's or the group's freedom from government control as to demand a divinely ordained authoritarian government. One, al-Banna, was an accomplished organizer and (if the Christian term be permitted) pastoral preacher. The other two were more intellectual. Mawdudi was more elitist and made no effort at mass political organization. Qutb, with a populist streak, worked within the framework of the most widespread religio-political movement in modern times—the Muslim Brethren.

Many other Sunni Islamist leaders could be mentioned. Some have attained political power, or some measure thereof, such as Pakistan's General Zia, Hasan Turabi of Sudan, or Malaysia's Anwar Ibrahim.[31] Others have assembled and led opposition groups: Abbasi Medani of the Algerian FIS (Islamic Salvation Front), Rashid Ghannoushi of the Tunisian MTI (Islamic Tendencies Movement), or Ahmad Yasin of the Palestinian Hamas. Some have been more radical and terrorist, others more prone to work within the system. For all, however, the ideas of al-Banna, Mawdudi, and Qutb provided the ideological bedrock of Sunni Islamism.

15.

Khomeini and Shi'ite Islamism

The most dramatic example of politics and Islam in this century is the Islamic Revolution in Iran, which overthrew the Pahlavi dynasty, rejected monarchy as un-Islamic, and established an Islamic Republic continuing to this day. This cataclysmic change brought about in 1978–1979 has fueled, more than any other, the American image of radical Islam. The dour visage of that elderly cleric, Ayatullah Khomeini, became in those years following 1978 as recognizable as that of the American president.

Sustaining the white heat of American-Iranian confrontation was the storming of the American Embassy in Tehran by radical Islamists on November 4, 1979, and its occupants taken hostage—in clear violation of international law and custom. Only 444 days later was this crisis resolved with the release of the remaining 52 American hostages on January 20, 1981, just hours after President Reagan's inauguration. Jimmy Carter—whose last years as president were clouded, and his reelection prospects probably dashed, by the challenges Islamic Iran had posed—was denied the solace of having the hostage release take place during his tenure.

President Reagan, too, was almost tripped up by Islamic Iran. The mid-eighties brought the "Iran-Contra" affair in which the administration, in violation of its stated policy, secretly provided arms to Iran in its war against neighboring Iraq. Then, when this undercover operation was revealed, the Reagan administration lurched in the opposite direction toward support of Iraq. This sufficed to force Ayatullah Khomeini into a decision "more deadly than taking poison" (as he put it) and sue for peace with Iraq on unfavorable terms.

Even the later crisis and war provoked by Iraq's invasion of Kuwait did not open the door for rapprochement between the United States and Iran. Although a few Americans now call for restored relations with Iran, evoking in some cases realist balance-of-power arguments and in others the belief that the Islamic Republic of Iran has mellowed, official U.S. policy continues to lump together Iraq and Iran as rogue states that must be held in check by a policy of "dual containment."

From the Iranian perspective the United States is the country that mounted a coup overthrowing a popular nationalist leader, Muhammad Musaddiq, as long ago as 1953 and thereafter supported an increasingly despotic shah. The U.S. is seen as the country that backed Iran's enemy, Iraq, during that brutal war lasting from 1980 to 1988 and has since been the principal outside power seeking to rein in, if not overthrow, its Islamic Republic. Ayatullah Khomeini's image of the U.S. as the "great Satan" still strikes a responsive chord among many Iranians.

The Islamic Revolution in Iran, in short, has had a distinctive impact on peoples and governments in Iran and elsewhere, Muslims and non-Muslims, because it was truly a revolution, not a coup and not simply a reshuffling of seats in the same old political game. And it was a revolution that succeeded and survived. The political system it brought into being has now lasted for some two decades.

Religio-political opposition movements may well threaten existing regimes, but their impact on history falls far short of what a revolutionary movement that seizes power will exert. The Islamic Republic of Iran has had a more substantial impact on both Muslims and even non-Muslims than those many religio-political opposition movements in this era that have never (or not yet) captured power. In sheer terms of effecting significant change, the Islamic Revolution in Iran may be compared to the radically different revolution achieved by Kemal Ataturk in creating the secular Republic of Turkey following the First World War. Both revolutions seized power and then implemented major changes.

The impact of the Islamic revolution in Iran not just in that country but throughout the Muslim world and beyond is even more striking given that it has taken place in the context of Shi'i Islam, which, it will be recalled, accounts for only roughly 15 percent of the world's Muslims. Moreover, many might claim—although the matter is not beyond dispute—that mainstream Shi'i political thought has been even more politically quietist than that of the majority Sunni community. Indeed, a principal thrust of Khomeini's writings was to counter this quietism and give high religious value to this-worldly political action. He presented such this-worldly political action as a religious requirement. And his words sparked and sustained a revolution.

An equally important characteristic of this successful seizure of power in the name of Islam is that the leadership came from the ranks of the established Shi'i religious clergy. This is in sharp contrast with Islamism in the Sunni world. Neither Hasan al-Banna nor Sayyid Qutb was an *'alim*. Even though Mawdudi had the religious training authorizing him to claim that title, he avoided so presenting himself. The many other leaders of Sunni Islamist radicalism have been, with almost no exceptions, recipients of essentially secular (Westernized) education and engaged in modern-sector occupations. The number of Sunni Islamists trained as engineers or scientists, for example, has often been noted.

Most Sunni Islamist movements have manifested more than a little "anticlericalism" in the form of scoring the Sunni religious establishment for toadying to government. In some cases, as in Egypt, high-ranking official ulama have been directly challenged, or even assassinated. Here in Iran one finds the great exception—a successful revolution led by establishment clergy. Leading this revolution was the quintessential Shi'i Muslim cleric, Ayatullah Ruhallah Khomeini.

Who was Ayatullah Khomeini?[1] He was born in 1902 in the village of Khomein, located roughly 180 miles southwest of Tehran.

His mother was the daughter of a well-regarded Shi'i cleric, a *mujtahid*. Both his father and paternal grandfather were religious scholars as well. The family had landholdings and was well off by provincial standards. Tragedy struck early. When Khomeini was only four months old his father was killed in an ambush that almost certainly resulted from a vendetta pitting the Khomeinis against another leading family of the region. His mother must have been an indominatable women, for she spent the next three years with wearying trips from Khomein to Tehran seeking justice, leaving the infant Khomeini in the care of a wet nurse. Eventually, the shah's government hanged one of the assassins.[2] Khomeini's mother died when he was fifteen.

Everything in Khomeini's family background pointed him toward a career of religious scholarship, and by all evidence this is precisely what he always wished to do. His early education was in his home town. Then at the age of eighteen he went to the nearby village of Arak to become a disciple of Ayatullah Ha'eri, the preeminent religious scholar of his time (*marja' al-taqlid*). A year later Ha'eri moved to Qum to revive a religious seminary (the Fayzieh) there that had fallen on hard times. Khomeini followed and was to remain with his mentor until Ha'eri's death in 1937. By the early 1930s Khomeini had become a teacher at the Fayzieh seminary.

In 1929 Khomeini married the daughter of a Tehran cleric. She was his only wife and they had seven children, five surviving infancy (two sons and three daughters). The daughters married into bazaar or clerical families. The sons assisted their father in his religious career of growing importance. The older son, Mustafa, died suddenly in 1977 while with his father in Najaf, Iraq.[3] The younger son, Ahmad, died in 1995. He had concerned himself with collecting and publishing the writings of his father.

Sometime after the death of Ayatullah Ha'eri, Khomeini's first mentor, Ayatullah Burujerdi, emerged as the preeminent Iranian Shi'i cleric. Khomeini accepted Burujerdi's religious leadership, remaining loyal to the man and his mission until Burujerdi's death in 1961. Interestingly, both Ha'eri and Burujerdi were classic examples of apolitical clerics. Both espoused accommodation with the existing Pahlavi regime. Yet, Khomeini had, it seems, so much internalized the operational code of the traditional Shi'i religious establishment that he accepted their leadership. His sustained political activism began only in the seventh decade of his life, after the death of the last of the two clerics who had served in turn as his marja' al-taqlid. Henceforth, he was available to become in his own right a marja' al-taqlid to others.

Yet, two decades earlier, a harbinger of Khomeini the political activist appeared. In August 1941 Britain and the Soviet Union intervened in Iran, forced Riza Shah into exile, and replaced him with his twenty-one-year-old son, Muhammad Riza Shah. Soon thereafter, Khomeini published an unsigned and undated tract entitled *Kashf al-Asrar* (Secrets Unveiled).[4] Ostensibly a defense of Shi'ism and the Shi'i religious establishment against a secularist-oriented book recently published, *Kashf al-Asrar* attacked the actions of Riza Shah—safe enough, it might be argued, following Riza's ouster by allied forces who remained to occupy Iran.

In *Kashf al-Asrar* Khomeini insisted that the only true model for worldly politics was "the government of God." God's law, i.e., Islam, is comprehensive. It covers everything "from the most general problems of all countries to the specifics of a man's family."[5] God, thus, is the only valid legislator, for He has given mankind all the legislation ever needed in His divine mandate, which are the rules of Islam.

Khomeini went on to give a more activist interpretation to that Qur'anic verse, "Oh ye who believe, Obey God, His Prophet and those in authority among you" (4:59), which has throughout the centuries been cited to buttress political quietism. Khomeini rebutted this venerable claim that one must obey one's rulers with exquisite irony:

> Now we ask our God-given reason for judgment: God sent the Prophet of Islam with thousands of heavenly laws and established His government on the belief in the uniqueness of God and Justice. . . . Would this same God order men to obey Ataturk who has disestablished state religion, persecuted believers, oppressed the people, sanctioned moral corruption, and, in general, opposed the religion of God? Moreover, would he order us to obey (Riza Shah) Pahlavi who, as we all know, did all that he could to uproot Islam?[6]

Khomeini, in this book, however, stopped short of insisting on rule by the religiously learned (*velayat-e faqih*). "We do not mean to say that the shah, the ministers, the soldiers, and the dustmen should all be faqihs." Still, he did suggest that the religiously learned might well be members of the parliament (the majlis), or supervise such a body, and "these religious men would then elect a just sultan who would not disobey divine law nor practice oppression nor trangress against people's property, life and honor."[7]

Khomeini, thus, did not then declare monarchy as such to be un-Islamic. Nor did he rule out limited cooperation with government. The ulama, he wrote, "consider even this rotten administration better than none at all."[8]

Khomeini in *Kashf al-Asrar* was at his satirical best in attacking Riza Shah and the secularists for aping Western ways, e.g.,

> The day everyone was forced to wear the Pahlavi cap, it was said, "We need to have a national symbol. Independence in matters of dress is proof and guarantee of the independence of a nation." Then a few years later, everyone was forced to put on European hats, and suddenly the justification changed: "We have dealings with foreigners and must dress the same way they do in order to enjoy greatness in the world." If a country's greatness depends on its hat, it would be a thing very easily lost!
>
> While all this was going on, the foreigners, who wished to implement their plans and rob you of one hat while putting another on our head, watched you in amusement from afar. . . . With a European hat on your head, you would parade around the streets enjoying the naked girls, taking pride in this "achievement."[9]

The tone of *Kashf al-Asrar*, the bold assertion of the right and responsibility of the ulama to monitor government in order to assure conformity with God's Law, the powerful appeal to Islamic authenticity, and the scornful dismissing of alien (Western) way all prefigure themes to be found in the powerful religio-political advocacy that Khomeini advanced from the 1960s until his death in June 1989.

At the same time, *Kashf al-Asrar* is restrained by comparison with Khomeini's ideology from the 1960s on. This tract reflected an effort by the ulama class, who had been badly battered by Riza Shah's Westernizing reforms, to regain some of the ground lost. Presented at a time when it was safe, even perhaps prudent, to attack Riza Shah, *Kashf al-Asrar* could be fitted into the accommodationist stance toward government that Burujerdi personified.[10] Indeed, Hamid Algar maintains that Ayatullah Burujerdi himself had asked Khomeini to write *Kashf al-Asrar*, and that seems plausible.[11]

Khomeini remained attuned to the Burujerdi quietist line during the hectic period (1951–1953) in which Prime Minister Muhammad Musaddiq by nationalizing Iranian oil challenged the British presence and Pahlavi rule only to be overthrown by a CIA-backed coup in August 1953. One leading cleric, Ayatullah Kashani, did become politically active, first supporting Musaddiq and then at a critical moment turning against him, but Khomeini was not tempted to follow suit. Continued loyalty to Ayatullah Burujerdi was surely sufficient to explain Khomeini's choice.

A retrospective view of Khomeini's entire life and thought suggests another, equally important motive. Musaddiq represented and was largely supported by the more modern secular and Westernized elements of Iran. He and his supporters, while deserving support for their nationalist resistance to foreign manipulation, would be just as intent on downgrading the ulama role in society as Riza Shah had been (and his son Muhammad Riza Shah would prove to be), and he was gaining backing from that bastion of ulama strength—the bazaar.

> The great popularity of Mosaddeq with the bazaar and his nationalist platform was making the bazaar-mosque political alliance obsolescent by providing the former with viable alternative secular leadership. . . . When Khomeini embarked on his bid for the overthrow of the Pahlavi regime around 1970, he had in mind to settle not one but two scores: to avenge himself and the Shi'ite hierocracy against the two Pahlavis, and to turn the tables on the Westernized intellectuals who, according to him, had cheated the hierocracy in all the important nationwide movements of the preceding century. As we now know, having ejected the Pahlavis, he wasted no time in initiating a massive *kulturkampf* against the Westernized intelligentsia.[12]

This tug of war between the ulama and the Westernizers (as old as the period of the Constitutional Revolution in the first decade of the twentieth century) surely shaped Khomeini's thought and action not just during the Musaddiq period but throughout his life.

By the time Ayatullah Burujerdi died in 1961 Muhammad Riza Shah was no longer the timorous young ruler of the 1940s or the man who had fled his country in 1953 only to be brought back by an American-sponsored coup. He felt strong enough to engage in yet one more example of the kind of autocratic modernization program that powerful Middle Eastern leaders have often undertaken since the days of Egypt's Muhammad Ali. What came to be known as the "White Revolution," or the "Shah and People Revolution," involved a broad range of reforms including land reform, moves toward increased rights for women, and a barrage of actions intended to the clip the wings of the ulama. To Khomeini and to other clerics the nightmare of the Riza Shah era was returning.

The Shi'i clerics, however, were by no means alone in their antipathy to the Pahlavi regime. The shah built an increasingly powerful state but never won over adequate constituencies of Iranians dedicated to support the regime out of either interest or loyalty. Thousands of Irans received advanced higher education at home and abroad at state expense, but these young beneficiaries of Pahlavi largesse were overwhelmingly opposed to the shah's police-state despotism. He coddled the armed forces but did not show trust in its leaders, nor they in him. Beneficiaries of the land reform program did not gel into a signficant group that could serve as a political asset.[13] Nor did the shah's measures in support of women's liberation produce any significant organizational muscle for the regime. It was a classic case of "uneven development," with massive and not totally ineffective social and economics changes alongside appalling "political underdevelopment."[14] In retrospect, it is easy to explain why the Pahlavi regime fell, but why was it an Islamic Revolution? And why was it led by Khomeini?

Khomeini entered the lists early against the shah's White Revolution. He was arrested, then released, then arrested again, and finally exiled from Iran in late 1964. He was away from Iran for somewhat more than fourteen years until February 1, 1979, when with the deliberation of a frail seventy-seven-year-old scholar he descended the ramp of the airplane that had brought him from Paris. Thereafter, he slowly made his way by motorcade from the Tehran Airport to the capital city along a route thronged with an estimated three million exultant Iranians. How did he do it? And from exile? Simply stated, "Khomeini is to the Islamic Revolution what Lenin was to the Bolshevik, Mao to the Chinese, and Castro to the Cuban revolutions."[15]

He possessed both ideology and organization. Even before the death of Burujerdi, Khomeini was gathering disciples from among the mullahs, and he shifted into high gear thereafter. In the mid-1970s the not implausible claim was advanced that he had trained no fewer than five hundred mujtahids.[16] That he had a following among the ulama is clear. In those few years from Burujerdi's death until Khomeini's exile (1961–1964), the latter's brave defiance of the regime, as contrasted with the more muted protests of other clerics, ensured his standing among those of his religious profession.

He also, more surprisingly, won the following of those outside the ranks of the clergy, and this for a variety of reasons. First, the secular nationalists—the followers of the ill-fated Musaddiq—were less than united, and their several leaders underestimated the importance of Khomeini and the clerics. That these black-frocked men of religion might greatly influence the masses was to be expected, but the secular elite never dreamed that the clerics could actually organize and lead a political movement.

Second, the strong sense felt throughout Iranian society of being manipulated by a domestic despot working arm in arm with alien forces prepared the ground for a blending together of xenophobic nationalism (which Iran's history since the early nineteenth century certainly cultivated), traditionalism, and religious feeling. Religion and nationalism are readily merged in a Shi'i Iran surrounded as it is by threatening non-Muslim and Sunni Muslim neighbors. Even those workers and peasants following the Tudeh (Communist) Party could easily be swayed by Khomeini's message combining religion, nationalism, and populism.

Third, the radical writings of Ali Shari'ati had conditioned the young, and more particularly the educated young, to countenance the idea of a revolutionary movement led by Khomeini. Shari'ati, the son of a reform-minded cleric, was born in 1933 in a village near Mashhad in the northeastern Iranian province of Khorasan. Shortly after his birth, the family moved to the city of Mashhad where Shari'ati was educated. After attending normal school in Mashhad he was by the age of nineteen embarked on a teaching career while being already heavily involved in pro-Musaddiq politics. He remained sufficiently active politically in the years after Musaddiq's overthrow to earn his first jail sentence in 1957. In these years, while continuing his teaching and writing, he had enrolled in the University of Mashhad, graduating in 1959 near the top of his class, which entitled him to a scholarship to study abroad. The government refused him permission to leave until a year later. He then enrolled in a graduate program at the Sorbonne, receiving his doctorate in 1964 and returning to Iran.[17]

Those Parisian years were crucial in the development of Shari'ati's ideology. He associated himself with the Algerian nationalist movement, the

Front de Liberation Nationale (FLN), and wrote for its newspaper, *El Moujahid*. He embraced the revolutionary ideas of Franz Fanon and even undertook to translate his *Les Damnées de la Terre* (in English, *The Wretched of the Earth*) into Persian. He also translated Che Guevera's *Guerrilla Warfare*. His contacts in person or through their writings with other Marxist, revolutionary, and third world ideologues shaped the development of his own thought. He presented a Shi'i Islam that was liberating and revolutionary by positing a distinction between "Alid" and "Safavid" Islam. The former was the pure Islam personified by Ali, the son-in-law of Muhammad and in Shi'i Islam the first in the legitimate line of succession (the imams). What Shari'ati called Safavid Islam, by contrast, was the debased, quietist, and obscurantist Islam cobbled together by later clerics.

By this formulation Shari'ati had managed to make Islam—Alid Islam— the appropriate matrix of a revolutionary struggle in Iran (and, for that matter, all the Muslim world, or at the least the Sh'i Muslim world) of his day. He had presented a program that rejected the "Safavid" clergy as supporters of a repressive social system without falling into the trap of seeming to propose alien ideas and ways. Instead, his Alid Islam managed to nationalize (or, better, Islamize) third world revolutionary doctrine.

In those twelve years from his return to Iran in 1964 to his death in 1977, Shari'ati emerged as the political thinker attracting many Iranians (especially the young exposed to modern education in Iran and abroad) eager to escape what they saw as the incubus of the shah's regime. And the Shari'ati ideology paved the way to acceptance of Khomeini as revolutionary leader. All those agonizing contradictions such as atheistic Marxism versus politically impotent Islam or alien modernity versus stultifying nativism or religious versus secular were swept away as avoidable misperceptions. The right kind of Sh'i cleric, an Alid Shi'i cleric, would be able to rally all Iranians in the liberation struggle. Ayatullah Khomeini was seen as just such a leader.

> By late 1978, such was Khomeini's popularity among Shari'ati supporters that it was they—not the clergy—who took the somewhat blasphemous step of endowing him with the title of Imam, a title that in the past Shi'i Iranians had reserved for the Twelve Holy Imams. Lacking both the theological concerns of the 'ulama and the sociological sophistication of their late mentor, Shari'ati's followers argued that Khomeini was not just an ordinary ayatollah but a charismatic Imam who would carry through the revolution and lead the community (*Ummat*) toward the long-awaited classless society (*Nezam-i Towhid*).[18]

What Ali Shari'ati himself would have thought of the Islamic Republic ushered in by Khomeini in 1979 was never to be tested. In and out of prison after his return from Paris, Shari'ati was finally banished from Iran in 1977. He flew to England where somewhat later he died under mysterious circumstances that strongly suggest a SAVAK assassination.[19]

Shari'ati's ideas not only disposed his many followers to embrace Khomeini but seemingly influenced Khomeini as well. Certainly Khomeini's own work increasingly emphasized the difference between the haves and the have-nots, the oppressors (*mustakbirin*) and the oppressed (*mustaz'ifin*). Moreover, Khomeini realized the need to appeal to other than the clerics, and he sensed the cardinal importance of Iran's secular educated youth. In one significant passage of his *Islamic Government* Khomeini preached:

> You must make yourselves known to the people of the world and also authentic models of Islamic leadership and government. You must address yourselves to the university people in particular, the educated class. . . . The students are looking to Najaf, appealing for help. Should we sit idle, waiting for them to enjoin the good upon us and call us to our duties?[20]

Khomeini's most famous writing and the culmination of his mature political thought was his *Islamic Government*, first given as a series of lectures to seminarians at Najaf in 1970 and then issued as a short book in Persian, Arabic, and, in time, many other languages—122 pages in Hamid Algar's very able English translation from the Persian.[21] Islamic Government, available in a good English translation and with a manageably short text written in a clear, forceful style, merits a careful reading. One can better appreciate how he could keep his class, and his readers, on their toes with his pungent irony. The following may serve as examples:

1. Foreigners and *akhunds* (his dismissing term for government-supported quietist clerics) try to teach that "Islam consists of a few ordinances concerning menstruation and parturition . . . the proper field of study for *akhunds*" (p. 30).
2. The Islamic tax (*khums*) is intended to support the broad political and social purposes of Islamic government, not just for the upkeep of *sayyids*. "How could the *sayyids* ever need so vast a budget?" (p. 45).
3. "Since the range of thought of some people is confined to the mosque we are now sitting in . . . when they hear the expression 'consumption of what is forbidden,' they can only think of some corner grocer who is (God forbid) selling his customers short . . . (while) our

public funds are being embezzled; our oil is being plundered; and our country is being turned into a market for expensive, unnecessary goods by the representatives for foreign companies" (p. 115).

4. Islamic meetings such as Friday prayer in the mosque and the *Hajj* have social and political as well as devotional purposes, but the unaware "are only concerned about the correct pronunciation of *wa la al-dallin*" (last words of the *Fatiha* [Opening] of the Qur'an) (p. 130).

One can also appreciate the impact of his jeremiads:

1. "Rulers who establish centers of vice and corruption, who build centers of vice and wine-drinking, and spend the income of the religious endowments constructing cinemas" and "these profligate royal ceremonies" (p. 58).

2. "Are you taking from the rich what they owe the poor and passing it on to them? For that is your Islamic duty, to take from the rich and give to the poor. Your answer will be, in effect: 'No, this is none of our concern! God willing, others will come and perform this task.' Then another part of the wall will have collapsed" (e.g., the wall of the "Islamic fortress," p. 74).

3. Concerning the governmental ulama, "Our youths must strip them of their turbans. The turbans of these *akhunds*, who cause corruption in Muslim society while claiming to be *fuqaha* and *'ulama*, must be removed. I do not know if our young people in Iran have died; where are they? Why do they not strip these people of their turbans?" (p. 145).

4. "O God, foreshorten the arms of the oppressors that are stretched out against the lands of the Muslims and root out all traitors to Islam and the Islamic countries" (p. 149).

The reader will also be struck by Khomeini's philippics against imperialism, Orientalists, Israel, and Jews. Given Iran's modern history, an ample measure of anti-imperialism is to be expected. Still, the exaggerated thrust of his many references offers a disturbing, if not indeed paranoid, image of a totally good Islam threatened since time out of mind by enemies from without and traitors from within. Examples:

1. "From the beginning the historical movement of Islam has had to contend with the Jews, for it was they who first established anti-Islamic propaganda. . . . This activity continues down to the present" (p. 27).

2. If Muslims had been properly prepared "a handful of Jews would never have dared to occupy our lands, and to burn and destroy the *Masjid al-Aqsa*" (p. 46). (It was, in fact, a deranged Australian Christian who set fire to the Al-Aqsa mosque in Jerusalem.)

3. "The imperialists, the oppressive and treacherous rulers, the Jews, Christians and materialists are all attempting to distort the truths of Islam and lead Muslims astray. . . . We see today that the Jews (may God curse them) have meddled with the text of the Qur'an. We must protest and make the people aware that the Jews and their foreign backers are opposed to the very foundations of Islam and wish to establish Jewish domination throughout the world" (p. 127).

4. "In our own city of Tehran now there are centers of evil propaganda run by the churches, the Zionists, and the Baha'is to lead our people astray and make them abandon the ordinances and teachings of Islam" (p. 128). See also p. 27 tracing imperialism against Islam back to the Crusades and pp. 139–142 claiming a British and then American imperialist masterplan over the past three hundred years.

Even complete neophytes to Islamic studies should also come away from a reading of *Islamic Government* with a feel for the author's closely argued scholastic style. They will see how the lectures, while filled with Islamic exegesis, work rigorously toward a here-and-now political agenda.

That political agenda can be simply stated: Islam provides a comprehensive sociopolitical system valid for all time and place. Thus, God is the sole legislator. Government is mandated in order to implement God's plan in this world. Individual believers are not permitted simply to suffer unjust rule in silence. They must actively work to realize God's plan in this world. The only acceptable form of this Islamic government is that directed by the most religiously learned. This is the guardianship of the faqih (velayat-e faqih). Thus monarchy or for that matter any other form of government is unacceptable. "Since Islamic government," Khomeini asserted, "is a government of law, those acquainted with the law, or more precisely, with religion—i.e., the *fuqaha*—must supervise its functioning. It is they who supervise all executive and administrative affairs of the country, together with all planning."[22]

The circle is complete. The case for an Islamic Republic ruled by the most learned faqih, or, failing an ability to determine at any time just who that might be, by a collective body of learned fuqaha is logically unanswerable given Khomeini's assumptions about God's plan for mankind and the ability of the just and learned faqih to administer that plan.

It remains only to point out what a radical change in traditional Shii political thought Ayatullah Khomeini managed to impose. The lasting impact on Iran and on Islam of Khomeini's message remains to be seen. This much can be affirmed now: Iranians responded to that message, and 1979 saw the birth of the Islamic Republic of Iran. That event and Iran's history since then deserve, for better or worse, the rubic *revolutionary*.

Conclusion

After sketching the Islamic heritage in politics and political thought in part 1, this study outlined in part 2 developments over the past two centuries leading to the present-day phenomenon of radical political movements (or, in a few cases, governments) claiming to be based on a true understanding of what Islam requires. The ideological dimension, concentrating on the representative Islamist religio-political thinkers and their ideas, has provided the organizational framework. The actual politics of these Islamist movements has received less attention. Nor have the several contemporary Muslim spokesmen for a more liberal interpretation of Islam in its relations to worldly affairs been given their due. That is another subject for another time.

One goal of this work has been to demonstrate that the history of Muslims and Islamic civilization is too rich, diverse, and ever changing to be reduced to a few eternal essentials. Comparisons with the Christian and, to a lesser extent, the Jewish experience were intended to highlight this point. No one suggests a timeless and unchanging Christian approach to politics. The same should hold for Islam. The possible difference in its worldly manifestations between the Christianity of Paul, Augustine, Aquinas, or Luther is readily accepted. Christianity has a history. So does Islam. Christianity also has its diversity. To take just modern American examples, one appreciates that Paul Tillich and Billy Graham both fit under the rubric *Christian*. The same holds for a high church Episcopal service and a revivalist tent meeting. Islam has its equivalents.

Accordingly, to sum up in overly simplified terms how today's Muslims are responding to politics risks defeating the larger goal of taking the measure of Muslims and Islam in all their variety. Even so, a few concluding generalizations may be warranted.

I have argued that the Muslim world has witnessed a dramatic change in politics and political thought in modern times. The last two centuries offer as decisive, and wrenching, a period of change for Muslims as any era in Islamic history since the worldly beginnings of Islam in Arabia over fourteen centuries ago. Muslims before the modern age had, with rare exceptions, lived in Muslim-ruled states. Over the centuries a Muslim civilization had developed in a context of self-sufficiency that justifies the oft-used phrase *Muslim world.* While the many different peoples living in these several Muslim polities were always in contact with others, the important concept of *Dar al-Islam* (the abode of Islam) was more than a theological construct. It reflected a historically shaped reality.

This Muslim cultural autonomy began to be challenged and ultimately almost overwhelmed in modern times, a process that began roughly two centuries ago in the Middle East and the Indian subcontinent (the Muslim heartland organized politically into the Ottoman, Safavid, and Moghul Empires, the last and in many respects most impressive of the many Muslim dynasties), somewhat earlier in the East Indies, somewhat later in the Maghrib, Africa, and Central Asia.

In this new era Muslim leaders sought, and are still seeking, strategies to cope with the new realities brought in large measure by the threatening/ attractive alien West. These strategies have ranged from accommodation to outright resistance. In the process the ideologies advanced have been presented in the terminology of classical Islamic political thought, which is based on a selective idealization of Islam's golden age, the time of the Prophet Muhammad and the early Muslim community.

These calls for being true to one's religious roots, so common of late, must not mislead, however. The radical Islamists offer not simply a "return of Islam" in the sense of a getting back to some history-defying Islamic essence. They also advance new ideas served up in familiar old terms. Although the radical Islamists, our major interest, claim to be restoring the golden age of the early Islamic period, they are, in many important respects, revolutionaries. Ayatollah Khomeini's *velayat-e faqih* advances a radical clerical control of political life outside the mainstream of classical Muslim political thought and even more removed from actual Muslim political history. Mawdudi and Qutb have radically reinterpreted *jahiliyya,* making it a normative standard to judge today's rulers rather than the historical period before God's revelation to Muhammad. The very idea that one Muslim can declare another to be an infidel is out of line with the classic Muslim disposition to leave such matters to God's judgment, not man's.

Both the selective use of the past and the intrusion of the new are to be expected. Dramatic historical changes always involve just such a choosing of bits and pieces from a culture's past. All the more reason, therefore, to understand that past. Such was the task set for part 1. It provided the background needed to gauge in part 2 what modern Muslims have chosen, as well as what they have passed over, from the Islamic political heritage. Covered in greatest detail were three Sunni Islamists (Al-Banna, Mawdudi, and Qutb) and one Shi'i, Ayatullah Khomeini. Although many others could be cited, it was suggested that these four had been the most influential. With rare exception, the thoughts and actions of other Islamists can be linked to the ideas of one or more of these four.

Will radical Islamism win out by seizing power in even more countries, or, no less important, will the ideas of the Islamists, Al-Banna, Mawdudi, Qutb, Khomeini, and their many followers, outlive them and thereby modify later thought and action in the Muslim world? Are we witnessing throughout the Muslim world a historic change as decisive as was the Reformation for the Christian West?

It is clearly too soon to know. Some observers believe that the political appeal of the Islamists has already peaked. Others regard the Islamists as still gaining strength.

This much can be said: the radical Islamists continue to dominate the debate in today's Muslim world. Any ideology that claims to have an all-embracing program, that answers all questions, has the potential to attract a following. This is even more the case when daily life is unsatisfactory and appears to be getting worse even as existing ways of doing things have been discredited. Chapter 12 presented the case for a generalized Muslim malaise that has deepened over the past several decades as harsh reality has shattered the dreams of decolonization, modernization, and a restored autonomy vis-à-vis the outside world. Most of all, in such circumstances, an ideology claiming divine mandate, that offers salvation both here and now and in the world to come, is a formidable opponent. Such is, and will always be, the strength of the fervent believer.

Yet, that historical storehouse of Islamic thought concerning politics (set out in part 1) contains themes that could be utilized by modern Muslim thinkers to present an Islam quite different from what the radical Islamists advance. In addition to a centuries-old tradition of political quietism, there is the venerable Muslim resistance to permitting government to impose religious doctrine. Political quietism is, admittedly, not a very solid foundation on which to build a political ideology in today's world. Modern developments (such as growing economic interdependence, the imposing increase in literacy, the communications revolution . . .) require greater organization and group interaction, not a loosely structured pattern of individuals and groups opting out. The strong and centralized state is as necessary as is an engaged citizenry if people are to avoid the harsh penalties imposed on underdeveloped economies. Still, a certain skepticism about government matched by resistance to governmental efforts to control religion are well represented in the Muslim tradition. All this can be drawn on for present-day purposes.

More generally, alongside the great emphasis on the community (*umma*) is the deep-seated sense that the individual's Islamic credentials are to be judged by God alone, not by other men, even less by government. Thus, as compared with the history of Christendom, there have been in Islam few heresy trials, nothing quite like excommunication or anathema and not nearly so many intra-Muslim religious wars. This tolerant legacy could also be woven into a political program quite different from that of the fundamentalists.

This, in turn, relates to those Islamists as well as some Western scholars who assert there is not—cannot be—any separation between religion and the state in Islam. To say this is to ignore much of what has actually happened throughout Islamic history. There are, in any case, many varieties of separation, and of integration, between religion and the state. Admittedly, the possible liberal Muslim response to fundamentalists is unlikely to take as a model the constitutionally mandated secular state found in the United States. Still, the Islamic legacy of resisting governmental efforts to impose religious doctrine—far more effectively than in the Christian West—surely offers a useful building block for a distinctive Muslim mode of shielding religious faith and practice from the clutches of political power.

Several observers dismiss such prospects for a liberal challenge to the Islamists by maintaining that all Muslims are at least potentially fundamentalists and thus will ever be attracted to the message of the Islamists. All Muslims, so this line of argument goes, are necessarily scriptural literalists, because the divine, uncreated nature of the Qur'an is an article of faith held by all from the most latitudinarian to the strictest Islamist. That being the case, the literal injunctions found in the Qur'an (e.g., the *hadd* punishments of amputation for stealing, stoning for adultery, or the acceptance of polygyny) cannot be set aside. Well, yes, the Muslim equivalent of the Reformation's *sola scriptura* can raise problems, but the ingenuity of political theorists and theologians, past and present, suggests that this problem has been resolved in the past and can be in the future. After all, "revelation is not God's word. Revelation is God's word in human words, and that is where the mess begins."[1]

Ironically, but ultimately offering some hope for all who harbor reservations concerning fundamentalists whether Muslims, Christians, or Jews, these scriptural literalist dreams are best broken up in the bright morning light of efforts to implement the proposed utopia. The Islamic Revolution is still alive and well in Iran after two decades, but in the eyes of Iranians and others it has necessarily been brought down from dream to reality.[2] Even more, the shaky performance of the Islamist government in Sudan or the earlier regime of Pakistan's General Zia gives fundamentalist government a very human face, warts and all.

Finally, all the world—and no part more than the Muslim world—confronts rapid vertiginous change. For Muslims, yesterday's colonial rule, today's poor performance in competing with or confronting the West, the shaky institutionalization of existing states, the stark divide between rich and poor, the massive demographic changes, and the great increase of political awareness and social expectations brought by massive increases in education set alongside a reality that frustrates this newly gained competence— all conspire to guarantee both disorientation and collective angst. The working out of problems Muslims face today will not be easy. Even a cursory look at revolutionary periods, past and present, Muslim and non-Muslim, indicates that a degree of violence and outrage (as the terrorist attacks) is, unfortunately, inescapable. With careful planning and good luck it can possibly be minimized.

How might that be done? The scholarly debate describing contemporary Muslim states and societies and predicting future developments has produced a spectrum of options. At one end are those insisting that Islam is the major factor explaining the situation of today's Muslims. Islam has so thoroughly molded them that they must be analyzed by different criteria. Islam is sui generis.

At the other end of the spectrum are found those maintaining that basic political, economic, and social factors—such as are found in all societies— account for the problems and the prospects of today's Muslim world. If the reality of daily life in these Muslim countries were more sanguine and secure, the Islamists would have scarcely a following.

When the spectrum of possible explanations is presented that baldly, the judicious would place themselves somewhere in between those two extremes. Fair enough, but at what point? As with all studies of society, past and present, giving the correct weight to the quantifiable and the material as opposed to the ideological and psychological is a challenge. This book, while concentrating almost exclusively on the "Islamic factor," adopts a position much closer to those who would insist that Muslims are very much like other people. Islam is not sui generis.

At the same time, certain differences clearly distinguish Islam and Muslims from other religions and peoples. Islam is not, as the fundamentalist would have it, "the solution," but Islam is very much a part of whatever solutions Muslim societies choose. This book has sought to identify the distinctive Muslim approach to politics, past and present, even while keeping in mind that we "are all from Adam."[3]

Notes

Introduction

1. The standard Arabic transliteration is *qismah* or *qismat* in combining form. Interestingly, the word appears only three times in the Qur'an and never in the sense of fate. Two verbal forms come closer to that meaning: 15:43–44 where the seven gates of hell have, each, their apportioned lot and 43:32 where God, blaming those who would "apportion" His mercy, proclaims that He has apportioned ranks in this world. Moreover, "God's mercy is better than worldly wealth."

2. *Maktub*, as such, appears just once in the Qur'an, but *kitab* (the Book, i.e., the Qur'an) and other forms of the k-t-b root conveying the ideas of what is written in the sense of being prescribed provide one of the most prominent Qur'anic motifs.

3. The Persian word is *gharbzadegi*, which was the title of an influential short book written in the early 1960s by the Iranian social critic Jalal Al-e Ahmad. *Gharbzadegi* soon became one of the preferred watchwords used against the Pahlavi regime in Iran. Ironically, Jalal Al-e Ahmad and many other opponents of Muhammad Riza Shah who bandied the word "Westoxification" were themselves quite "Westernized," especially so when set alongside the mullahs who seized control in 1979.

4. An oft-cited slogan that has rather convincingly been shown to have been coined no earlier than the late nineteenth century.

5. Qur'an 2:143: "We have appointed you a community of the middle way, so that you might be witness before all mankind." This is the translation of Abu A'la Mawdudi, who figures prominently later in this book as a leading Islamist.

He is not usually thought to be flexible or moderate. Yet, his commentary on that verse, while giving Muslims a leadership role in the world (but not unlike the Christian "light for revelation to the Gentiles and for glory to thy people Israel," Luke 2:32), adds this touching sentence, "What is expected of this community is that it should be able to make known, both by word and deed, the meaning of godliness and righteousness, of equity and fair play." *Towards Understanding the Qur'an*, vol. 1 (Surahs 1–3), English version of Mawdudi's *Tafhim al-Qur'an*, pp. 120–121. Caution in classifying the good and the bad (from whatever perspective) in religio-political confrontations is advisable.

1. Setting the Stage: Islam and Muslims

1. These estimates and those in the following three paragraphs are taken (rounded) from the table on p. 315 of the 1999 *Encyclopaedia Britannica Book of the Year*.

2. For the 1994 pilgrimage season, for example, roughly 2.5 million Muslims are reported to have come. *Encyclopaedia Britannica Book of the Year*, 1995, p. 274.

3. Estimates a few decades ago usually advanced a 90 percent/10 percent Sunni-Shi'a split. It can be speculated that the number of Shi'a in countries of majority Sunni populations, or of non-Shi'a political control (e.g., Iraq or Lebanon), were often underreported and that present estimates are more accurate. Neither conversions to Shi'ism nor significant birth rate differentials would appear to be a factor. High birth rates among Shi'a (as in Lebanon) are more than matched globally by high or even higher birth rates among Sunnis (as in Jordan). A cautionary note on all such speculation: most of the essential demographic and quantitative research and analysis on such issues remains to be accomplished.

4. It was the Fatimids who founded Cairo (*Al-Qahira*, "the victorious," in Arabic) in 969 C.E. and soon thereafter built the celebrated al-Azhar mosque-university. After the end of Fatimid rule (definitely achieved two centuries later in 1169) and Egypt's return to Sunnism, al-Azhar became and has remained the most famous Sunni religious seminary in the world.

5. Egyptian President Anwar al-Sadat labeled his Muslim fundamentalist opponents Kharijites, perhaps an appropriate tag for those uncompromising, puritanical religious radicals whose tactic of assassination later extended to the president himself. Sadat's evoking the name of this earliest of Muslim schisms, the Kharijites, also underscores how very important the early history of Islam remains in today's political lexicon.

6. One might add, for example, the Ahmadiyya movement in the Indian subcontinent, named after Hazrat Mirza Ghulam Ahmad (d. 1908), who is seen as

the promised mahdi or messiah. They consider themselves to be Muslim but are not so regarded by many Muslims and have suffered considerable political oppression in Pakistan. Another example is the American Black Muslim movement, which in its origins was demonstrably a syncretist religion, but in the intervening years many have come to embrace "orthodox" Sunni Islam. Such was the case with the late Malcolm X.

2. Islam, Judaism, and Christianity in Comparative Perspective: An Overview

1. Bowles, *The Spider's House*, p. 6. Bowles, alas, is not usually "right on target" about Moroccans or Muslims. In most of his fiction they are presented as the "Other" who are just not like us. See Coury, "Paul Bowles and Orientalism."

2. Hodgson is author of the monumental three-volume *The Venture of Islam*.

3. In recent years it has become chic in certain circles to deny the possibility of value-free scholarship. Of course, value-free scholarship is a goal that can only be approximated, never achieved. It is a methodological convention, but one that enhances cross-cultural communication.

4. Crone, "Islam, Judeo-Christianity, and Byzantine Iconoclasm," *Jerusalem Studies in Arabic and Islam*, p. 63.

5. Seyyed Hossein Nasr, "Comments on a Few Theological Issues," p. 463.

6. Hodgson, "A Comparison of Islam and Christianity," pp. 56–60.

7. And yet there is something of the deathbed conversion syndrome deep in Christian culture. Remember Mistress Quickly in reporting the last mortal moments of Shakespeare's classic rogue, Falstaff: "So a' cried out 'God, God, God!' three or four times: now I, to comfort him, bid him a' should not think of God. I hoped there was no need to trouble himself with any such thoughts yet." *Henry V*, 2.3.9.

8. Hashmi, "Interpreting the Islamic Ethics of War and Peace," pp. 164–165. A useful compilation is Peters's *Jihad in Classical and Modern Islam: A Reader*.

9. Perhaps even more than in Judaism with such images as "The lord is my shepherd" (23d Psalm)?

10. In traditional pious formulations of the majority Sunnis, Islam's golden age came to a close after the time of the "four rightly guided caliphs" who immediately succeeded Muhammad (the minority Shi'is maintain that the fourth caliph, Ali, should have immediately assumed the caliphate followed thereafter by his descendants). Thereafter, under the Umayyads, came *mulk* (kingship) and a falling away from Islamic political virtues. In any case, whether the early Muslim community was to remain centered in Arabia was never the issue. The fourth caliph and Muhammad's son-in-law, Ali, had already moved to Basra in Iraq. Even if Ali had won the civil war rather than Mu'awiya, the

founder of the Umayyad dynasty, the political center of gravity would have left Arabia, not to return.

11. The singular is *faqih*, a term brought to Western attention by the Ayatullah Khomeini, who insisted that a religiously learned individual, the *faqih*, should serve as principal guide to the conduct of government among Muslims. This was *wilayat al-faqih*, or, in Persian transliteration, *velayat-e faqih*, which is the stewardship or guardianship exercised by one learned in Islam. In its comprehensiveness and legalistic rigor the Khomeini ideal is reminiscent of John Calvin's plans for Geneva.

3. Muslim "Church Government"

1. The Sufi brotherhood leaders (shaykkhs or *pirs* or *babas* . . .), as noted in the previous chapter, are religious specialists in a different sense, being guides to a more gnostic approach to God. As such, they run the gamut from learned intellectuals to uneducated "seers."

2. It was technically only a military occupation from 1882 until 1914 when Britain declared a protectorate. These nuances, important for diplomatic history, can be disregarded here. More important for our subject was the option that Abduh represented of cooperation with foreign non-Muslim power in the conviction that this policy, rather than active or even passive resistance, would best serve the long-term interests of Egypt and of Islam.

3. Followers of this doctrine reject the label *Wahhabi* as implying a partial transfer to a mere mortal of the veneration due exclusively to God. They use, instead the term *Muwahhidun*, which translates literally as "unitarians" (i.e., accepting the oneness of God), but given the theologically liberal sense of *Unitarian* in the Christian context that translation would occasion different misunderstandings.

4. Note the parallel with English constitutional history: Trevelyan in his *History of England* writes, "James and Charles held, with the students of Roman Law, that the will of the Prince was the source of law, and that the Judges were 'lions under the throne,' bound to speak, as he directed them. (Sir Edward) Coke, on the other hand, in the spirit of the English Common Law, conceived of law as having an independent existence of its own, set above the King as well as his subjects." Richard H. Nolte, after citing Trevelyan, added, "To borrow Coke's metaphor, the ruler in classical Islam had lions under the throne in the form of his Islamic law judges. But he could not command them. He could leash them and unleash them, but they listened to the command of the sacred law, which was beyond his control." Nolte, "The Rule of Law in the Arab Middle East." Writing at a time when secularization seemed unstoppable and the ulama in full retreat, Nolte continued that the modern Middle Eastern ruler "has equipped

himself with powerful new lions borrowed from the West who are fully subservient to his command and has also asserted his control over the sacred law
itself." This interpretation from the 1950s offers a stimulating backdrop to the
different situation Middle East political authority confronts today.

5. Ibn Khaldun (1332–1406) was author of the justly celebrated philosophy
of history that has been translated in its entirety by Franz Rosenthal, *The
Muqaddimah*. A convenient selection of short passages illustrating Ibn
Khaldun's principal ideas is *An Arab Philosophy of History* translated and
arranged by Charles Issawi.

6. An apparent exception was the action of the Egyptian Higher Committee
of al-Azhar ulama in 1925 against Shaykh Ali Abd al-Raziq, whose celebrated
book, *Al-Islam wa Usul al-Hukm*, argued for separation of religion and state.
They voted to expel him from the ranks of Azhar ulama and to deprive him of
his judgeship. They were acting as a "church," but this was no "church-state"
confrontation. King Fuad and the Azhari ulama were cooperating in this very
political decision. Interestingly, Abd al-Raziq's supporters argued, inter alia, that
the action resembled "religious courts in the Middle Ages" and the Egyptian
intellectual Taha Husayn insisted that the Sunni Azhari ulama were acting like
Shi'is (which is somewhat like a Baptist accusing his opponent of popery). See
Smith, *Islam and the Search for Social Order*, pp. 77–79.

7. For details on each case see Green, "A Tunisian Reply to a Wahhabi
Proclamation"; Ali Mahjoubi, *Les Origines du mouvement national en Tunisie*,
pp. 486–510; *Al-Ahram*, May 10, 1979; and *Middle East Journal* (Autumn
1960), pp. 452–453. See also the many examples cited in the article "Shaikh al-
Islam" in the *Shorter Encyclopaedia of Islam*.

8. In this treaty the Ottomans lost control over the Crimean Tatars, but article 3 stated that these Muslims should follow the Ottoman sultan "in his capacity of Grand Caliph" in religious matters. This was balanced by the Russian
claim to protect Orthodox Christian Ottoman subjects (article 7). See Hurewitz,
The Middle East and North Africa in World Politics, pp. 92–101, for the English
text of the treaty. European claims to intervene on behalf of non-Muslim subjects (a leitmotif of "Eastern Question" diplomacy, with France and Austria
vying to protect the Catholic and Uniate Christians, Britain supporting the few
Protestants, plus, interestingly, the Druze, and Russia championing the
Orthodox Christians) has as its logical corollary the Ottoman right to speak for
Muslims under non-Muslim political authority. See also pp. 108 ff., this volume.

9. See "Shaikh al-Islam," in the *Shorter Encyclopaedia of Islam*.

10. More precisely, the twelfth imam went into occultation in 874 C.E.
Thereafter, he was deemed to have contacted the Shi'i community by means
of a representative or agent (*wakil*) who upon his death was replaced by
another *wakil*. The fourth wakil announced just before his death in 941 that
henceforth the imam would not communicate with the community through

human mediation until his return as the mahdi. Shi'is call the period from 874 to 940 the lesser occultation (*al-ghayba al-sughra*). Thereafter, the Shi'a community has been living in the period of greater occultation (*al-ghayba al-kubra*).

11. Unlike the various groups stemming from Sevener or Ismaili Shi'ism, who were politically active. Thus, the Fatimid challenge to the Abbasid caliphate and the Fatimid offshoot that became the Druze community.

12. *Akhbar* (sing. *khabar*) is identical to *hadith* (pl. *ahadith*) as used in Sunni Islam. Both Sunnis and Shi'is use maxims and sayings from the Prophet and from those living during the Muslim patristic age, but their collections of such material to guide the faithful differ somewhat. In Shi'ism the tracing of *akhbar* to Ali and the imams predominates.

13. Cole, "Imami Jurisprudence and the Role of the Ulama," p. 40.

14. Arjomand, *The Shadow of God and the Hidden Imam*, p. 265.

15. In 1890 the Shah granted a British subject a monopoly over the production, sale, and export of all tobacco. Dismay from within Iran at this sellout to foreign control and an appeal from Jamal al-Din al-Afghani (recently deported from Iran), in neighboring Iraq, ignited action. The order of the leading Shi'i 'alim of the day, Hajj Mirza Hasan Shirazi, to boycott all use of tobacco forced the Iranian government to cancel the concession. See Keddie, *Roots of Revolution*, pp. 66–67, plus the same author's *Sayyid Jamal ad-Din "al-Afghani,"* chapter 12: "The Tobacco Protest of 1891–1892." The classic study of the constitutional revolutionary period in Iran is Browne, *The Persian Revolution of 1905–1910*. A summary account is given in *Roots of Revolution*. Note also chapter 2, "The Constitutional Revolution," in Abrahamian, *Iran Between Two Revolutions*.

16. In a short introduction to his translation of Khomeini's writings and declarations, Hamid Algar observed that Khomeini was called "imam" and not "ayatullah" in Iranian usage, adding, "The title 'Ayatullah' in Shi'i Islam is generally bestowed on high-ranking religious scholars, and has also been applied to Imam Khomeini. However, since his role has been unique among the religious scholars of Iran and has exceeded what is implied in the title 'Ayatullah,' he has received the designation of Imam in recent years. It is important to note that the word *imam* applied to Khomeini has its general and original sense of leader, and not the particular and technical sense it has acquired when applied to the Twelve Imams believed by Shi'i Muslims to be the successors of the Prophet." Algar buttresses the distinction between the two uses of "imam" by two citations from Khomeini's celebrated *Islamic Government*. See *Islam and Revolution*, p. 10. There is every reason to accept that Khomeini, precise Islamic scholar that he was, intended just such a distinction to be made. He was not presuming to be *the* imam returning from his long occultation. Even so, given the apocalyptic atmosphere prevailing in Iran during the period that brought down the shah and created the Islamic Republic, and given the charismatic quality of Khomeini's

leadership, the two meanings of *imam* may well have become somewhat con-
flated in the popular mind.

4. The Historical Bases of Traditional Muslim and Christian Political Theory

1. Lest this very worldly interpretation and the use of the lowercase *he* in
speaking of Jesus appear abusive to (my fellow) Christians, let me explain that
it stems from an effort to study human history in strictly human terms without
reference to divine purpose or divine intervention, always differently understood in different religions. The different religions and their relations to politics
and history can and should be studied comparatively, but not from the dogmat-
ics of any particular religion. Scholarship is necessarily earthbound. Religious
faith is something else.

2. The historical development among Orthodox and Eastern churches was
different, but since the Western experience in the long run has had a decidedly
greater *political* impact on the world it seems appropriate to discuss just the
two—Western Christendom and the Muslim umma for comparison.

3. Exceptions that test the rule are the Kharijites during the time of the early
Muslim community and the *Takfir wa al-Hijra* movement in modern Egypt.

4. Abd al-Raziq, *Al-Islam wa Usul al-Hukm*. Khalid, *Min Huna Nabda*.

5. That is, the tradition of deriving political theories from an examination of
how humans actually behave rather than how they ought to behave. As Francis
Bacon insisted, "We are much beholden to Machiavel and others, that write what
men do, and not what they ought to do."

6. Luther, *Secular Authority*, 3:237.

5. Unity and Community

1. Even the Shi'a community had reached this point by 869 C.E. with the
ghayba of the twelfth imam. Thereafter, Twelver Shi'ism, like Sunnism, could
avoid the political problems that come with a divinely guided leader present in
this world. Ismaili or Sevener Shi'ism took a different development, as seen in
the messianic religio-political movement of the Fatimids or, for that matter, the
position of the Agha Khan among present-day Ismailis.

2. Qur'an 4:59

3. Al-Suhrawardi, *Kitab Adab al-Muridin*, p. 29.

4. Ibn Jama'a, *Tahrir al-Ahkam fii Tadbir Ahl al-Islam*, p. 357: "Jurists in
Morocco have summed up the rule in the brief maxim: 'To him who holds power
obedience is given.' " Santillana, "Law and Society," p. 303.

5. For example, the Westernizing Tunisian statesman, Khayr al-Din al-Tunisi, cited this as part of his argument for constitutionalism. See *The Surest Path*, p. 83.

6. Abu Yusuf, *Kitab al-Kharaj*, extracted and translated by Lewis, *Islam from the Prophet Muhammad*, p. 161.

7. Ibn Batta, *Kitab al-Sharh wa al-Ibana 'ala Usul al-Sunna wa al-Diyana*, cited in Lewis, *Islam from the Prophet Muhammad* p. 171.

8. Cahen, "The Body Politic," p. 157.

9. Arguing, as I do, for a greater cultural uniformity among the world's Muslims than among Christians requires careful footwork lest I contribute to the Western penchant for depicting Islamic civilization as a monotony that scarcely changes in time or place. A good antidote to such "essentializing" of Islam is Clifford Geertz's classic *Islam Observed*. The conclusions presented in *Two Worlds of Islam* by von der Mehden should also be mentioned. Still, I would emphasize—even while accepting the elusiveness of accurate measurement—the striking degree of shared cultural values and mores by Muslim world as compared with Christians.

10. Quran 3:103–104, 3:110, and 2:143.

11. The first, third, and fifth of these hadiths are from the *Sahih* of Muslim, the second from *Mishkat al-Masabih*, and the fourth from *Sunan al-Tirmidhi*. As an indication of the extent to which such hadiths are still very much part of the living political tradition, all five were cited by the well-known Pakistani fundamentalist Abu al-A'la al-Mawdudi in his booklet *Al-Da'watu al-Qawmiyya wa al-Rabita al-Islamiyya* (The Ideology of Nationalism and the Islamic Tie).

6. The Roots of Political Pessimism

1. H. A. R. Gibb, "An Interpretation of Islamic History," in Gibb, *Studies on the Civilization of Islam*, p. 22.

2. Wittfogel, *Oriental Despotism*.

3. Weber, *The Theory of Social and Economic Organization*, p. 347.

4. Cited in Turner, *Weber and Islam*, p. 77. This book as well as Turner's *Marx and the End of Orientalism* offer useful discussion of this general subject.

5. "For the greater part of the Middle Ages and over most of its area, the West formed a society primarily agrarian, feudal, and monastic, at a time when the strength of Islam lay in its great cities, wealthy courts, and long lines of communication." Southern, *Western Views of Islam in the Middle Ages*, p. 7. Southern continues, illuminating a comparative point we have discussed earlier: "To Western ideals essentially celibate, sacerdotal, and hierarchical, Islam opposed the outlook of a laity frankly indulgent and sensual, in principle egali-

tarian, enjoying a remarkable freedom of speculation, with no priests and no monasteries built into the basic structure of society as they were in the West."

6. Levi-Provençal, *Conferences sur l'Espagne Musulmane*, p. 90.

7. This view is forcefully presented in chapter 3, "Ethnicity, Social Class, and the Mosaic Model" of Turner's *Marx and the End of Orientalism*.

8. "Kitab al-Imara," *Sahih Muslim*, 3:1033. In another hadith Muhammad is reported to have said, "There will be leaders who will not be led by my guidance and who will not adopt my ways. There will be among them men who will have the heart of devils in bodies of human beings." When asked what should the believers then do, the Prophet answered, "You will listen to the amir and carry out his orders, even if your back is flogged and your wealth is snatched you should listen and obey." Ibid., p. 1029.

7. *Muslim Attitudes Toward the State: An Impressionist Sketch*

1. Grafftey-Smith, *Bright Levant*, p. 67.

2. A part of the oral tradition from Ottoman days that Geoffrey Lewis recalls having first heard many years ago from a Turkish elder who grew up during the last decades of the Ottoman Empire. The same sense of remoteness from government is also conveyed throughout Ivo Andric's celebrated novel, *The Bridge on the Drina*. For example, Ottoman grand vizier Mehmed Sokolli ordered the building of a bridge over the river in his native Bosnia. At first viewed as a boon by all the villagers, Muslims and Christians, the disorder caused by the actual building of the bridge brought second thoughts. As for the Muslims, "It was a fine thing, they thought, to belong to the pure ruling faith; it was a fine thing, to have as a countryman the Vezir in Stambul, and still finer to imagine the strong, costly bridge across the river . . . (but) their town had been turned into a hell." Indeed, they "in private among themselves, avowed that they were fed up to the teeth with lordship and pride and future glory and had had more than enough of the bridge and the Vezir. They only prayed Allah to deliver them from this disaster." The Christians felt the same, but "no one asked their opinion about anything." Andric, *The Bridge on the Drina*, pp. 31–32.

3. In addition to Andric's *The Bridge on the Drina*, note the following passage from Eric Ambler's *Judgment on Deltchev*, p. 57:

" 'Did you notice our wall?'

'It's very fine.'

'You will see such walls round most of our houses. In Bulgaria, and in Greece, in Yugoslavia, in all the countries of Europe that lived with Turkish rule it is the same. To put a wall around your house then was not only to put up a barrier against the casual violence of foreign soldiers, it was a way to deny their existence. Then our people lived behind their walls in small worlds of illusion that did not include the Ottoman Empire.' "

Although these two novels are set in the Balkans—which did have appreciable Muslim minorities—the interaction with political authority would hold for Ottoman Afro-Asia as well. Nor was such blocking out of the state and the public more characteristic of non-Muslims. Indeed, the penchant for privacy was more in evidence among Muslims.

4. Munif al-Razzaz, *Ma'alim al-Hayat al-'Arabiyya al-Jadida*, 3d ed. (Beirut, 1956), as cited in Vatikiotis, *The Egyptian Army in Politics*, p. 245. Note also the following:

"Throughout the Arab world the citizen has only a narrow choice: obedience or submission. He ends up regarding the state and its representatives as a sort of fate that enchains him and lies in wait for him or fills and satifies him." Masmoudi, *Les Arabes dans le Tempete*, p. 77.

5. Gamal Abdel Nasser, *Egypt's Liberation*, p. 65. It is now generally accepted that Nasser's friend, the journalist Mohamed Heikal, actually wrote the book. This does not, however, detract from the value of the book as a portrait of the Nasserist self-image.

6. Pellissier de Reynaud, *Description de la Regence de Tunis*, p. 45.

7. Adapted from the translation from al-Jabarti that appears in Gibb and Bowen, *Islamic Society and the West*, p. 205.

8. Batatu, *Syria's Peasantry*, p. 112.

9. Ibn Abi Diyaf, *Ithaf Ahl al-Zaman fi Akhbar Muluk Tunis wa 'Ahd al-Aman*, 2:172–173.

10. Lybyer, *The Government of the Ottoman Empire*.

11. A clear, short statement of these major modifications of the Lybyer thesis is chapter 2, "Ottoman Society and Institutions," in Itzkowitz, *Ottoman Empire and Islamic Tradition*. For a cogent review of this historiographical dispute concerning the nature of the Ottoman state, with a convincing resolution of the issue, see chapter 1 in Findley, *Bureaucratic Reform in the Ottoman Empire*, especially pp. 44–58.

12. Ismail Urbain, in the French official publication *Tableau de la situation des Etablissements francais dans l'Algerie*, published in the late 1830s and 1840s. Cited in Boyer, *L'Evolution de l'Algerie mediane*, p. 49.

13. Cited in Charles-Andre Julien, *Les Techniciens de la colonisation*, p. 65.

14. Note the following example of modern political thinking: "When Mr. Gladstone was making up to the Irish and Cromwell was mowing them down, they were both applying democratic diplomacy. They recognized that a subject race must ultimately either be enfranchised or enslaved, and they faced the facts accordingly." Young, *Diplomacy Old and New*, p. 18. In a traditional bureaucratic empire, on the other hand, the subjects are neither enfranchised nor enslaved, but controlled, more or less, in a strictly limited arena of governmental activity.

8. Islam and Politics in Modern Times: The Great Transformation

1. *Jahiliyya* in traditional Muslim theology was the historical period prior to mankind's receiving God's final revelation, the Qur'an (the seal of prophecy), through the instrumentality of Muhammad. It has been adapted by Muslim radicals to designate the status of those deemed to have so fallen away from Islamic belief and practice as to lose their status as Muslims. This significant reworking of a venerable Islamic term, *jahiliyya*, was first advanced by the Indian (later Pakistani) Abu al-A'la Mawdudi as long ago as the 1930s and developed in the l950s and 1960s by the Egyptian Sayyid Qutb.

2. Karl Marx, *The Eighteenth Brumaire of Louis Bonaparte* in Tucker, *The Marx-Engels Reader*, p. 437. Marx continued, "Thus Luther donned the mask of the Apostle Paul." Comparisons between the thoughts and actions in today's Muslim world and those of the Reformation in Europe will be developed later. Marx's reference to "costume" is especially apt in the light of attention among Muslims today to such matters as beards and "Islamic dress."

3. The two classic battles that sealed Muslim success took place at Yarmuk (636 against the Byzantines) and Qadisiyya (637 against the Sassanids) and occurred within the first five years following the death of Muhammad. Both battles have figured often in later religio-political symbolism. During the Iraq-Iran War (1980–1988), for example, Saddam Husayn's regime depicting Iraq as the legatee of both Arabism versus Persia and Islam versus Manichaeanism.

4. The Mongol onslaught was finally halted by the Mamluks of Egypt, under Baybars, at the Battle of Ain Jalut in 1260. Ain Jalut is thus a powerful symbol that can be used to good effect by contemporary Egyptian leadership, even though scholarly purists could protest that the Mamluks were scarcely "Egyptian." It is related that Baybars restored the Abbasid caliphate, bringing to Cairo a surviving family member who was given the throne title of *al-Mustansir lil-Allah*.

5. A partial exception, certain Ottoman ideas of statecraft can be traced to Mongol influence, but, then, the original Ottomans were themselves nomadic warriors from Inner Asia.

6. The tendency in all religions is to make the period of origins paradigmatic and ahistorical. The scientific study of religions needs to both understand the importance of "golden ageism" in a religion and probe the worldly reality of what actually transpired. Thus, it is not surprising—and certainly not a derogation of Islam—to point out that three of the four "rightly guided caliphs" met a violent death. Similar stresses and strains can be identified in other religions, certainly in Judaism and Christianity.

7. The mutineers from various army units, after having captured Delhi in 1857, declared Bahadur emperor of all India. With the suppression of the mutiny in the following year, the last Moghul emperor's fate was sealed. That, however,

was already a foregone conclusion. Moghul emperors had ceased to appear on Indian coinage in the 1820s and even before the Sepoy Rebellion Bahadur had been informed by the British that he was to be the last emperor. In 1858 the British government assumed direct control over India, taking over from the East India Company.

8. Texts and commentaries of the two treaties are in Hurewitz, *The Middle East and North Africa in World Politics*, pp. 197–199, 231–237.

9. Text and commentary ibid., pp. 92–101.

10. Generally successful from the European perspective except for the Crimean War. Not at all a success story when viewed through the lens of Ottoman or Middle Eastern history.

11. In my *International Politics and the Middle East* I argue that the confrontation between the dominant Western state system and the vulnerable Ottoman system, beginning some two centuries ago, has produced a distinctive "diplomatic culture" that, surviving the death of the Ottoman Empire, continues to this day.

12. Southeast Asia includes, it is true, the Muslim states of Indonesia and Malaysia plus tiny Brunei. Yet, ironically, for the latter two the major domestic issue is the Muslim majority's perception that the non-Muslim minority (mainly Chinese) is too dominant in business, the professions, and administration. Indonesia, with an encouraging economic performance—not lacking in ups and downs, however—in recent decades remains in the group of "low-income economies," ahead of China and India and just below Egypt. See World Bank, *World Development Report* (1992) "Table I: Basic Indicators," p. 218.

9. Meeting the Western Challenge: The Early Establishment Response

1. Akbar was one of the rare Muslim rulers of an established dynasty (not a challenger in the process of establishing a dynasty as with the Abbasids, Fatimids, Safavids, and others) who sought to impose religious doctrine. His plans came to naught. A later Moghul emperor, Aurangzib (1618–1707, r. 1658–1707) went to the other extreme and attempted to impose an austere Sunni Islam, alienating Shi'is and actively persecuting Hindus and Sikhs. His actions, following the earlier flip-flops of Moghul religious policy, contributed to the dynasty's rapid decline following his reign. Given the minority status of Muslims throughout the Moghul Empire, a de facto secularism, bestowing religious and communal autonomy to India's diverse population, offered the best prospect of holding things together.

2. Several general studies of the entire Muslim world in modern times can be

recommended: the appropriate chapters treating the last two centuries in the two-volume *Cambridge History of Islam* and in Lapidus, *A History of Islamic Societies*, plus volume 3, "The Gunpowder Empires and Modern Times," in Hodgson's three volume *The Venture of Islam*. Not quite so comprehensive but readable and reliable is Mortimer, *Faith and Power*. Among the classic interpretations of Islam and Muslims in the modern period, but with scant historical narrative, are Gibb, *Modern Trends in Islam*, and Smith, *Islam in Modern History*. All are available in later paperback editions.

3. The last vestige of Ottoman Turkish rule in Algeria was represented by Ahmad Bey, who held out in Constantine until 1837. Interestingly, French military authorities soon came to realize that their conquest of Algeria would have been easier had they chosen to co-opt rather than banish the Ottoman Turks.

4. Ibn Abi Diyaf (Bin Diyaf), *Ithaf*, 3:182–183. Other examples are cited in chapter 7, "The Encroaching Outside World," of my *The Tunisia of Ahmad Bey*.

5. The imagery of a "game" deftly captures a significant aspect of the British—and, in general, Western—mindset during the heyday of European imperialism. Didn't the Duke of Wellington assert that "the battle of Waterloo was won on the playing fields of Eton"? To this should be added the impact of Thomas Arnold, headmaster of Rugby, on British imperial thinking. Much later, in this century, a friend of mine who grew up in Egypt and worked in Sudan in the period immediately before and after Sudanese independence in 1956 labeled the British officers of the elite Sudan Political Service "Boy Scouts who never grew up." The Muslims, however, living in these territories of the "great game" and the later cold war saw it differently. They were at best very subordinate players and at worst no more than the playing field.

6. Colonial and imperial historiography is filled with (usually pejorative) accounts of divide-and-rule tactics employed by the dominant powers. That the weaker powers just as often adopt the opposite tactic is often overlooked. To ignore this ongoing dialectic is to view modern history too much in terms of a dynamic West and a largely inert non-West—ironically, just what those of adamant anticolonialist orientation most seek to transcend.

7. On "defensive modernization" see Black, *The Dynamics of Modernization*, pp. 119–123. See also Black and Brown, *Modernization in the Middle East*.

8. My translation, with introduction and commentary, *The Surest Path*, is of the *Muqaddima* (or "introduction"), which amounts to a scant 110 pages in English. The *Muqaddima* is followed by what can properly be described as a textbook on comparative governments and societies treating twenty-one different European countries, 366 pages in the original Arabic.

9. An earlier English translation was later discovered by the Tunisian historian Moncef Chenoufi, but since this translation was not cited by any contempo-

rary or later sources known to me it must be assumed that only the Arabic original plus the French and Turkish translations reached a significant readership.

10. Sadiqi College, actually a secondary school, almost died of neglect after Khayr al-Din's dismissal but was resusitated and became the flagship of the bilingual, bicultural "Franco-arabe" educational system installed during the French Protectorate period (1881–1956). Eight of the eleven members of an early postindependence Tunisian cabinet, for example, were Sadiqi alumni. A thorough study of this one school that played such a major role in modern Tunisian history is Sraieb, *Le College Sadiki de Tunis.*

11. Two good biographies exist: Troll, *Sayyid Ahmad Khan*, and Malik, *Sir Sayyid Ahmad Khan.* See also Smith, *Modern Islam in India*, especially pp. 8–26. This book offers a sound presentation of the several Indian Muslim orientations in modern times.

12. Cited in Malik, *Sir Sayyid Ahmad Khan* p. 96.

13. This assertion, defensible as a general guideline, does require some modification. First, it is inaccurate to write of the ulama as a monolith (the same could be said for the Christian clergy or other religious specialists). There were "establishment ulama" holding high position and generally supporting government. At the other end of the ulama spectrum were Muslim equivalents of the poor parish priest often of limited formal education and identifying with the needs and lifestyles of those they served. Second, the former group were, in the Ottoman context, virtually members of the ruling group. As such, some of them became involved quite early in the Westernizing activities. Even so, for the establishment ulama to support government was consistent with traditional behavior and did not necessarily indicate conversion to Westernization. See the pioneering article by Heyd, "The Ottoman Ulema and Westernization."

14. He used the rubric *al-Afghani* as part of his false claim of having been born in Afghanistan and raised as a Sunni Muslim, for he was intent on being an effective political activist in Sunni circles. It is now clearly established that he was born into a Shi'i family in Iran.

15. Unrelenting in his attacks on Sir Sayyid Ahmad Khan, seeing him as simply a tool of British imperialism, Afghani was, however, was no religious mossback. Most of his ideas were radical and modernist, often shockingly so in the context of the times. Yet in attacking Sir Sayyid Ahmad Khan's pro-British modernism Afghani used many traditionalist themes. This is but one more aspect of the convoluted Afghani legend resulting in later traditionalists, secular nationalists, and others all claiming him as their own.

16. Haim, *Arab Nationalism*, p. 18.

17. *Shura* appears just once, in the Qur'an 42:36 (*wa 'amruhum shura—their affair being counsel between them*). The verbal form—to take counsel—

also appears just once, in Qur'an 3:159. Such is often the case with scriptural proof texts. Witness the major role played in Christian political thought by the one verse, Matthew 22:21: "Render therefore to Caesar the things that are Caesar's and unto God the things that are God's." Traditional Islamic political thought did enjoin rulers to consult with community leaders who were, in turn, expected to offer advice. Still, "there was no clear idea *who* exactly should be consulted and should warn, and how far the ruler should be bound by what they said." Hourani, *Arabic Thought in the Liberal Age*, p. 6.

18. See, for example, the perceptive article by Reid, "Arabic Thought in the Liberal Age," especially pp. 550–552, a critique of Albert Hourani's classic study which—as the title indicates—emphasizes the contribution of the liberal, Weseternizing Arabs in the nineteenth century and after. Hourani, himself, in introducing his *The Emergence of the Modern Middle East*, felt that his earlier work had perhaps exaggerated the "impact of the West": "Intermingled with the movement of acceptance of new ideas were other movements, of thinkers who still lived within one or other of the ancient traditions of Islamic piety and learning and tried to preserve them. . . . Throughout the nineteenth century, the movements of thought in which social and political change was reflected had to be seen in terms not only of the tensions between 'Islam and the West,' but also of an older tension between different Muslim ideals, those of personal devotion and legal correctness." Ibid., p. xvii.

19. Including both indigenous and alien political leadership. Thus, Sayyid Ahmad Khan or Shaykh Muhammad Abduh could influence the policy of their alien colonial overlords just as Khayr al-Din al-Tunisi or the men of the Tanzimat could work within still independent governing structures.

10. The Early Antiestablishment Response to the Western Challenge

1. Involving, of course, both Hindus and Muslims.

2. This school grew out of the earlier School of Languages and Administration founded by Muhammad Ali in 1835 and first led by al-Tahtawi. Closed by Abbas in 1850, it was reopened by Ismail and then developed into a law school with a French jurist, one Vidal Pasha, as director. Vatikiotis, *The History of Egypt from Muhammad Ali to Mubarak*, p. 102.

3. See Lewis, *The Emergence of Modern Turkey*, pp. 114 and 102.

4. See Minault, "Islam and Mass Politics," pp. 170–171. She notes that the Islamic modernists (such as the graduates of Sir Sayyid Ahmad Khan's Aligarh) were at one with the conservative ulama on this issue.

5. See Ben Achour, *Categories de la Societe Tunisoise*, pp. 443–444.

6. See Shaw, *Between Old and New,* part 5, "The Triumph of Reaction," and especially pp. 378–383 and 404–405.

7. Bin Diyaf, *Ithaf,* vol. 7, biography no. 138.

8. Mahdism can usefully be compared with equivalent movements in Judaism and Christianity. See my "The Sudanese Mahdiya," especially pp. 146–149.

9. This entire period looms large in late Victorian British history. The death of General Charles "Chinese" Gordon when Khartoum fell stunned the British government, and Queen Victoria violated emerging constitutional practice by sending Prime Minister Gladstone a telegram *en clair* expressing her dismay. Then, the Anglo-Egyptian Reconquest (Britain, having occupied Egypt since 1882) led by General Kitchener had, as a very young officer, Winston Churchill, who later wrote of the campaign in his *The River War.* Later movies such as *The Four Feathers* (1939, 1978 remake) and *Khartoum* (1966 with Charlton Heston as Gordon and Lawrence Olivier as the mahdi) have kept alive the sense of exoticism and high adventure.

10. This continuing social dynamic pitting prudence against passion can shed light on the mass support throughout the Muslim world given such wildly different twentieth-century leaders—some not even religious in personal orientation or political program—as Kemal Ataturk, Ibn Saud, Ayatollah Khomeini, Nasser, and, yes, even Saddam Husayn. All, at least for a time, were viewed as standing up to the foreign oppressor. This is a very human reaction. It would be erroneous to attribute it to some characteristic of Islamic culture.

11. The best scholarly studies are Keddie, *Sayyid Jamal ad-Din "al-Afghani"* and Pakdaman, *Djamal-ed-Din Assad Abadi dit Afghani.* The classic, and controversial, depiction of Afghani (plus his early disciple, Abduh) as dissimulators is Kedourie, *Afghani and 'Abduh.* Appraisals by most Muslim writers continue to be overwhelmingly favorable. An influential earlier example was the chapter on al-Afghani is Amin's *Zu'ama al-Islah fi 'Asr al-Hadith.*

12. Keddie, "Pan-Islam as Proto-Nationalism."

13. See Shaw and Shaw, *History of the Ottoman Empire and Modern Turkey,* 2:191.

14. Article 3 of the text in Hurewitz, *The Middle East and North Africa in World Politics,* p. 94.

15. Pan-Islamic ideas were "a reaction against the Tanzimat doctrine of fusing Muslims and non-Muslims into an Ottoman nation. Only Muslims, according to Pan-Islamists, should unite to form the national basis of the Ottoman Empire under the caliph who was also head of that Empire. Even Muslims outside the Empire should rally round the caliph in their struggle for independence from European domination." Berkes, *The Development of Secularism in Turkey,* p. 267. Berkes adds that the caliph "began to appear as the actual or potential

ruler of Muslims everywhere. The caliphate was not merely a spiritual power; it was a state. Islam was not merely a religion; it was a nationality, a political community, a civilization." Ibid., p. 268.

16. The title the pope had granted Henry VIII in 1521, just thirteen years before the Act of Supremacy set in motion the creation of a national church separated from Rome.

11. From World War I to the 1960s: The Years of Muted Islamist Politics

1. Not just territorially a single political unit under French rule beginning in 1830 but an autonomous Ottoman polity since the late sixteenth century. Under nonindigenous rulers, of course, but such has been the pedigree of many states that later became nation states.

2. Somewhat surprisingly, the Berbers of Morocco and Algeria (there are only minuscule pockets of Berber speakers in Tunisia) could well have been another such group, but developments in the colonial period actually fostered reasonably good Berber-Arab relations. In simplest terms, the French "Berber policy" seeking to split the two backfired. See Gellner and Micaud, *Arabs and Berbers*.

3. Babur, a descendant of Tamerlane and founder of the celebrated Moghul dynasty, used Kabul as the base for his conquest of India. Then, in the early eighteenth century, it was invaders from Afghanistan who overthrew the Safavid dynasty in Iran.

4. Pakistan, a neologism, means "Land of the Pure" in Urdu and is said to have been popularized by Indian Muslim students in Britain during the 1930s responding especially to the appeal launched by the poet and intellectual Muhammad Iqbal for a distinctive Muslim nation. The political union of Westernized secularists and pious traditionalists is a common theme in modern nationalist movements based on religion. There are, for example, several striking points of comparison between Zionism and the movement creating Pakistan. Both leaders (Herzl and Jinnah) were secular, for both movements the basic problem concerned absorption into a larger cultural unity (assimilation for Jews, becoming a minority component in a majority Hindu state), and both succeeded because they managed to win over—almost in spite of themselves—the support of a constituency embracing more traditional religious loyalties.

5. Interestingly, the struggle of would-be modernists to implement change, which in religious terms was usually presented as going back to a pristine golden age, was often depicted in terms of youth against age. This, moreover, took

place in societies that had traditionally offered great respect to age. In Tunisia, for example, the image was that of "young Tunisians" against "old turbans."

6. "Tribalism" and "clan rule" are terms often used to mean "primitive" and not ready for "statehood." Reacting against such supercilious dismissals (often, it is true, expressed by adamant apologists for European colonial rule), scholars have perhaps glossed over the difficulty of converting such polities into nation states. So-called tribal or clan political systems have a considerable stability that is not easily overcome. Witness recent developments in Somalia and Afghanistan.

7. The last Ottoman sultan, Muhammed VI, fled from Istanbul on a British ship. His cousin, Abdulmajid, replaced him as caliph.

8. Kemal, *Nutuk*, p. 433, English translation, pp. 591–593, cited in Berkes, *The Development of Secularism in Turkey*, p. 459. The "speech," given on successive days on October 15 to 22, 1927, serves as a major statement of Ataturk's political philosophy.

9. This is convincingly argued by Minault in her *The Khilafat Movement*.

10. It has been plausibly suggested that after the 1857 Indian Mutiny and the deposition of the last Moghul emperor the Ottoman sultan, as the last significant Sunni Muslim head of state, could readily be embraced as caliph by Indian Muslims. See Landau, *The Politics of Pan-Islam*, pp. 184–185, where he also notes that the name of the sultan/caliph "was proclaimed in the Friday sermons." He adds that there is some doubt about when this practice began and implies that it may not have been all that widespread. Mention of the ruler's name in the Friday sermon is the established Muslim means of recognizing political legitimacy, and throughout the centuries dropping the name of an existing ruler has signaled revolt.

11. See Arnold J. Toynbee, "The Islamic World Since the Peace Settlement," 1:571ff. See also the solid (strongly pro-Ataturk) account in Berkes, *The Development of Secularism in Turkey*, pp. 446–460. Berkes archly dubs this Indian intervention a "gift of British diplomacy" (p. 458).

12. Ibid., pp. 458–459, and the sources cited there.

13. Text in Kramer, *Islam Assembled*, appendix 4, pp. 181–182. Kramer's book studied the evolution of the Islamic international congresses that he convincingly argues replaced the caliphate as symbol and instrument of Islamic unity. On the general subject of Pan-Islam see the thorough study with a very rich bibliography by Landau, *The Politics of Pan-Islam*.

14. The Khilafat movement had earlier (in late March, only days after Ataturk's abolition of the caliphate) cabled Egyptian prime minister Sa'd Zaghlul warning against hasty action (i.e. announcing the appointment of King Fuad). It was just the message that Zaghlul and his Wafd Party wished to hear, for they were fighting a two front nationalist struggle against 1. the British and 2. the king and his entourage. See Kedourie, "Sa'd Zaghlul and the British."

15. Shaukat Ali, the Khilafat movement leader, was still concerned about the caliphate, and his candidate was the last Ottoman caliph living in exile. This upset the Egyptian, Saudi, and Turkish governments and the Hashimites ruling in Transjordan and Iraq—one of the few issues those governments could agree on. See Kramer, *Islam Assembled*, pp. 125ff.

16. The British, reacting to pressure from Ibn Saud, would not let Sharif Husayn establish himself with his sons either in Transjordan or Iraq. When he became mortally ill he was allowed to join his son, Abdullah, amir of Transjordan, for his final months. He died on June 4, 1931, at the age of seventy-eight. See Wilson, *King Abdullah, Britain, and the Making of Jordan*, pp. 88–89.

17. Good general works on this subject include Porath, *In Search of Arab Unity*, and Pipes, *Greater Syria*. A solid monograph on the principal nationalist party pushing Fertile Crescent unity, with good analysis of that party's founder, the charismatic and mercurial Anton Sa'adeh, is Zuwiyya Yamak, *The Syrian Social Nationalist Party*.

18. Banani, *The Modernization of Iran*, p. 94.

19. Avery, *Modern Iran*, p. 275. Chapter 17, "The New Order," pp. 269–303, is a good brief account of Riza Shah's forced draft modernization program. For the Turkish equivalent (and Riza was often inspired by Ataturk) the classic account is Lewis, *The Emergence of Modern Turkey*, especially chapter 8, "The Kemalist Republic," but all of part 2, "Aspects of Change," offers a "before and after" breakdown according to different subjects. Especially relevant to the general theme of this book is chapter 12, "Religion and Culture."

20. Hardly an accurate count, for there had been no Persian monarchy from 640 C.E. (at the time of the Arabo/Islamic conquest) to 1501 (the rise of the Safavid dynasty). See Keddie, *Roots of Revolution*, p. 180. Chapters 5 through 7 offer a good narrative of the Pahlavi period.

21. Dahm, *Sukarno and the Struggle for Indonesian Independence*, p. 342.

22. See the very evocative appraisal of the Wafd in Lacouture and Lacouture, *Egypt in Transition*, in chapter 10, "The Wafd," pp. 86–96. Note also, p. 240, the following valedictory for the Wafd: "The Wafd stands for a certain mob appeal, a certain dynamic and nationalist view of the State: it stands also for parliamentarians, and free thought. It is everything that the military leaders (i.e., the Free Officers who came to power by coup in 1952) are not. . . . It is an Egypt of cafe terraces, where eloquence is more important than results, where principles count for more than effectiveness, and where there is a fairly sincere and generous basis of respect for the will of the people. It stands for freedom of the Press, questions in the House, student gatherings, congresses and back-slapping. . . . It is also a form of liberalism, a typically Egyptian tolerance in the approach to religious and racial problems."

12. The Return of Islam?

"The Return of Islam" was the title of an article by Bernard Lewis that first appeared in *Commentary* and has since been reprinted in several different collections. Lewis is among the most eminent of those insisting on the importance of Islam as a factor molding the attitudes and actions of Muslims past and present.

1. See my "Nasser and the June War." See also Parker, *The Six-Day War*, especially the introduction and chapter 1, "Origins of the Crisis."

2. For the argument that the June War did not radically change the underlying systemic structure of politics and diplomacy even in the Middle East, see my "The June 1967 War," in the volume edited by Lukacs and Battah, *The Arab-Israeli Conflict*. The opposite view is presented in the following chapter by Tibi, "Structural and Ideological Change."

3. This is after the breakaway of East Pakistan to form Bangladesh. The 1980 estimated population of Bangladesh was 88,678,000. For 1990 the figure was 109,291,000. The population increase, thus, from 1950 to 1990 for the original Pakistan (and after 1971 the remaining Pakistan plus Bangladesh) would be

1950	1960	1970	1980	1990
75.04	93.73	114.19	170.82	221.34

4. See my "Tunisia."

5. Malcolm Kerr, "Egypt," p. 173.

6. World Bank, *World Development Report* 1980, 1984. 1994, 1995. This figure, the World Bank explains, "is calculated by dividing the number of pupils enrolled in all post-secondary schools and universities by the population in the 20–24 age group." The higher education figures are not broken down by gender. Some rough adjustments have been made in producing this table. For example, the 1980 column is drawn from data given for 1981 in comparison with 1979 and other years (no figures for 1980 appearing in any *World Development Report* annual). Moreover, later year reports often modify earlier reports. The figures given in the 1990 column are in line with those given in the 1995 *Report*, which lists results for the year, 1992, with one interesting exception. The higher educational enrollment percentage for Iran is listed as double that of 1990, jumping from 6 percent to 12 percent. Tunisia's percentage rose from 9 percent to 11 percent, while Bangladesh and Turkey each rose one percent to 4 percent and 15 percent respectively.

7. Cited in Charles Issawi, "Economic Growth and Development," p. 233, and Szyliowicz, *Education and Modernization in the Middle East*, pp. 464–465 (correcting the figure for Turkey in 1945).

8. Kitchen, *The Educated African*, p. 367; *Britannica Book of the Year 1996* p. 683.

9. Mahmud Messadi in *Al-Mabahith* (October 1947). Cited in my "Tunisia," p. 158.

10. Ministry of Education, *Perspectives decennales de l'enseignement* (Tunis, c. 1958). Cited in ibid., p. 157.

11. Cited in my "Tunisia: Education, 'Cultural Unity,' and the Future," originally a report to the Institute of Current World Affairs, December 1, 1960. Reprinted in Zartman, *Man, State, and Society in the Contemporary Maghrib.*

12. The first phrase figures in the title of the book by Daniel Lerner, *The Passing of Traditional Society,* which was very influential in its day. The notion of a society being able to attain, if the right modernizing steps are taken, a "take-off" stage of economic development was advanced by W. W. Rostow. See his *The Stages of Economic Growth.*

13. Writing soon after the three countries of French North Africa had received their independence, Roger Le Tourneau (who had served in the French educational administration of all three during his long Maghribi career) described the impact of the "European ideas" in these terms: the North Africans "have experienced a bewilderment at once terrible and enervating in losing their intellectual security, of having everything again put in question even to the very foundations of their civilization, to see opening before their curiosity immense new horizons that their fathers never even suspected. . . . The old Islam of North Africa has been profoundly shaken. . . . Many Muslims of the Maghrib no longer believe as their ancestors did. . . . For many Islam is no longer a spiritual conviction but only a principle of social organization deemed superior to others." *Evolution politique de l'Afrique du Nord Musulmane,* pp. 39–40.

14. That is, 1948–1949 (the creation of Israel and the ensuing failed Arab military effort), 1956 (Suez War), 1967 (Six Day War), 1969–1970 (War of Attrition), 1973 (Ramadan or Yom Kippur War), and the 1982 Israeli invasion of Lebanon. The Suez War was a political victory for Nasser's Egypt, as was the 1973 war, being a near military victory that turned sour but a sharp demonstration to Israel and the United States that the existing "no war, no peace" status was unstable and unacceptable to the Arabs. In strictly military terms, however, all wars were Arab defeats. Perceptive Arabs realized as much.

15. The undeclared war between India and Pakistan over Kashmir (1947–1949), with India maintaining control, the short 1965 war that ended in a draw, and the decisive 1971 Indian intervention supporting East Pakistani secession and the creation of Bangladesh.

16. Afghanistan ultimately prevailed against the Soviet invasion beginning in December 1979, the last Soviet troops leaving nine years later, in February 1989. The Somalia case was quite different. Essentially, UN and U.S. efforts beginning in 1992 to provide humanitarian aid to the Somalis facing mass starvation resulting from civil war ran afoul of the continued tribal divisons. UN

losses of seventy-four and American losses of eighteen in 1993 led to with-drawals in early 1994.

13. The Radical Muslim Discourse

1. Martin Marty and Scott Appleby, "Conclusion: Remaking the State: The Limits of the Fundamentalist Imagination" in Marty and Appleby, *Fundamentalisms and the State*, 3:620. This is volume 3 of the five volumes published—over thirty-five hundred pages on fundamentalism worldwide.

2. Several have suggested this comparison. See the compelling presentation by Goldberg, "Smashing Idols and the State." Such a comparison is not intend-ed to suggest that the Islamists modeled themselves on the Reformation. That an earlier generation of reformist Muslims did is quite a different matter. Writing in the 1950s, Wilfred Cantwell Smith observed that Republican Turkey might be "accused of aping the West even in religion, in seeking to reproduce in Islam a Reformation that Christendom effected in earlier times and different circumstances. Certainly it is startling to hear the name of Luther on many Turkish lips that could scarcely discourse on the works of al-Ash'ari or al-Ghazzali or Iqbal." *Islam in Modern History*, p. 206.

3. Beginning with Frederick Engels, in 1850, who in *The Peasant War in Germany* argued that Luther moved from an early "revolutionary stance" only to later join "the train of the middle-class, the nobility and the princes." See Aland, *Four Reformers*, pp. 13–15.

4. I claim no Olympian impartiality and confess to a distaste for the harsh rhetoric and actions of today's Islamists. If transported back to the sixteenth cen-tury, I would probably have sided with Erasmus over Luther. Indeed, I rather like the ingenuous remarks attributed to the Duke of Buckingham in the eighteenth century (after religious confrontation in England had, admittedly, somewhat cooled): "I have not faith enough to be a Presbyterian, nor good works enough to be a Papist, and therefore I am an honest old Protestant without either faith or good works." Cited in Stone, "The Results of the English Revoluton," pp. 72–73.

5. Luther completed his translation of the New Testament in 1522 and the rest of the Bible by 1534. Tyndale's translation of the New Testament (1525–1526) was the first to appear in print.

6. The claim that the several Arabic dialects are so different from each other and from classical Arabic as to constitute separate languages is a touchy subject provoking both scientific and—even more—religious disputes. Although it is foolhardy for a layman to enter the linguist's lair, personal experience indicates that while, for example, an illiterate Moroccan would have difficulties under-standing an illiterate Iraqi, educated native Arabic speakers can communicate

easily with their educated peers. Moreover, the educated native Arabic speaker can pick up the Arabic of the Qur'an as well as the corpus of material from the premodern period (certainly the earliest Arabic poetry) far more readily than the educated native English speaker can make sense of Chaucer. The linguistic history of modern Arabic speakers and modern Hebrew speakers (cognate languages, moreover) would be a fruitful study with just enough similarities and differences to provide useful findings.

7. From the early years of the sixteenth century to at least 1648 (the end of the Thirty Years War) but, more meaningfully, until the late 1680s (the 1685 Revocation of the Edict of Nantes in France and the 1688 "Glorious Revolution" in England).

8. Weber adopts a four-part system of religious options: asceticism (or mastery) and mysticism (or resignedness) are given either otherworldy or innerworldy orientations. Both otherworldy options devalue activity in the here and now. Innerworldly mysticism accepts the world but gives it slight positive value. The innerworldly ascetic, in Talcott Parsons's summary of Weber, "seeks mastery over the worldly component of his individual personality, and seeks in principle to extend this mastery to *all* aspects of the human condition." Weber saw Protestantism as the purest example of innerworldly asceticism. Weber, *The Sociology of Religion*, pp. l–lii.

9. See the classic study by Walzer, *The Revolution of the Saints*, where in the preface he writes of the Calvinist saint as "the first of those self-disciplined agents of social and political reconstruction who have appeared so frequently in modern history. He is the destroyer of an old order for which there is no need to feel nostalgic. He is the builder of a repressive system which may well have to be endured before it can be escaped or transcended. He is, above all, an extraordinarily bold, inventive, and ruthless politician."

10. Not to mention the many examples of governmental cooperation within the Muslim world that are more readily explained by realpolitik than religion. The best example might well be the Ba'thist government of Syria lined up with Iran in order to better confront the Ba'thist government of neighboring Iraq.

14. Al-Banna, Mawdudi, and Qutb

1. Treatment of al-Banna draws largely on Mitchell's excellent study, *The Society of Muslim Brothers*.

2. British military presence in the canal zone remained well beyond Egypt's ostensible independence (1936) and admission into the League of Nations (1937). Britain finally evacuated its canal zone military bases only in June 1956. One month later, Nasser nationalized the canal, setting in motion the diplomat-

ic crisis that briefly brought back British troops, allied with France and Israel, in attacking Egypt that fall.

3. Mitchell, *The Society of Muslim Brothers* p. 328.

4. Indeed, his early mission was "at first misinterpreted as merely another *sufi* (mystic) order about to take its place with all the other *sufi* orders." J. Heyworth-Dunne, *Religious and Political Trends in Modern Egypt*, p. 33.

5. These data from Mitchell, *The Society of Muslim Brothers* and Husaini, *The Moslem Brethren*, but following Mitchell's more detailed account where they diverge.

6. A replay, one might say, of the all-or-nothing Kharijite claim that Ali had betrayed the good cause by compromising with the enemy, and it will be remembered that the assassination attempt against Ali was successful. The uncompromising fanatic turning violently against those who might consider negotiating with the enemy stands out as a constant, transcending centuries and cultures. Even Oliver Cromwell was led to caution his more adamant followers, "I beseech you, in the bowels of Christ, think it possible you may be mistaken."

7. Paul in 1st Corinthians 9:22. Al-Banna's "pastoral letters" (a good way to characterize much of his writing) are in style and substance rather like Paul's letters to the early Church. They both deal with very down-to-earth issues of human relations and make their points with homely images.

8. "Islamist" is chosen rather than "Muslim" to escape implicit conflation with many other Muslim approaches that certainly cannot be dubbed totalitarian. The Muslim Brethren, of course, has had a continued existence since 1928, but it has been presented in the past tense here (i.e., during the time of al-Banna). This leaves open the question of whether today's Muslim Brethren has, as its leaders maintain, become moderate and accepting of establishment rules.

9. Nasr, "Mawdudi and the Jama'at-i Islami," p. 99.

10. Ibid., citing Mawdudi's autobiography. Qasim Amin was an Islamic modernist championing women's liberation. That the young man would translate this work, so out of harmony with Mawdudi's later very traditionalist views concerning women in Islam, would seem to buttress the image of him as a liberal nationalist in his earliest years.

11. Ibid., p. 101.

12. Adams, "Mawdudi and the Islamic State," pp. 100–101.

13. Ibid., pp. 104–105.

14. Nasr, "Mawdudi and the Jama'at-i Islami," pp. 114–115.

15. The death sentence, a classic example of judicial excess, undercut the very strong case demonstrating the danger of the harsh Islamist ideology Mawdudi presented. A thorough study of these tragic days is the official *Report of the Court of Inquiry Constituted Under Punjab Act II*. Usually referred to as the Munir Report, after the presiding judge, Muhammad Munir, this "unusually revealing and at times brilliant" official study set alongside the 1949 Objectives

Resolution of the Constituent Assembly offers "in polar fashion much of the fundamentals of Pakistan's early religious development." Smith, *Islam in Modern History*, pp. 232 and 218.

16. From Mawdudi's *Islam ka Mazriyah Siyasi* (Islam's Political Views), Delhi 1967, as cited in Nasr, "Mawdudi and the Jama'at-i Islami," p. 108.

17. Adams, "Mawdudi and the Islamic State," p. 123.

18. The best treatment of that talented group of thinkers, including al-'Aqqad, Taha Husayn, Muhammad Husayn Haykal, Ahmad Amin, and Tawfiq al-Hakim, who helped shape Egyptian intellectual life during the interwar years is Safran, *Egypt in Search of Political Community*, especially part 4. See also Lutfi al-Sayyid Marsot, *Egypt's Liberal Experiment*, in particular, chapter 8, "Intellectual Eddies and Currents."

19. A point stressed in Safran, *Egypt in Search of Political Community*, pp. 165ff, and Lutfi al-Sayyid Marsot, *Egypt's Liberal Experiment*, 230ff. See also the perceptive portrayal by Tripp, "Sayyid Qutb."

20. Sayyid Qutb's letters and articles have been brought together in *Amirika min al-Dakhil bi-Mundhar Sayyid Qutb*.

21. *Amirika*, p. 135, and Qutb, "Aduwunna al-Awwal: Al-Rajul al-Abyad" (Our Primary Enemy, the White Man), *Al-Risala* 2, 1009 (November 3, 1952), p. 1217. Cited in Abu-Rabi', *Intellectual Origins of Islamic Resurgence*, p. 134 and p. 301, note 150.

22. Qutb, *Social Justice in Islam*, pp. 132–133.

23. A point caught by Abu-Rabi', *Intellectual Origins of Islamic Resurgence*, p. 296, note 73.

24. Exemplified in such works as *Ma'rakat al-Islam wa al-Ra'smaliyyah* (The Struggle Between Islam and Capitalism) and *Al-Salam al-'Alami wa al-Islam* (World Peace and Islam), both appearing as early as 1951.

25. Translating Qutb's *hakimiyya* as sovereignty best reveals his sense of the Qur'anic meaning, but the Arabic root used in each case, H-K-M, more accurately conveys the sense of judging or judgment. Thus, the Pickthall translation of Qur'an 12:40 reads, "The decision rests with Allah only" and of Qur'an 5:47, "Whoso judgeth not by that which Allah hath revealed; such are evil-livers." Ahmad S. Moussali makes the point that Qutb, "like the Kharijites" in the early days of Islam, managed to give the Qur'anic *hukm* a political as well as a juridical meaning. See his *Radical Islamic Fundamentalism*, pp. 150–151.

26. Qutb, *Fi Zilal al-Qur'an*.

27. See on this and for Sayyid Qutb in general the excellent chapter by Tripp, "Sayyid Qutb." See also Moussali, *Radical Islamic Fundamentalism*, a major source for Tripp's interpretation.

28. Haddad, "Sayyid Qutb," p. 73, relying on the account in Mahdi Fadlallah, *Ma' Sayyid Qutb fi Fikratihi al-Siyasi wa al-Dini* (With Sayyid Qutb in His Political and Religious Thought) (Beirut, 1978), p. 91. Fadlallah seems to be the

source of accounts relating Qutb's warm contacts with the Free Officers in those early months.

29. This, too, is from Fadlallah, *Ma' Sayyid Qutb fi Fikratihi al-Siyasi wa al-Dini*. The Liberation Rally, created in January 1953, was the first of the Nasserist efforts to create an overarching political movement that would eliminate the need for political parties, which were, accordingly, banned. It was succeeded by the National Union (1957–1961) and the Arab Socialist Union (1962).

30. Even more than was the case with the massive trials following the October 1954 assassination against Nasser. Then, at least, bullets had been fired and conspirators identified, even though the Nasserist government seized the opportunity to try many others, including the brotherhood leader Hasan al-Hudaybi, almost certainly innocent of and opposed to acts of violence.

31. Ibrahim was the dynamic leader of the Malaysian Muslim Youth movement. In the early 1980s he joined the ruling political party, assumed increasingly important government positions, and as deputy prime minister was poised to succeed the longtime prime minister, Dr. Mahathir bin Mohammed. In September 1998 Mahathir, apparently jealous of his rising importance, had him fired and later jailed on what most consider trumped up charges.

15. Khomeini and Shi'ite Islamism

1. The best short biographical sketch is found in Abrahamian, *Khomeinism*, pp. 5–12. See also Khomeini, *Islam and Revolution*, translated and edited by Algar, pp. 13–21, and two chapters in Keddie, *Religion and Politics in Iran*: Tabari, "The Role of the Clergy," and Rose, "*Velayat-e Faqih* and the Recovery of Islamic Identity."

2. Abrahamian, *Khomeinism*, p. 6. Algar mentions only that the father was "murdered by bandits." Khomeini, *Islam and Revolution*, p. 13.

3. "Assassinated by the Shah's U.S.-instituted security policy, *Savak*," according to Algar, who adds, "Imam Khomeini bore this blow stoically, but the tragedy inflamed the public in Iran." Khomeini, *Islam and Revolution*, p. 19.

4. There is disagreement concerning the publication date, ranging from 1941 to as late as 1944.

5. Cited and translated (from p. 184 in the 1979 Persian edition of *Kashf al-Asrar*) by Tabari, "The Role of the Clergy," p. 61. Tabari provides a stimulating summary of *Kashf al-Asrar* on pp. 60–64.

6. Ibid., p. 62.

7. Ibid., p. 62. (Persian, p. 189). Compare with the extract translated by Hamid Algar from pp. 221–224 of the 1941 edition (? see note 4): "We do not say that the government must be in the hands of the *faqih*; rather we say that government must be run in accordance with God's law, for the welfare of the country

and the people demands this, and it is not feasible except with the supervision of the religious leaders." Khomeini, *Islam and Revolution*, p. 170.

8. Cited in Bakhash, *The Reign of the Ayatollahs*, p. 23 (p. 186, Persian edition—date not specified).

9. Khomeini, *Islam and Revolution* p. 172. The association of Westernization with wanton sexuality is a persistent theme in Khomeini's writings and, for that matter, in the writings of many radical Islamists. Of course, strictly defined gender roles and rigidly puritanical sexual codes characterize fundamentalist movements, Muslim and non-Muslim.

10. Khomeini's slap (Khomeini, *Islam and Revolution*, p. 170) at Hitler for having invaded Poland served, of course, to denigrate Riza Shah for his Nazi leanings (which cost him his throne), but it is not perhaps overly cynical to note that such a reference would go over well with the British and Soviet occupying powers.

11. Ibid., p. 169.

12. Arjomand, *The Turban for the Crown*, p. 87.

13. A program not all that successful, but, then, few third world land reforms have been. See on this subject Kazemi, *Poverty and Revolution in Iran*, and Lambton, *The Persian Land Reform*.

14. Abrahamian, *Iran Between Two Revolutions*, especially pp. 435–446.

15. Abrahamian, *Iran Between Two Revolutions*, p. 531.

16. Arjomand, *The Turban for the Crown*, p. 98.

17. Shari'ati is usually described as a sociologist and certainly saw himself as a social theorist. Still, his dissertation was in medieval Persian philology. See Richard, "Modern Iranian Political Thought," p. 215. Pp. 215–228 of Richard's chapter offer a solid summary of Shariati's life, thought, and influence. Another fine account is Akhavi, "Shariati's Social Thought."

18. Abrahamian, *Iran Between Two Revolutions*, p. 534. It must be pointed out, however, that Khomeini himself in his *Islamic Government*, pp. 83–84, distinguished between an "imam" who is leader or guide or judge and any of the succession of twelve imams after Prophet Muhammad (the twelfth and last imam being "hidden" only to return at the end of time). The former usage of imam is, according to Khomeini, the just *faqih*.

19. The death of Ayatullah Khomeini's oldest son, Mustafa, and now Ali Shari'ati both assassinated by SAVAK? A superficial cynicism might see in these allegations the Middle Eastern penchant for conspiracy theories overlaid with the Shi'i emphasis on martyrdom. The SAVAK record for brutality must not, however, be minimized. Shari'ati left for England with the understanding that his wife and daughters would be permitted to follow. When he later went to meet the plane bringing his family he found that his wife and one of his daughters had been refused permission to leave Iran. He died soon thereafter in June 1977. Richard, "Modern Iranian Political Thought," p. 216.

20. Khomeini, *Islam and Revolution*, p. 129. The last sentence in the original text uses the Islamic injunction *al-'amr fi al-ma'ruf wa al-nahya 'an al-munkar* (command the good and resist the evil), which is the classic text used to buttress the claim that each believer must strive to achieve the divinely mandated good society in this world. A nice touch, that, asking these fledgling clerics if they are to await receiving instructions concerning their religious duties from those educated in secular institutions.

21. The first entry in Algar's collection of Ayatollah Khomeini's writings, *Islam and Revolution*, pp. 26–149, with translator's notes pp. 150–166. There remains some disagreement concerning whether the original lectures were given in Persian or Arabic. Algar and also Abrahamian, *Khomeinism*, p. 11, insist on the former. Abrahamian adds, "Khomeini, like many Iranian senior clerics, never attained fluency in spoken Arabic." Others insist that lectures at the Najaf religious seminary would necessarily have been given in Arabic.

22. Khomeini, *Islamic Government*, p. 79.

Conclusion

1. John P. Meier challenging Robert Gorham Davis's criticism of his review of Robin Lane Fox, *The Unauthorized Version*, in the *New York Times Book Review*, August 2, 1992, p. 27.

2. Iran just may be evolving from Islamist rigor to a more moderate and humane polity. The surprising election of Muhammad Khatami as president in May 1997 followed by the sweeping victory of the liberals in the February 2000 elections to the Majlis are positive signs of such. See on these developments during the past few years Wright, *The Last Great Revolution* and Adelkhah, *Being Modern in Iran*.

3. "O People, all of you are from Adam and Adam is from dust. There is no special distinction among mankind. There is no boasting for the Arab over the Persian, nor the Persian over the Arab. The noblest to God is the most Godfearing." Hadith of the Prophet Muhammad, cited in Ibn Hisham, 4:32.

Islam and Politics Past and Present:
A Bibliographical Essay

Islamic studies specialists often dismiss the many works on radical Islam as much chaff and little wheat. Yes, there is no lack of the shrill, the sensational, and the superficial. Make no mistake, however. Many well-researched and thoughtful books and articles has been produced. So much has been written on this subject during the past several decades that any attempt at an an exhaustive listing would result in a book-length compilation. Indeed, such a compilation already exists—in two volumes, *The Contemporary Islamic Revival* (1991) and *The Islamic Revival Since 1988* (1997), both edited by Yvonne Yazbeck Haddad and others.

Even the limited selections made in this essay have produced more pages than many readers may wish to review and certainly more titles than all but those planning to write their own books on the subject require. To accommodate the busy reader I have sought out shorter works (slim books, journal articles, or chapters in books), but a sufficient number of the big books have also been included to satisfy those seeking greater detail on one aspect or another of this large and protean subject.

Discussing the literature on Islamist thought and action in today's Muslim world is a large enough assignment in itself, but this subject can be set in proper context only with some background knowledge of Islamic history throughout its fourteen-plus centuries. A few general works are cited to serve the needs of those readers with little knowledge of Islamic history.

Full bibliographical information is to be found in the alphabetically arranged list of works cited that follows this essay.

General Studies of Islamic History and Civilization

For overall orientation the two-volume *Cambridge History of Islam*, the three-volume *Venture of Islam*, by Marshall G. S. Hodgson, or the large one-volume *A History of Islamic Societies* by Ira Lapidus can be recommended. All three have the advantage of treating the entire Muslim world and not just the Middle East. By contrast, André Miquel's *L'Islam et sa civilisation*, in spite of the name, deals essentially with the Middle East from the rise of Islam to this century. Miquel does, however, offer a 72-page "Tableaux chronologiques" divided into four concurrent categories—"Histoire politique et militare," "Histoire religieuse," "Histoire economique, social et culturelle," and "En dehors de l'Islam"—which are very useful for ready chronological orientation.

Hodgson's *Venture of Islam* is by no means an introductory text. It is perhaps best read by those possessing more than rudimentary knowledge of the subject. His was a pioneering work in seeing Islamic civilization as a whole, in challenging the longstanding interpretation of Muslims as having been in a state of decline since the time of the Prophet Muhammad and the early community (volume 3 is significantly entitled "The Gunpowder Empires and Modern Times," referring to those impressive Muslim polities: the Ottoman, Safavid, and Moghul Empires).

Hodgson also sought to distinguish between Islam as religion, the political arrangements of Muslims past and present, and the overall culture of Muslims. For the first, he used the terms *Islam* or *Islamic*. For the second, he coined *Islamdom*, comparable to *Christendom*, and for the latter, *Islamicate* (as one might speak of Italianate architecture or art). The terminology has caught on only fleetingly, but the substantive importance of such distinctions must be appreciated. The reductio ad absurdum of labeling all aspects of life among Muslim peoples as "Islamic" is reached, so the story goes, with the monograph written on "Atheism in Islam." The extent to which the values and institutions of the religion called Islam shape the institutions, attitudes, and mores of Muslims is precisely what needs to be examined. The profligate use of the adjective *Islamic* for all aspects of life among Muslims obscures what most needs to be analyzed.

Lapidus divides his *History of Islamic Societies* into three parts treating 1. the origins of Islamic civilization in the Middle East c. 600 to c. 1200, 2. the worldwide diffusion of Islamic societies from the tenth to the nineteenth centuries, and 3. "The Modern Transformation: Muslim Peoples in the Nineteenth and Twentieth Centuries." The modern period (part 3) get fuller coverage. It is almost one-half of the book. At the same time, those earlier twelve centuries are well covered. This book is perhaps more accessible than Hodgson's, and it is equally learned. Both Hodgson and Lapidus provide excellent annotated bibliographies.

The multiauthored *Cambridge History of Islam* offers chronological coverage of the world of Islam divided into "The Central Islamic Lands" (volume 1), essentially the Middle East, and "The Further Islamic Lands" (volume 2), everything else (including, surprisingly, the Maghrib). Volume 2 also contains fifteen separate chapters on all aspects of Islamic civilization. Chapters 2 through 7 treat "The Sources of Islamic Civilization," "Economy, Society, Institutions," "Law and Justice," "Religion and Culture," "Mysticism," and "Revival and Reform in Islam." A thematic chapter in volume 1 on "The Political Impact of the West" should be noted.

Islamic Political Thought

Both present-day Islamists and their opponents appeal to an earlier tradition of political thought, emphasizing especially the time of the Prophet Muhammad and the early community as the appropriate model but actually drawing on a much more extensive chronological chain of writers such as Ibn Taimiyya (1263–1328) or Ibn Khaldun (1332–1406). For this body of Islamic thought one can consult E. I. J. Rosenthal's *Political Thought in Medieval Islam* or Ann Lambton's *State and Government in Medieval Islam*, which I find more satisfying. W. M. Watt has written a number of short books on aspects of Islam. One of these, entitled *Islamic Political Thought*, can serve as a primer.

Those seeking to get a general sense of what might be called classical Islamic thinking regarding government and politics might well consult some combination of the following shorter pieces:

> David de Santillana, "Law and Society" in the original *The Legacy of Islam*;
> Ann Lambton, "Islamic Political Thought" in the new *Legacy of Islam*;
> plus two writings, both entitled "The Body Politic," the first by Claude Cahen in *Unity and Variety in Islamic Civilization* and the second constituting two chapters in Gustave von Grunebaum's *Medieval Islam*.

Ira Lapidus, "State and Religion in Islamic Societies," as well as his earlier "The Separation of State and Religion in the Development of Early Islamic

Society" are also important in challenging the oft-stated idea that there can never be a separation between state and religion in Islam.

A useful way to study political thought is by probing the meaning and content of the terminology used. Here, we are especially well served by the splendid *The Political Language of Islam* by Bernard Lewis. This meaty little book is divided into five chapters—"Metaphor and Illusion," "The Body Politic," "The Rulers and the Ruled," "War and Peace," and "The Limits of Obedience"—all clearly relevant. This is a book to read and reread.

No one scholar did more than H. A. R. Gibb to present an interpretation of Islamic political thought that remains generally accepted to this day. Several of his seminal writings on this subject are conveniently collected in his *Studies on the Civilization of Islam.*

The above works treat essentially the political thought of the ulama. The Muslim philosophers, reluctant to challenge Islamic orthodoxy, usually chose a compartmentalized intellectual existence and had less direct impact on shaping the Muslim *umma's* approach to politics. Still, their ideas did filter into the mainstream. An appealing book for this aspect of classical Islamic thought is that edited by Ralph Lerner and Muhsin Mahdi, *Medieval Political Philosophy: A Sourcebook*, which has the added advantages of offering examples and commentary concerning the three religious traditions, Judaism, Christianity, and Islam. In addition to the several selections and commentaries found in Lerner and Mahdi, one can consult an interesting article by Charles Butterworth. In "Prudence Versus Legitimacy: The Persistent Theme in Islamic Thought" he distinguishes the legalistic tradition of the ulama from that of the philosophers.

As for that third strand in premodern Islamic political thought, the mirrors for princes literature, a number of representative "mirrors" have been translated into English. An important example is *The Book of Government or Rules for Kings*, a translation of the *Siyasat-name* written by the celebrated vizier, Nizam al-Mulk (1018–1092). A good quick description of this more pragmatic princely tradition in political thought is set out in chapter 3, "The Islamic Intellectual Heritage of the Young Ottomans," of Serif Mardin's *The Genesis of Young Ottoman Thought.*

Mardin's book also serves as a bridge to studies on political thought (not just Islamist political thought) in modern times, which is very much tied up with the response of the several different Muslim societies to the impact of the West. This is a huge subject, and only a few titles can be mentioned. *The Emergence of Modern Turkey* by Bernard Lewis traces the Ottoman efforts to respond to the new world imposed by the West during almost a century and a half from the late eighteenth century until after the First World War, when there emerged out of the ashes of this long-lived empire a Turkish nation-state in Anatolia plus a number of would-be nation-states through the Arab world. Lewis's account, which treats much more than political ideas, offers a model for equivalent states such as Egypt and Tunisia (technically part of the Ottoman but autonomous and virtually independent) or Morocco and Iran. Yet another study of the same period is *The Development of Secularism in Turkey* by the Turkish scholar, Niyazi Berkes. The title is significant: Berkes presents secularism as a great achievement.

Dealing only with the Arab world but revealing an intellectual ferment not unlike that throughout the entire Muslim world in modern times is Albert Hourani's *Arabic Thought in the Liberal Age*. Nationalism (Arab or other) and Islamism are, of course, at one and the same time in contention and thoroughly intertwined. An excellent short statement is the seventy-page introduction by Sylvia G. Haim to her *Arab Nationalism: An Anthology*. Note that both Hourani and Haim treat al-Afghani and Muhummad Abduh. Bernard Lewis has much to say on the linkages between nationalism and religion in his *The Shaping of the Modern Middle East*, especially the chapters "Patriotism and Nationalism" and "The Revolt of Islam."

E. I. J. Rosenthal, some years after his book *Political Thought in Medieval Islam* (1958), followed with *Islam in the Modern National State* (1965). This book thus appeared several years before the great outburst of Islamist activity and the scholarly monitoring of that phenomenon, which was in large measure unexpected. This book presents different case studies, e.g., "Islam and Turkish Nationalism," "Islam and Arab Nationalism," and "For and Against the *Khilafa*." It also has the advantage of treating Islam east and west of the Middle Eastern core with coverage not only of Pakistan but also of Malaya (later Malaysia) plus Morocco and Tunisia.

The best single book on modern Islamic political thought is Hamid Enayat's work by that title. Enayat also gives considerable attention to political thought in Shi'ism and offers as well a separate chapter on "Shi'ism and Sunnism: Conflict and Concord."

Islamic Fundamentalism

Turning now to works treating more directly Islamist thought and action in modern times, first a word about terminology. Many object to the term *fundamentalism*, seeing it as a borrowing from another time and place (the word was used first to describe American Protestant scriptural literalists early in this century). Others maintain that the term has no utility since the dogma of the uncreated Qur'an makes all Muslims fundamentalists. They necessarily embrace the "inerrancy" of their scripture. The scholarly debate over terminology itself, which continues, can provide insights into several contending ways of understanding what is being studied. I find the term *fundamentalism* useful, and like the way it evokes the comparative approach. *Islamist* is increasing accepted, it would seem, as a word that avoids debate over terminology, but that term has its problems, too, implying that those so designated are somehow more "Muslim" than others. In any case, the most convincing argument I have found for describing the subject of our study as fundamentalism is in the first several pages of "Islamic Fundamentalism Reconsidered: A Critical Outline of Problems, Ideas, and Approaches" by Sadik J. al-'Azm. That entire long article, which goes on to offer comparative insights into Protestant, Catholic, and Islamic fundamentalism, merits a careful reading. On defining fundamentalism see also Bruce Lawrence's *Defenders of God: The Fundamentalist Revolt Against the Modern Age*, passim, and especially his listing of five fundamentalist traits (pp. 100–101).

No scholarly consensus exists about how to describe and explain Islamic radicalism. In simplest terms, interpretations range from those seeing Islamists as largely nonthreatening to established order, or, at least, capable of being co-opted by established order, to those lumping all Islamists as revolutionaries bent on replacing the status quo with an authoritarian Islamic state. To the former, the hard-core terrorists are unrepresentative exceptions. To the latter, those same terrorists simply express more openly what all Islamists believe and aspire to achieve. There are, as well, interpretations opting for some middle point between these two extremes (as I have done in this book). I will try to present a sampling of these contending interpretations.

John Voll's *Islam: Continuity and Change in the Modern World* is a good way to begin our listing. It is by no means confined to Islamists and modern Islamic fundamentalism. It is, rather, a solid text treating just what the title states. Only the penultimate chapter zeros in on "The Resurgence of Islam." Voll also provides equal treatment to all parts of the Muslim world. Anyone lacking the time to select readings from the many books and articles listed earlier can rely on this one book to set the general context.

John Esposito has, like Voll, devoted his scholarly attention almost exclusively to Islamic studies. Among his many publications, the two that most directly treat our subject are his *Islam and Politics* and *The Islamic Threat: Myth or Reality?* Esposito has also edited several books on this subject including *Political Islam: Revolution, Radicalism, or Reform? Islam and Development: Religion and Sociopolitical Change, Voices of Resurgent Islam,* and *Islam in Transition: Muslim Perspectives* (coedited with John J. Donohue). The latter is a very able selection of writings by Muslims themselves, covering a spectrum ranging from such liberal Muslim thinkers as Sadik al-Azam, Hichem Djait, and the late Muhammad Nuwayhi to adamant Islamists Mawdudi and Qutb. *Voices of Resurgent Islam* contains a mix of writings by non-Muslim and Muslim scholars. Esposito and Voll have also collaborated on a work, *Islam and Democracy,* that is relevant to our subject.

Are Islam and nationalism incompatible? This is a subject about which even Islamists differ. Hasan al-Banna, for example, held that nationalism and Islamism could be reconciled. James Piscatori's stimulating *Islam in a World of Nation-States* argues that most Muslim states have accommodated themselves to the prevailing nation-state system quite well. See also Nikki Keddie's "Pan-Islam as Proto-Nationalism," which, while treating the earlier period of Pan-Islam, deftly indicates the possibility of blending together Islamism and nationalism.

Edward Mortimer's *Faith and Power* (1982) is a very readable early account that sets the stage with a good chapter on "Traditional Muslim Attitudes to Power," and then sketches the "Western Impact and Muslim Responses" before turning to six twentieth-century cases studies of the interaction of Islam and politics, Turkey, Saudi Arabia, Pakistan, Iran, plus an overview chapter entitled "Arab Nationalism and Muslim Brotherhood."

A year later, Daniel Pipes, a scholar well-versed in Islamic studies, both premodern and modern, provided a penetrating account in his *In the Path of God: Islam and Political Power.* His early chapters take the customary vantage point as adopted by Mortimer (and, for that matter, this book and most studies) of describing an Islamic civilization that developed over the centuries its own approach to politics and then was obliged to confront in modern times a threatening but also enticing West. His chapter "The Islamic Revival: A Survey of Countries" gets much said in few pages. Nothing mincing about the Pipes approach, his is a well-informed, hard-eyed study enriched by many comparative insights. Pipes, in a penultimate chapter, also ties in the availability of oil wealth as a factor facilitating Islamic revivalists movements across national borders.

Another forceful writer whose natural intelligence and scholarly flair was enriched by his having grown up as a Greek Christian insider/outsider in Egypt and Palestine was the late P. J. Vatikiotis (he died in December 1997). His little book, *Islam and the State,* is stimulating but, in my view, overly inclined to view Islam (not just Islamists) as incapable of adjusting to the basic requirements of modernity. Read the book and read as well Abbas Kelidar's excellent obituary appreciation of Vatikiotis, which also sums up the major points raised in *Islam and the State*. Let one example suffice:

> Vatikiotis was constantly conscious of the clash between religion, with its extensive cultural complex or ethos, and secular modernity under which the national secular state emerged. . . . For him "the essence of secularism, apart from the separation between religion and state, is the acceptance of the proposition that there is no finality to forms, no exclusive possession of absolute and indivisible truth. A corollary of this is the recognition of alternative notions about man and the world and, more significantly, the toleration of these alternative views."
> (Kelidar, *Islam and the State*, p. 98)

It is a position that he did not believe either Islam could sustain or the traditional jurists and their modern Islamist counterparts would ever entertain.

My own review of *Islam and the State* sets out my reservations.

Youssef M. Choueiri's *Islamic Fundamentalism* (London 1990) offers another overview with thoughtful insights. He sees Islamic fundamentalism as the

> latest and perhaps the last attempt to establish a totalitarian Islamic state. . . . Its ideology is closely related to the anxieties and ambitions of certain strata of society: small merchants, middle traders, artisans, students, teachers and state employees. Hence, it is an ideology shot through with the precarious position of these social groups. (p. 12)

Choueiri also explicates one of those seemingly minor points that actually is very revealing (pp. 142–149). This is the extent to which Sayyid Qutb was influenced by Alexis Carrel (1873–1944). Carrel, a medical doctor, received the Nobel Prize in 1912, but his importance here was his later book, *Man, the Unknown* (a best-seller in the 1930s and 1940s) and his easily fitting as an official in the government of Vichy France. Carrel put himself forward as a social philosopher (if not, indeed, a prophet) deploring the presumed dehumanizing impact of modern Western materialism (especially capitalism). A social Darwinist elitist, he went all the way into advocating eugenics and euthanasia to breed the best and weed out the unfit. Qutb, Choueri argues, adapted Carrel's ideas (not, in fairness, eugenics and euthanasia) to come up with "a Third World version of fascism." Choueiri shrewdly suggests that what Carrel called modern Western "barbarism" could be transposed into Qutb's *jahiliyya*. An excellent insight, which also demonstrates that even Islamists most intent on rejecting the "other" in favor of a postulated cultural authenticity often rely on theories and ideologies advanced by outsiders.

One of the most insightful studies is Nazih Ayubi's *Political Islam: Religion and Politics in the Arab World*. Although, as the title indicates, he deals only with the Arab world, Ayubi addresses major themes relevant elsewhere in the Muslim world. His first chapter on "Theory and Practice of the Islamic State" is an excellent survey, consistent with the main lines of the works cited above treating Islamic political thought but offering thoughtful new twists. Other chapters treat "The Politics of Sex and the Family," discuss Islamic banking, and survey both the intellectual sources and the socioeconomic bases of political Islam. He even has a stimulating chapter entitled "The Islamic Liberals Answer Back."

Islam and Revolution in the Middle East by Henry Munson Jr. is another good general study. Munson elsewhere offers an entrée into the scholarly debate over comparative fundamentalisms. These exchanges took place in the short-lived and regrettably now defunct journal *Contention*. In "Not all Crustaceans Are Crabs: Reflections on the Comparative Study of Fundamentalism and Politics" Munson critically reviewed the multivolume fundamentalisms project edited by Martin E. Marty and R. Scott Appleby (to be noted later). There followed in later issues exchanges with Appleby, who took issue with Munson's criticism. Then came Munson's longer "Intolerable Tolerance: Western Academia and Islamic Fundamentalism," a hard-hitting critique of what he saw as a tendency among several Western scholars to condone or turn a blind eye to the seamier side of the Islamists in word and deed. This is a core issue, and Munson handles it bluntly but fairly. In an effort to give fair treatment to the "Other," do scholars risk falling into a double standard, explaining away or passing over statements or deeds that they would not, for a moment, countenance at home?

A more recent book is *The Future of Islam and the West: Clash of Civilizations or Peaceful Coexistence?* (1998) by Shireen T. Hunter. As the subtitle suggests, this book was written in the wake of the "clash of civilizations" argument initiated by Harvard political scientist Samuel Huntington. Hunter's book is a very readable general essay, which offers a sanguine interpretation by arguing that today's Muslim world contains much more than the Islamists. Two interesting case studies on "the role of Islam in shaping foreign policy" treat Iran and Saudi Arabia.

Also taking their distance from the "clash of civilizations" school are

Scott W. Hibbard and David Little in their short book *Islamic Activism and U.S. Foreign Policy*. In greater detail, and more recently still, Fawaz A. Gerges addresses this subject in *America and Political Islam: Clash of Cultures or Clash of Interests?* Gerges's major focus is American perceptions of and policies toward Islamism, but that in itself is an interestingly different way to study the subject.

The just published *Jihad: Expansion et déclin de l'islamisme* by Gilles Kepel is an excellent, in-depth study concluding that Islamism as a political force has peaked. An English translation is planned.

Writings by Islamists

A number of writings by the several different Islamists are available in English. The very influential *Islamic Government* by Ayatullah Khomeini along with others of his writings have been translated by Hamid Algar in *Islam and Revolution: Writings and Declarations of Imam Khomeini*. For al-Banna, see Charles Wendell's translation entitled *Five Tracts of Hasan al-Banna*. There is also a Pakistani translation of his memoirs, *Memoirs of Hasan al-Banna, Shaheed*. Sayyid Qutb's first major Islamist book, *Social Justice in Islam*, has been twice translated, earlier by J. B. Hardie (1970) and then again in 1996 by William E. Shephard, *Sayyid Qutb and Islamic Activism: A Translation and Critical Analysis of Social Justice in Islam*. Shephard's bibliography lists translations available of other works by Qutb, including his celebrated *Milestones*.

Many of Mawdudi's works have been translated into English, often distributed as small inexpensive pamphlets. To select just two examples: *First Principles of the Islamic State* and *Political Theory of Islam*. The latter lists another fourteen of Mawdudi's books translated into English.

Certainly one of the more chillingly extremist Islamist writings was Muhammad 'Abd al-Salam Faraj's *Al-Faridah al-Gha'ibah*, a short pamphlet setting out the justification for taking extreme action, including political assassination, to replace *jahiliyya* government with true Islamic government. A translation is available in Johannes J. G. Jansen, *The Neglected Duty: The Creed of Sadat's Assassins and Islamic Resurgence in the Middle East*. The first 157 pages of Jansen's book provides a thorough assessment of the background to the book and to Sadat's assassination as well as a responses to *The Neglected Duty* by Al-Azhar ulama, Sufis, and other religious figures.

Other short readings (usually excerpts from longer works) available in English, covering the range of Muslim opinion from liberal to fundamentalist, are conveniently grouped in *Liberal Islam: A Sourcebook* edited by Charles Kurzman. Esposito's *Voices of Resurgent Islam* and Esposito and Donohue, *Islam in Transition*, noted earlier, also contain short selections from Muslim writers, again of all leanings but including such Islamists as Sudan's Hasan Turabi.

Reportage

One of the offsetting ironies concerning the professoriate and the media professionals is the use of the terms *academic* to mean lacking relationship with the real world and *journalistic* conveying the sense of superficial. In fact, academics and journalists can be equally relevant and profound or irrelevant and slipshod. Their professional standards differ in modalities but not in rigor. Useful insights into the world of Islamists can be obtained from those who rely largely on interviews and in-area encounters with Islamists and the Muslim world. Several such books can be recommended: Judith Miller's *God Has Ninety-Nine Names: Reporting from a Militant Middle East* offers a somber appraisal of the Islamists, with short studies of ten different Middle Eastern countries. Milton Viorst's *In the Shadow of the Prophet: The Struggle for the Soul of Islam,* in spite of the title, deals largely with the Arab world plus to some extent Iran. His interpretation of Arab society over the centuries is perhaps best skipped in favor of such works as Hourani's *Arab Peoples* or Lewis's *The Middle East,* but when he get to what he does best— interviewing selected Middle Easterners—he has much to offer in his account of religion and politics in Egypt, Sudan, Iran, Saudi Arabia, Algeria, and Jordan. Note also his fine chapter on the Muslims in France.

Mary Anne Weaver in her *A Portrait of Egypt: A Journey Through the World of Militant Islam* has the advantage of concentrating on a single country that she knows well. Interviewing, as all Westerners do, those in power plus the usual handful of Egyptian experts, Weaver also took on the more daunting assignment of seeking out representative Islamists living outside the law. The result is a sad, gripping story of violence and mutual miscomprehension between government and the Islamists. Old Egyptian hands will cluck approvingly from time to time, "Yes, she's got it right." Try this test: read the last four pages. Chances are that you will want to sit right down and read the book through.

V. S. Naipaul has two books that can be recommended. His *Among the Believers: An Islamic Journey* appeared in 1981. His "journey" put him in touch with selected representatives of the great and, even more, the less than great in Iran, Pakistan, Malaysia, and Indonesia. Then, almost two decades later, in *Beyond Belief: Islamic Excursions Among the Converted Peoples* he revisited the same countries and often the same people. Naipaul thus concentrates on the Muslim peoples from Iran eastward, compensating for the greater Western coverage of the Middle East. Those familiar with his writing (I think especially of his novel, *A Bend in the River*) will not be surprised by his critical, even supercilious, appraisal of his subjects. Perhaps unfair on balance, these are nevertheless insightful accounts.

The Fundamentalisms Project and Encyclopedias

Five fat volumes comparing fundamentalist movement worldwide were published between 1991 and 1995. Edited by Martin Marty and Scott Appleby there were:

> Volume 1, *Fundamentalisms Observed* (1991)
> Volume 2, *Fundamentalisms and Society* (1993)
> Volume 3, *Fundamentalisms and the State* (1993)
> Volume 4, *Accounting for Fundamentalisms* (1994)
> Volume 5, *Fundamentalisms Comprehended* (1995)

That is an intimidatingly large corpus of writings, and even the most diligent scholar may balk at reading them all. Yet, it must be pointed out that the quantity of this undertaking is matched by its quality. It might appear that volume 3, *Fundamentalism and the State*, is most relevant, but equally important articles are found in the other volumes. Perhaps the most convenient way to approach these five tomes is to see them as a high-quality anthology of writings of encyclopedic proportions and breadth. One can find detailed coverage of specific topics (e.g., Hizbullah in Lebanon or the Tajdid movement in Nigeria, both in volume 3, or Shi'ite fundamentalism in Iraq and the Jama'at-i-Islami in South Asia, both in volume 4). One way to decide on what to read and in what order would be to start with the four final chapters (105 pages) of volume 5, coauthored by Gabriel Almond, Emmanuel Sivan, and R. Scott Appleby, an impressive effort to sum up the findings of this ambitious project.

The fundamentalisms project, it was suggested, is somewhat like an encyclopedia. Two recent encyclopedias are directly relevant to our subject. They are the four-volume *Oxford Encyclopedia of the Modern Islamic World*, John L. Esposito, editor in chief, and Robert Wuthnow, editor, *The*

Encyclopedia of Politics and Religion (two volumes). The former, larger and confined to the Islamic world, offers more extensive coverage. The latter, treating Islam along with all other religions, provides a comparative perspective. Both have good short bibliographies following most of the entries. The basic reference work for the specialist in Islamic studies is, of course, the multivolumed *Encyclopaedia of Islam*.

Several collected works have already been mentioned, and a few others are worthy of note. *Pioneers of Islamic Revival*, edited by Ali Rahnema, provides especially well-done short biographies of the principal modern Islamists thinkers. *Islamic Fundamentalism*, edited by Abdel Salam Sidahmad and Anoushiravan Ehteshami, offers several stimulating general studies and eight separate country case studies. The gender issue looms large in Islamist thought and actions. Another useful chapter is "Women and Islam: The Case of Rashid al-Ghannushi of Tunisia."

The journal *Middle East Report* presents articles by scholars that can be described as tough-minded critics of Western "establishment" thinking concerning the Middle East who, as secular leftists, have no great predilection for religious fundamentalism either. The thirty-two articles collected from different issues of *Middle East Report* in *Political Islam*, edited by Joel Beinen and Joe Stork, thus deliver useful perspectives. The subsections include "Islam, Democracy, and Civil Society" (including a stimulating article by Yahya Sadowski and Gudrun Kramer), "The Contest for the State and the Political Economy," "Political Islam and Gender Relations," "The Struggle Over Popular Culture," and "Movements and Personalities."

Spokesmen for the Despised: Fundamentalist Leaders of the Middle East, edited by R. Scott Appleby, has chapters on fundamentalisms in all three religions, Judaism, Christianity, and Islam, but the latter clearly gets the greatest coverage, with solid chapters on Khomeini's legacy, the Lebanese Shi'i spokesman for Hizbullah, Shaykh Muhammad Husayn Fadlallah, Shaykh Ahmad Yasin of the Palestinian Hamas, and the Sudanese Hasan Turabi. In addition, Patrick Gaffney, who has done in-depth research on the actual text of Muslim preachers in Egypt, has an interesting chapter on "Fundamentalist Preaching and Islamic Militancy in Upper Egypt."

Political Islam, edited by Charles E. Butterworth and I. William Zartman, is highly recommended, offering especially coherent coverage treating the usual major themes (e.g., Islamic political thought, the Muslim brotherhoods, Islam and democracy) as well as good area coverage, including such less covered topics as Islam in Nigeria or the states of the former Soviet Union.

An earlier collected work, *Islamic Resurgence in the Arab World*, edited by Ali E. Hillal Dessouki, which appeared in 1982, has stood the test of time well and deserves continued attention.

The Islamism Debate, edited by Martin Kramer, offers usefully contrasting views, addressing the topics "Are Islamists for or Against Democracy?" "Are Islamists Ideological or Pragmatic?" "Should the West Promote Rights or *Realpolitik*?" and "Is Islamism the Future?"

Islamism and Egypt has not only received surely the most coverage but also some of the best. The pioneering article by Egyptian sociologist Saad Eddin Ibrahim, "Anatomy of Egypt's Militant Islamic Groups," which appeared in 1980, provided just the kind of detailed and organized examination of the individuals directly involved that can lead to understanding of what is taking place. A few years later the French scholar, Gilles Kepel, wrote his forceful study, translated into English as *Muslim Extremism in Egypt: The Prophet and the Pharaoh* (1985). That same year brought what stands out in my judgment as the best single monograph on Islamism, Emmanuel Sivan's *Radical Islam: Medieval Theology and Modern Politics*. Sivan scoured the bookstores and, even more, the small open-air stalls in Cairo where the many pamphlets, tracts, and sermons of the Islamists could be found. He studied this material—so often slighted if not quite ignored by outside scholars—and fitted it into a compelling interpretation of Islamism in Egypt.

There are many other single-country or single movement studies, but only one more will be cited here. That is Ziad Abu-Amr's *Islamic Fundamentalism in the West Bank and Gaza: Muslim Brotherhood and Islamic Jihad*. Whither Palestine and whether a viable settlement between Israel and the Palestinians can be reached is a subject of interest to Muslims and non-Muslims alike, in the region and beyond. How Islamic fundamentalism fits into all this cries out for attention. Abu-Amr's carefully constructed monograph is the place to begin in exploring such issues. Islamism in the West Bank and Gaza also offers a compelling case study of such questions as whether and, if so, how fundamentalist movements can be co-opted or won over to the politics of negotiated compromise.

Finally, a concluding word about the two-volume bibliography compiled by Yvonne Haddad and others, mentioned at the beginning of this essay. The first volume, *The Contemporary Islamic Revival*, covers works published between 1970 and 1988. The number of works published between 1988 and 1997 (the date *The Islamic Revival Since 1988* appeared) required yet another volume. These are substantial books: 230 and 298 pages respectively. The first volume begins with three bibliographical essays by Haddad, and then John Voll followed by John Esposito. The breakdown of the work thereafter is, first, a category of "General Studies" further broken down into:

A. Interpretive Studies
B. Economics
C. Women

The remainder of the book is divided according to area. The second volume follows the same format but adds to "General Studies" a category D entitled "Democracy."

It might be of more than passing interest to note that the first volume (covering 1970–1988) needed only eight pages to list the writing dealing with "Women." That same category in the second volume (1988–1997) had swelled to 40 pages. The considerably greater number of writings on the Middle East is also borne out in this two-volume bibliography as follows:

Total Pages

	Middle East	Asia
Volume 1 (1970–1988)	57	40
Volume 2 (1988–1997)	27	19

Many, but not all, of the writings listed are annotated as well. A spot check of the two volumes would seem to indicate that annotation is somewhat more in evidence and longer in the second volume. Author, title, and subject indexes are to be found as well in both volumes. This two-volume work is an important research tool. May the editor and her collaborators be encouraged to continue this good work with later volumes.

Is it, however, overkill to have two books of bibliography? Is it too much even in this book to have filled fifteen pages with this avowedly selective bibliographical essay? Shall we conclude that "of making many books there is no end; and much study is a weariness of the flesh" (Ecclesiastes 12:12)?

Much better, surely, to see these many books and articles as indicating that a major issue concerning the somewhat more than one billion of the world's peoples is at least receiving the attention it deserves. Much better to realize that even though little consensus prevails there are many solid works from which to choose.

Works Cited

Abd al-Raziq, Ali. *Al-Islam wa Usul al-Hukm*. Cairo, 1925. Trans. L. Bercher, "L'Islam et les bases du pouvoir." *Revue des Etudes Islamiques* 7 (1930), pp. 353–391 and 8 (1934), pp. 163–222.

Abdul Nasser, Gamal. *Egypt's Liberation: The Philosophy of the Revolution*. Washington, D.C.: Public Affairs, 1955.

Abrahamian, Ervand. *Iran Between Two Revolutions*. Princeton: Princeton University Press, 1982.

— *Khomeinism: Essays on the Islamic Republic*. Berkeley and Los Angeles: University of California Press, 1993.

Abu-Amr, Ziad. *Islamic Fundamentalism in the West Bank and Gaza: Muslim Brotherhood and Islamic Jihad*. Bloomington: Indiana University Press, 1994.

Abu-Rabi', Ibrahim M. *Intellectual Origins of Islamic Resurgence in the Modern Arab World*. Albany: State University of New York Press, 1996.

Adams, Charles J. "Mawdudi and the Islamic State." In John L. Esposito, ed., *Voices of Resurgent Islam*. New York and Oxford: Oxford University Press, 1983.

Adelkhah, Fariba. *Being Modern in Iran*. New York: Columbia University Press, 2000.

Akhavi, Shahrough. "Shariati's Social Thought." In Nikki R. Keddie, ed., *Religion and Politics in Iran: Shi'ism from Quietism to Revolution*. New Haven: Yale University Press, 1983.

Aland, Kurt. *Four Reformers: Luther-Melanchthon-Calvin-Zwingli*. Trans. James L. Schaaf. Minneapolis: Augsburg, 1979.

Ambler, Eric. *Judgment on Deltchev*. New York: Bantam, 1964.

Amin, Ahmad, *Zu'ama al-Islah fi 'Asr al-Hadith* (Leaders of Reform in the Modern Period). Cairo: Maktabat al-Nahda, 1965.

Andric, Ivo. *The Bridge on the Drina*. Trans. Lovett F. Edwards. New York: Signet/New American Library, 1967.

Appleby, R. Scott, ed. *Spokesmen for the Despised: Fundamentalist Leaders of the Middle East*. Chicago: University of Chicago Press, 1997.

Arjomand, Said. *The Shadow of God and the Hidden Imam: Religion, Political Order, and Societal Change in Shi'ite Iran from the Beginning to 1890*. Chicago: University of Chicago Press, 1984.

— *The Turban for the Crown: The Islamic Revolution in Iran*. New York and Oxford: Oxford University Press, 1988.

Arnold, Sir Thomas and Alfred Guillaume, eds. *The Legacy of Islam*. 1st ed. London: Oxford University Press, 1933.

Avery, Peter. *Modern Iran*. New York: Praeger, 1965.

Ayubi, Nazih. *Political Islam: Religion and Politics in the Arab World*. London and New York: Routledge, 1991.

Al-'Azm, Sadik J. "Islamic Fundamentalism Reconsidered: A Critical Outline of Problems, Ideas, and Approaches." *South Asia Bulletin, Comparative Studies of South Asia, Africa and the Middle East* 13/1 and 2 (1993) and 14/1 (1994).

Bakhash, Shaul. *The Reign of the Ayatollahs: Iran and the Islamic Revolution*. New York: Basic, 1984.

Banani, Amin. *The Modernization of Iran, 1921–1941*. Stanford: Stanford University Press, 1961.

al-Banna, Hasan. *Five Tracts of Hasan al-Banna*. Trans. Charles Wendell. Berkeley and Los Angeles: University of California Press, 1975.

— *Memoirs of Hasan al-Banna, Shaheed*. Karachi: International Islamic, 1981.

Batatu, Hanna. *Syria's Peasantry, the Descendants of Its Lesser Rural Notables, and Their Politics*. Princeton: Princeton University Press, 1999.

Beinen, Joel and Joe Stock, eds. *Political Islam: Essays from Middle East Report*. Berkeley and Los Angeles: University of California Press, 1997.

Ben Achour, Mohamed El-Aziz. *Catégories de la société tunisoise dans la deuxième moitié du XIXème siecle*. Tunis: Institut National d'Archeologie et d'Art, 1989.

Berkes, Niyazi. *The Development of Secularism in Turkey*. Montreal: McGill University Press, 1964.

Black, Cyril E. *The Dynamics of Modernization: A Study in Comparative History*. New York: Harper and Row, 1966.

Black, Cyril E. and L. Carl Brown, eds. *Modernization in the Middle East: The Ottoman Empire and Its Afro-Asian Successors*. Princeton: Darwin, 1992.

Bowles, Paul. *The Spider's House*. New York: Random House, 1955.

Boyer, Pierre. *L'Evolution de l'Algerie mediane (ancien departement d'Alger) de 1830 a 1956*. Paris: Adrien, 1960.

Brown, L. Carl. "Tunisia." In James S. Coleman, ed., *Education and Political Development*. Princeton: Princeton University Press, 1965.

— "The Sudanese Mahdiya." In Robert I. Rotberg and Ali A. Mazrui, eds., *Power and Protest in Black Africa*. Oxford University Press, 1970.

— *The Tunisia of Ahmad Bey*. Princeton: Princeton University Press, 1974.

— *International Politics and the Middle East: Old Rules, Dangerous Game*. Princeton: Princeton University Press, 1984.

— "The June 1967 War: A Turning Point?" In Yehuda Lukacs and Abdalla M. Battah, eds., *The Arab-Israeli Conflict: Two Decades of Change*. Boulder and London: Westview, 1988.

— "Review: *Islam and the State* by P. J. Vatikiotis." *Middle Eastern Studies* 25/3 (July 1989).

— "Nasser and the June War: Plan or Improvisation?" In S. Seikaly, R. Baalbaki, and P. Dodd, eds., *Quest for Understanding: Arabic and Islamic Studies in Memory of Malcolm H. Kerr*. Beirut: American University of Beirut Press, 1991.

Browne, Edward G. *The Persian Revolution of 1905–1910*. Cambridge: Cambridge University Press, 1910.

Butterworth, Charles E. "Prudence Versus Legitimacy: The Persistent Theme in Islamic Political Thought." In Ali E. Hillal Dessouki, ed., *Islamic Resurgence in the Arab World*. New York: Praeger, 1982.

Butterworth, Charles E. and I. William Zartman, eds. *Political Islam*. Annals of the American Academy of Political and Social Science, no. 524 (November 1992). Newbury Park, Cal.: Sage, 1992.

Cahen, Claude. "The Body Politic." In Gustave von Grunebaum, ed., *Unity and Variety in Muslim Civilization*. Chicago: University of Chicago Press, 1955.

Cambridge History of Islam. 2 vols. Cambridge: Cambridge University Press, 1988.

Choueri, Youssef M. *Islamic Fundamentalism*. London: Pinter, 1990.

Cole, Juan. "Imami Jurisprudence and the Role of the Ulama: Mortaza Ansari on Emulating the Supreme Exemplar." In Nikki R. Keddie, ed., *Religion and Politics in Iran*. New Haven: Yale University Press, 1983.

Coury, Ralph. "Paul Bowles and Orientalism." In R. Kevin Lacey and Francis Poole, eds. *Mirrors on the Maghrib: Critical Reflections on Paul and Jane Bowles and Other American Writers in Morocco*. Delmar, N.Y.: Caravan, 1996.

Crone, Patricia. "Islam, Judeo-Christianity, and Byzantine Iconoclasm." *Jerusalem Studies in Arabic and Islam* 2 (1980).

Dahm, Bernhard. *Sukarno and the Struggle for Indonesian Independence*. Trans. Mary F. Somers Heidhues. Ithaca: Cornell University Press, 1969.

Dessouki, Ali E. Hillal, ed. *Islamic Resurgence in the Arab World*. New York: Praeger, 1982.

Enayat, Hamid. *Modern Islamic Political Thought*. Austin: University of Texas Press, 1982.

Encyclopedia of Islam.

Esposito, John L. *Voices of Resurgent Islam*. Oxford and New York: Oxford University Press, 1983.

— *The Islamic Threat: Myth or Reality?* 2d ed. New York: Oxford University Press, 1995.

— *Islam and Politics* 4th ed. Syracuse: Syracuse University Press, 1998.

Esposito, John L, ed. *Islam and Development: Religion and Sociopolitical Change*. Syracuse: Syracuse University Press, 1980.

— *The Oxford Encyclopedia of the Modern Islamic World*. 4 vols. New York: Oxford University Press, 1995.

— *Political Islam: Revolution, Radicalism, or Reform?* Boulder: Lynne Rienner, 1997.

Esposito, John L. and John J. Donohue, eds. *Islam in Transition: Muslim Perspectives*. New York: Oxford University Press, 1982.

Esposito, John L. and John Voll. *Islam and Democracy*. New York: Oxford University Press, 1996.

Fadlallah, Mahdi. *Ma'Sayyid Qutb fi Fikratihi al-Siyasi wa al-Dini* (With Sayyid Qutb in His Political and Religious Thought.) Beirut, 1978.

Findley, Carter V. *Bureaucratic Reform in the Ottoman Empire: The Sublime Porte, 1789–1922*. Princeton: Princeton University Press, 1980.

Gellner, Ernest and Charles A. Micaud, eds. *Arabs and Berbers: From Tribe to Nation in North Africa*. London: Duckworth, 1973.

Geertz, Clifford. *Islam Observed: Religious Development in Morocco and Indonesia*. Chicago: University of Chicago Press, 1968.

Gerges, Fawaz A. *America and Political Islam: Clash of Cultures or Clash of Interests?* Cambridge: Cambridge University Press, 1999.

Gibb, H. A. R. *Modern Trends in Islam*. Chicago: University of Chicago Press, 1947.

— *Studies on the Civilization of Islam*. Boston: Beacon, 1962.

Gibb, H. A. R. and Harold Bowen. *Islamic Society and the West*. Vol. 1, part 1. Oxford: Oxford University Press/Royal Institute of International Affairs, 1950.

Goldberg, Ellis. "Smashing Idols and the State: The Protestant Ethic and Egyptian Sunni Radicalism." *Comparative Studies in Society and History* 33/1 (1991).

Grafftey-Smith, Lawrence. *Bright Levant*. London: John Murray, 1970.

Green, Arnold H. "A Tunisian Reply to a Wahhabi Proclamation: Texts and Contexts." In Arnold H. Green, ed., *In Quest of an Islamic Humanism: Arabic and Islamic Studies in Memory of Mohamed al-Nowaihi*. Cairo: American University in Cairo Press, 1984.

Haddad, Yvonne. "Sayyid Qutb: Ideologue of Islamic Revival," In John L. Esposito, ed. *Voices of Resurgent Islam*. Oxford University Press, 1983.

Haddad, Yvonne Yazbeck and John L. Esposito. *The Islamic Revival Since 1988: A Critical Survey and Bibliography*. Westport, Conn.: Greenwood, 1997.

Haddad, Yvonne Yazbeck, John Obert Voll, and John L. Esposito. *The Contemporary Islamic Revival: A Critical Survey and Bibliography.* Westport, Conn.: Greenwood, 1991.

Haim, Sylvia. *Arab Nationalism: An Anthology.* Berkeley and Los Angeles: University of California Press, 1962; pbk. ed., 1976.

Hashmi, Sohail H. "Interpreting the Islamic Ethics of War and Peace." In Terry Nardin, ed., *The Ethics of War and Peace: Religious and Secular Perspectives.* Princeton: Princeton University Press, 1996.

Heyd, Uriel. "The Ottoman Ulema and Westernization in the Time of Selim III and Mahmud II." *Scripta Hierosolymitana* 9 (1961).

Heyworth-Dunne, J. *Religious and Political Trends in Modern Egypt.* Washington, D.C.: self-published, 1950.

Hibbard, Scott W. and David Little. *Islamic Activism and U.S. Foreign Policy.* Washington, D.C.: United States Institute of Peace, 1997.

Hodgson, Marshall G. S. "A Comparison of Islam and Christianity as Framework for Religious Life." *Diogenes* 32 (Winter 1960).

— *The Venture of Islam.* 3 vols. Chicago: University of Chicago Press, 1974.

Hourani, Albert. *Arabic Thought in the Liberal Age, 1798–1939.* Oxford University Press, 1962.

— *The Emergence of the Modern Middle East.* Berkeley and Los Angeles: University of California Press, 1981.

— *A History of the Arab Peoples.* Cambridge: Harvard University Press, 1991.

Hunter, Shireen T. *The Future of Islam and the West: Clash of Civilizations or Peaceful Coexistence?* Westport, Conn.: Praeger, 1998.

Hurewitz, J. C. *The Middle East and North Africa in World Politics* Vol. 1. New Haven: Yale University Press, 1975.

Husaini, Ishak Musa. *The Moslem Brethren.* Beirut: Khayat's, 1956.

Ibn Abi Diyaf, Ahmad. *Ithaf Ahl al-Zaman fi Akhbar Muluk Tunis wa 'Ahd al-Aman.* 8 vols. Tunis: Kitabat al-Dawla lil-shu'un al-Thaqafa wa al-Akhbar, 1963–1966.

Ibn Jama'a, Badr al-Din Muhammad. *Tahrir al-Ahkam fi Tadbir Ahl al-Islam.* In *Islamica* 6 (1934), ed. Hans Koflet.

Ibn Khaldun, *The Muqaddimah: An Introduction to History.* Trans. Franz Rosenthal. 3 vols. 2d rev. ed. Princeton: Princeton University Press, 1967.

— *An Arab Philosophy of History.* (Selections from Ibn Khaldun's *Muqaddimah.*) Trans. Charles Issawi. Princeton: Darwin, 1987 [1950].

Ibrahim, Saad Eddin, "Anatomy of Egypt's Militant Islamic Groups," *International Journal of Middle Eastern Studies* 12/4 (December 1980).

Issawi, Charles. "Economic Growth and Development." In Cyril E. Black and L. Carl Brown, eds., *Modernization in the Middle East: The Ottoman Empire and its Afro-Asian Successors.* Princeton: Darwin, 1992.

Itzkowitz, Norman. *Ottoman Empire and Islamic Tradition.* New York: Knopf, 1972.

Jansen, Johannes J. G. *The Neglected Duty: The Creed of Sadat's Assassins and Islamic Resurgence in the Middle East.* New York: Macmillan, 1986.

Julien, Charles-Andre, ed. *Les Techniciens de la colonisation.* Paris: Presses Universitaires de France, 1946.

Kazemi, Farhad. *Poverty and Revolution in Iran.* New York: New York University Press, 1980.

Keddie, Nikki R. "Pan-Islam as Proto-Nationalism." *Journal of Modern History* 41/4 (March 1969).

— *Sayyid Jamal ad-Din "al-Afghani": A Political Biography.* Berkeley and Los Angeles: University of California Press, 1972.

— *Roots of Revolution: An Interpretive History of Modern Iran.* New Haven: Yale University Press, 1981.

— *Religion and Politics in Iran: Shi'ism from Quietism to Revolution.* New Haven: Yale University Press, 1983.

Kedourie, Elie. *Afghani and 'Abduh: An Essay on Religious Unbelief and Political Action.* New York: Humanities Press, 1966.

— "Sa'd Zaghlul and the British." In Elie Kedourie, *The Chatham House Version and Other Middle-Eastern Studies.* Hanover, N.H. and London: University Press of New England, 1984 [1970].

Kelidar, Abbas. "P. J. Vatikiotis: An Appreciation," *Middle Eastern Studies* 34/2 (April 1998).

Kepel, Gilles. *Muslim Extremism in Egypt: The Prophet and the Pharaoh.* Berkeley and Los Angeles: University of California Press, 1985.

— *Jihad: Expansion et déclin de l'islamisme.* Paris: Gallimard, 2000.

Kerr, Malcolm. "Egypt." In James S. Coleman, ed., *Education and Political Development.* Princeton: Princeton University Press, 1965.

Khalid, Khalid Muhammad. *Min Huna Nabda.* Cairo, 1950. Trans. I. Faruqi, *From Here We Start.* Washington, D.C.: American Council of Learned Societies, 1953.

Khayr al-Din al-Tunisi, *Aqwam al-Masalik li Ma'rifat Ahwal al-Mamalik.* Tunis, 1867. Trans. and ed. Leon Carl Brown, *The Surest Path: The Political Treatise of a Nineteenth-Century Muslim Statesman.* Cambridge: Harvard Middle East Monograph Series, 1967.

Khomeini, Ayatollah Ruhallah. *Islam and Revolution: Writings and Declarations of Imam Khomeini.* Trans. and ed. Hamid Algar. Berkeley: Mizan, 1981.

Kitchen, Helen, ed., *The Educated African.* New York: Praeger, 1962.

Kramer, Martin. *Islam Assembled: The Advent of the Muslim Congresses.* New York: Columbia University Press, 1986.

Kramer, Martin, ed. *The Islamism Debate.* Dayan Center for Middle East and African Studies, Tel Aviv University, 1997.

Kurzman, Charles. *Liberal Islam: A Sourcebook*. Oxford University Press, 1998.

Lacouture, Jean and Simonne Lacouture. *Egypt in Transition*. Trans. Francis Scarfe. New York: Criterion, 1958.

Lambton, Ann K. S. "Islamic Political Thought." In Joseph Schacht and C. E. Bosworth, eds., *The Legacy of Islam*. 2d ed. Oxford and New York: Oxford University Press, 1979.

— *The Persian Land Reform*. Oxford: Clarendon Press, 1969.

— *State and Government in Medieval Islam*. Oxford and New York: Oxford University Press, 1981.

Landau, Jacob. *The Politics of Pan-Islam: Ideology and Organization*. Oxford: Clarendon Press, 1990.

Lapidus, Ira M. "The Separation of State and Religion in Early Islamic Society." *International Journal of Middle Eastern Studies* 6/4 (October 1975).

— *A History of Islamic Societies*. Cambridge University Press, 1988.

— "State and Religion in Islamic Societies." *Past and Present*, no. 151 (May 1996).

Lawrence, Bruce. *Defenders of God: The Fundamentalism Revolt Against the Modern Age*. New York: Harper and Row, 1989.

Lerner, Daniel. *The Passing of Traditional Society: Modernizing the Middle East*. Chicago: Free Press, 1958.

Lerner, Ralph and Muhsin Mahdi, eds. *Medieval Political Philosophy: A Sourcebook*. Ithaca: Cornell University Press, 1963.

Le Tourneau, Roger. *Evolution politique de l'Afrique du nord musulmane, 1920–1962*. Paris: Librairie Armand Colin, 1962.

Levi-Provençal, E. *Conferences sur l'Espagne Musulmane*. Cairo: Imprimerie Nationale, 1951.

Lewis, Bernard. *The Emergence of Modern Turkey*. 2d ed. Oxford and New York: Oxford University Press, 1968.

— "The Return of Islam." *Commentary* 12/1 (Fall 1979).

— *The Political Language of Islam*. Chicago: University of Chicago Press, 1988.

— *The Shaping of the Modern Middle East*. Oxford and New York: Oxford University Press, 1994.

Lewis, Bernard, ed. *Islam from the Prophet Muhammad to the Capture of Constantinople*. Vol. 1. New York: Harper and Row, 1974.

Lutfi al-Sayyid Marsot, Afaf. *Egypt's Liberal Experiment, 1922–1936*. Berkeley and Los Angeles: University of California Press, 1977.

Luther, Martin. *Secular Authority: To What Extent Should It Be Obeyed? Works of Martin Luther*. Vol. 3. Philadelphia: Muhlenberg Press, 1930.

Lybyer, A. H. *The Government of the Ottoman Empire in the Time of Suleiman the Magnificent*. Cambridge: Harvard University Press, 1913.

Mahjoubi, Ali. *Les Origines du mouvement national en Tunisie: 1904-1934*. Tunis: Publications de l'Université de Tunis, 1982.

Malik, Hafiz. *Sir Sayyid Ahmad Khan and Muslim Modernization in India and Pakistan*. New York: Columbia University Press, 1980.

Malouf, Amin. *The First Century After Beatrice*. Trans. Dorothy S. Blair. London: Quartet, 1993.

Mardin, Serif. *The Genesis of Young Ottoman Thought*. Princeton: Princeton University Press, 1962.

Marty, Martin E. and R. Scott Appleby, eds. *Fundamentalisms Observed*. Vol. 1. 5 vols. Chicago: University of Chicago Press, 1991.

— *Fundamentalisms and Society*. Vol. 2. 5 vols. Chicago: University of Chicago Press, 1993.

— *Fundamentalisms and the State: Remaking Polities, Economies, and Militance*. Vol. 3. 5 vols. Chicago: University of Chicago Press, 1993.

— *Accounting for Fundamentalisms*. Vol. 4. 5 vols. Chicago: University of Chicago Press, 1994.

— *Fundamentalisms Comprehended*. Vol. 5. 5 vols. Chicago: University of Chicago Press, 1995.

Masmoudi, Muhammad. *Les Arabes dans le tempete*. Paris: Simeon, 1977.

Mawdudi, Abu al-A'la. *Bayn al-Da'watu al-Qawmiyya wa al-Rabita al-Islamiyya* (Between the Ideology of Nationalism and the Islamic Tie). Beirut: Dar al-'Arabiyya, 1967.

— *Political Theory of Islam*. 5th ed. Lahore: Islamic, 1976.

— *First Principles of the Islamic State*. 5th ed. Lahore: Islamic, 1978.

— *Towards Understanding the Qur'an (Tafhim al-Qur'an)*. Trans. and ed. Zafer Ishaq Ansari. London: Islamic Foundation, 1988.

Miller, Judith. *God Has Ninety-Nine Names: Reporting from a Militant Middle East*. New York: Simon and Schuster, 1997.

Minault, Gail. "Islam and Mass Politics: The Indian Ulama and the Khilafat Movement." In Donald Eugene Smith, ed., *Religion and Political Modernization*. New Haven: Yale University Press, 1974.

— *The Khilafat Movement: Religious Symbolism and Political Mobilization in India*. New York: Columbia University Press, 1982.

Miquel, André. *L'Islam et sa civilisation*. Paris: Librairie Armand Colin, 1968.

Mitchell, Richard P. *The Society of Muslim Brothers*. London: Oxford University Press, 1969.

Mortimer, Edward. *Faith and Power: The Politics of Islam*. New York: Vintage, 1982.

Moussali, Ahmad S. *Radical Islamic Fundamentalism: The Ideology and Political Discourse of Sayyid Qutb*. Beirut: American University of Beirut Press, 1992.

Munson, Henry Jr. "Comparing 'Fundamentalisms': A Review Article." Unpublished ms.

— "Not All Crustaceans Are Crabs: Reflections on the Comparative Study of Fundamentalism and Politics." *Contention* 4/3 (Spring 1995).

— "Intolerable Tolerance: Western Academia and Islamic Fundamentalism." *Contention* 5/3 (Spring 1996).

— *Islam and Revolution in the Middle East* New Haven: Yale University Press, 1989.

Muslim b. al-Hajjaj. *Sahih Muslim: Being Traditions and the Sayings and Doings of the Prophet Muhammad as Narrated by His Companions and Compiled Under the title "Al-Jami'-us-Sahih."* Trans. Abdul Hamid Siddiqi. Lahore: Ashraf, 1973.

Naipaul, V. S. *Among the Believers: An Islamic Journey.* New York: Knopf, 1981.

— *Beyond Belief: Islamic Excursions Among the Converted Peoples.* New York: Random House, 1998.

Nasr, Seyyed Hossein. "Comments on a Few Theological Issues in the Islamic-Christian Dialogue." In Yvonne Yazback Haddad and Wadi Haddad, eds., *Christian-Muslim Encounters.* Gainesville: University Press of Florida, 1995.

Nasr, Seyyed Vali Reza. "Mawdudi and the Jama'at-i Islami: The Origins, Theory and Practice of Islamic Revivalism." In Ali Rahnema, ed., *Pioneers of Islamic Revival.* London: Zed, 1994.

— *Mawdudi and the Making of Islamic Revivalism.* New York: Oxford University Press, 1996.

Nizam al-Mulk. *The Book of Government or Rules for Kings: The Siyar al-Muluk or Siyasatname of Nizam al-Mulk.* 2d ed. Trans. Hubert Drake. Boston: Routledge and Kegan Paul, 1978.

Nolte, Richard H. "The Rule of Law in the Arab Middle East." *Muslim World* (October 1958).

Pakdaman, Homa. *Djamal-ed-Din Assad Abadi dit Afghani.* Paris, 1969.

Parker, Richard B., ed. *The Six-Day War: A Retrospective.* Gainesville: University Press of Florida, 1996.

Pellissier de Reynaud, E. *Description de la Regence de Tunis: Exploration scientifique de l'Algerie.* Vol. 6. Paris: Imprimerie Imperiale, 1853.

Peters, Rudolph, ed. *Jihad in Classical and Modern Islam: A Reader.* Princeton: Markus Weiner, 1996.

Pipes, Daniel. *In the Path of God: Islam and Political Power.* New York: Basic, 1983.

— *Greater Syria: The History of an Ambition.* New York and Oxford: Oxford University Press, 1990.

Piscatori, James P. *Islam in a World of Nation-States.* Cambridge: Cambridge University Press, 1986.

Porath, Yehoshua. *In Search of Arab Unity, 1930–1945.* London: Frank Cass, 1986.

Qutb, Sayyid. *Al-Salam al-'Alami wa al-Islam* (World Peace and Islam). Cairo: Maktatat Wahba, 1951.

— *Fi Zilal al Qur'an* (In the Shadow of the Qur'an). Rev. ed. Beirut, Dar al-Shuruq. 1974.

— *Ma'rakat al-Islam wa al-Ra'smaliyya* (The Struggle Between Islam and Capitalism). Beirut: Dar al-Shuruq, 1974.

— *Milestones*. Beirut: Holy Koran, 1978; Karachi: International Islamic, 1981.

— *Social Justice in Islam* (*Al-'Adala al-Ijtima'iyya fi al-Islam*). Trans. John B. Hardie. New York: Octagon, 1980.

— *Amirika min al-Dakhil bi-Mundhar Sayyid Qutb* (America from within in the view of Sayyid Qutb). Ed. Salah al-Khalidi. Jiddah: Dar al-Manard. 1986.

Rahnema, Ali, ed., *Pioneers of Islamic Revival*. London and New Jersey: Zed, 1994.

Reid, Donald M. "Arabic Thought in the Liberal Age: Twenty Years After." *International Journal of Middle Eastern Studies* 14/4 (November 1982).

Report of the Court of Inquiry Constituted Under Punjab Act II of 1954 to Enquire into the Punjab Disturbances of 1953. Lahore, 1954.

Richard, Yann. "Modern Iranian Political Thought." In Nikki R. Keddie, *Roots of Revolution: An Interpretive History of Modern Iran*. New Haven: Yale University Press, 1981.

Rose, Gregory. "*Velayat-e Faqih* and the Recovery of Islamic Identity in the Thought of Ayatollah Khomeini." In Nikki R. Keddie, ed., *Religion and Politics in Iran: Shi'ish from Quietism to Revolution*. New Haven: Yale University Press, 1983.

Rosenthal, E. I. J. *Political Thought in Medieval Islam*. Cambridge: Cambridge University Press, 1958.

— *Islam in the Modern Nation State*. Cambridge: Cambridge University Press, 1965.

Rostow, Walt Whitman. *The Stages of Economic Growth*. Cambridge: Cambridge University Press, 1960.

Safran, Nadav. *Egypt in Search of Political Community*. Cambridge: Harvard University Press, 1961.

Santillana, David de. "Law and Society." In Sir Thomas Arnold and Alfred Guillaume, eds., *The Legacy of Islam*. London: Oxford University Press, 1931.

Shaw, Stanford J. *Between Old and New: The Ottoman Empire Under Sultan Selim III, 1789–1807*. Cambridge: Harvard University Press, 1971.

Shaw, Stanford J. and Ezel Kural Shaw. *History of the Ottoman Empire and Modern Turkey*. 2 vols. Cambridge: Cambridge University Press, 1977.

Shephard, William E. *Sayyid Qutb and Islamic Activism: A Translation and Critical Analysis of Social Justice in Islam*. Leiden: Brill, 1996.

Sidahmad, Abdel Salam and Anoushiravan Ehteshami, eds. *Islamic Fundamentalism*. Boulder: Westview, 1996.

Sivan, Emmanuel. *Radical Islam: Medieval Theology and Modern Politics*. New Haven: Yale University Press, 1985.

Smith, Charles D. *Islam and the Search for Social Order in Modern Egypt: A Biography of Muhammad Husayn Haykal*. Albany: State University of New York Press, 1983.

Smith, Wilfred Cantwell. *Islam in Modern History*. Princeton: Princeton University Press, 1957.

— *Modern Islam in India: A Social Analysis*. New Delhi: Usha, 1946.

Southern, R. W. *Western Views of Islam in the Middle Ages* Cambridge: Harvard University Press, 1962.

Sraieb, Noureddine. *Le College Sadiki de Tunis, 1875–1956: Enseignement et nationalisme*. Paris: CNRS, 1995.

Stone, Lawrence. "The Results of the English Revolution of the Seventeenth Century." In J. G. A. Pocock, ed., *Three British Revolutions: 1641, 1688, 1775*. Princeton: Princeton University Press, 1980.

Al-Suhrawardi, Abu al-Najif. *Kitab Adab al-Muridin*. Trans. Menahem Milson. *A Sufi Rule for Novices*. Cambridge: Harvard University Press, 1979.

Szyliowicz, Joseph. *Education and Modernization in the Middle East*. Ithaca: Cornell University Press, 1973.

Tabari, Azar, "The Role of the Clergy in Modern Iranian Politics." In Nikki R. Keddie, ed., *Religion and Politics in Iran: Shi'ism from Quietism to Revolution*. New Haven: Yale University Press, 1983.

Tibi, Bassam. "Structural and Ideological Change in the Arab Subsystem Since the Six Day War." In Yehuda Lukacs and Abdalla M. Battah, eds., *The Arab-Israeli Conflict: Two Decades of Change*. Boulder: Westview, 1988.

Toynbee, Arnold J. "The Islamic World Since the Peace Settlement." *Survey of International Affairs, 1925*. London: Oxford University Press/Royal Institute of International Affairs, 1927.

Tripp, Charles. "Sayyid Qutb: The Political Vision." In Ali Rahnema, ed., *Pioneers of Islamic Revival*. London: Zed, 1994.

Troll, Christian W. *Sayyid Ahmad Khan: A Reinterpretation of Muslim Theology*. New Delhi: Vikas, 1978.

Tucker, Robert C. *The Marx-Engels Reader*. New York: Norton, 1972.

Tunisian Ministry of Education, *Perspectives decennales de l'enseignment*. Tunis: Tunisian Ministry of Education [1958?].

Turner, Byran S. *Weber and Islam: A Critical Study*. London: Routledge and Kegan Paul, 1974.

— *Marx and the End of Orientalism*. London and Boston: Allen and Unwin, 1978.

Vatikiotis, P. J. *The Egyptian Army in Politics*. Bloomington: Indiana University Press, 1961.

— *The History of Egypt from Muhammad Ali to Mubarak.* 3d ed. Johns Hopkins University Press, 1985.

— *Islam and the State.* New York: Croom Helm, 1987.

Viorst, Milton. *In the Shadow of the Prophet: The Struggle for the Soul of Islam.* New York: Anchor, 1998.

Voll, John Obert. *Islam: Continuity and Change in the Modern World.* Boulder: Westview, 1982.

von der Mehden, Fred. *Two Worlds of Islam: Interaction Between Southeast Asia and the Middle East.* Gainesville: University Press of Florida, 1993.

von Grunebaum, Gustave. *Medieval Islam.* Rev. ed. Chicago: University of Chicago Press, 1953.

Walzer, Michael. *The Revolution of the Saints: A Study of the Origins of Radical Politics.* Cambridge: Harvard University Press, 1965.

Weaver, Mary Anne. *A Portrait of Egypt: A Journey Through the World of Militant Islam.* New York: Farrar, Straus and Giroux, 1999.

Weber, Max. *The Sociology of Religion.* Trans. Ephraim Fischoff, intro. Talcott Parsons. Boston: Beacon, 1963.

— *The Theory of Social and Economic Organization.* Ed. Talcott Parsons. New York: Free, 1964.

Wilson, Mary C. *King Abdullah, Britain and the Making of Jordan.* Cambridge: Cambridge University Press, 1987.

Wittfogel, Karl A. *Oriental Despotism: A Comparative Study of Total Power.* New Haven: Yale University Press, 1957.

World Bank. *World Development Report.* Selected years of this annual volume.

Wright, Robin. *The Last Great Revolution: Turmoil and Transformation in Iran.* New York: Knopf, 2000.

Wuthnow, Robert, ed. *The Encyclopedia of Politics and Religion.* 2 vols. Washington, D.C.: Congressional Quarterly, 1998.

Young, George. *Diplomacy Old and New.* London: Swarthmore, 1921.

Zartman, I. William, ed., *Man, State, and Society in the Contemporary Maghrib.* New York: Praeger, 1973.

Zuwiyya Yamak, Labib. *The Syrian Social Nationalist Party: An Ideological Analysis.* Cambridge: Harvard Middle East Monograph Series, 1966.

Index